Working With C

Yashavant Kanetkar

bpb
www.bpbonline.com

FIRST EDITION 1994
REPRINTED 2025

ISBN: 978-81-7029-301-9

Distributors:

BPB PUBLICATIONS
20, Ansari Road, Darya Ganj
New Delhi-110002
Ph: 23254990/23254991

DECCAN AGENCIES
4-3-329, Bank Street,
Hyderabad-500195
Ph: 24756967/24756400

MICRO MEDIA
Shop No. 5, Mahendra Chambers,
150 DN Rd. Next to Capital Cinema,
V.T. (C.S.T.) Station, MUMBAI-400 001
Ph: 22078296/22078297

BPB BOOK CENTRE
376 Old Lajpat Rai Market,
Delhi-110006
Ph: 23861747

To View Complete BPB Publications Catalogue Scan the QR Code:

Published by Manish Jain for BPB Publications, 20 Ansari Road, Darya Ganj, New Delhi-110002 and Printed at Manipal Technologies Limited, Manipal

www.bpbonline.com

Dedicated to ammi and dada

About The Author

Yashavant Prabhakar Kanetkar obtained his M.Tech. from IIT, Kanpur in 1987 and since then has been Director of ICIT, a Training and Software development firm which he set up at Nagpur. Already an author of the books 'Let Us C', 'Exploring C', 'C Projects' and 'Programming Expertise in Basic', these days he is writing a few more books on C and Unix with his team at ICIT. Mr. Kanetkar also writes 'The C Column' in Express Computer every week.

Acknowledgments

Writing a book in isolation has its own pitfalls. The book cannot tell you whether what you are saying makes sense and if you are, whether you are getting that sense across to the reader. Such is the time when you need technically competent colleagues to review what you are saying.

And I have been particularly lucky to have Niranjan Bakre who belongs to that rare genre of people who are well versed in both computers and book lore. His insights helped me mold the contents of the book in numerous ways. My sincere thanks to him for his attention for detail - in particular, for spotting all the missing semi-colons, undeclared variables and redundant commas. However, I accept the blame (albeit reluctantly, I confess) for any errors that may have escaped him.

Sunil Bang is another colleague who worked on this book project from the beginning. He ran all the programs in the book and helped hammer out many trivias.

Pravin Bagde joined me when I was through with the first few chapters. With nobody around to do the DTP work Pravin put his best foot forward and was soon drawing figures, creating tables, preparing indexes like a true professional.

Thanks are also due to Manish Jain of BPB Publications who has a magic formula of getting the books that I write onto the book-shelves all over India and across the seas in shortest possible time.

And finally many many thanks to all those Cfarers who kept company during this long travel.

COMBATING MENACE OF PIRACY

Dear Readers, Publishers, Booksellers, all College & University Administrations, & Librarians,

The Federation of Publishers' & Book Sellers' Associations in India (FPBAI) would like to bring a matter of great importance to your urgent notice. Though possession of pirated copies is a cognizable and non-bailable offence, punishable by law and carries stiff penalties including imprisonment, it continues to thrive in markets, bookshops and photocopy shops. This is a matter of grave concern for all of us in the education and publishing community. Let us all do our bit in combating this crime against creation and spread of knowledge. If you come across a pirated book, photocopies pages from a book or are in any kind of doubt about the genuineness of a copy, please contact Chairman, Anti Piracy Committee, FPBAI, 84, Second Floor (Opp. Cambridge Primary School), Daryaganj, New Delhi-110 002.

Your co-operation and help in bringing the culprits to book will help the publishing industry combat piracy and facilitate the continued availability of good books of quality production at reasonable prices.

RELEVANT PORTIONS OF THE COPYRIGHT ACT ARE GIVEN BELOW:

INFRINGEMENT OF COPYRIGHT

The owner of the copyright has the exclusive right in respect of the reproduction of the work and such other acts which enables the owner to get the financial benefits by exercising such rights. If any of these acts relating to the work is carried out by a person other than the owner without a license from the owner or competent person/authority under the Copyright Act 1957, it constitutes infringement of copyright in the work.

PIRACY

It is a kind of illegal activity which has been caused by rapid technological advancement. Latest techniques of photocopying and printing have made it easy to produce unauthorized copies of a book within a short span of time at a relatively low cost on a large scale. This offence deprives the author of the work from getting his legitimate due and ultimately hampers the growth of original and creative work by the pursuit of hard work and intellectual skill and national economy as well.

COPYRIGHT LEGISLATION

The Principal Act (Copyright Act, 1957) was amended in 1984 to incorporate anti-piracy legislation to check widespread piracy of books, etc. and it has been made a cognizable and non-bailable offence.

The punishment for various offences have been enhanced by amending sections 63 and 65 and by inserting new sections 63A & 63B.

SECTION 63:

Any person who knowingly infringes or abets the infringement of the copyright work shall be punishable with:

(i) Imprisonment for a term which shall not be less than 6 months but which may be extended up to 3 years;

(ii) Fine of not less than Rs. 50,000/- but up to Rs. 2 lakhs.

SECTION 63A:

The quantum of enhanced penalty on second or subsequent conviction shall be:

(i) Imprisonment for not less than 1 year but up to 3 years; and

(ii) Fine of not less than rupees 1 lakh but may be extended up to Rs. 2 lakhs.

SECTION 63B:

The quantum penalty for the offence of knowing use of infringing copy of computer program shall be:

(i) Imprisonment for not less than 7 days but up to 3 years; and

(ii) Fine of not less than Rs. 50,000/- but may be extended up to Rs. 2 lakhs.

More powers have been given to the police for prompt action and speedy apprehension of the offender by amending section 64, as any police officer not below the rank of Sub-Inspector may seize without warrant all infringing copies or the work if he is satisfied that the offence is under section 63 in respect of the infringement of copyright. The Economic Offence (Inapplicability of Limitation) Act, 1974 was amended by incorporating in the Schedule the clause (a) of section 63 of the Copyright Act, 1957 which declared infringement of copyright as an economic offence.

Contents

Introduction *xv*

1 Overview Of Programming **1**

Steps In Program Development 2
Programming Language Classification 4
Machine Language 5
Assembly Language 6
Third Generation Languages 7
Fourth Generation Languages 8
Characteristics of 3GLs and 4GLs 9
Language Translators 10
Programming Techniques 12
Exercise 16

2 An Overview of C language **19**

History of C language 21
Structure of a C program 23
Exercise 26

3 Data types, Variables and Constants **29**

The C Character Set 31
Data Types 31
Constants And Variables 33
C Constants 34
Rules For Constructing Integer Constants 34
Rules For Constructing Real Constants 35
Rules For Constructing Character Constants 36
Logical Constants 37
String Constants 37

C Variables 39
Rules For Constructing Variables Names 39
Variable Declaration 40
Scope of Variables: Local & Global 40
C Keywords 41
The First C Program 42
Type Modifiers 46
Integers, Long & Short 47
Integers, Signed & Unsigned 48
Chars, Signed & Unsigned 49
Storage Class Specifiers 51
Automatic Storage Class 52
Register Storage Class 55
Static storage Class 56
External Storage Class 58
Which To Use When 61
Exercise 63

4 Operators, Expressions, and Assignment Statements **67**

Operators 68
Arithmetic Operators 69
Increment and Decrement Operators 69
Modulo Division Operator 71
Relational Operatiors 72
Logical Operators 74
Bitwise Operators 76
One's Complement Operator 78
Right Shift Operator 80
Left Shift Operator 81
Bitwise AND Operator 82
Bitwise OR Operator 85
Bitwise XOR operator 86
Conditional Operator 87
The Comma Operators 88
sizeof operator 89
Precedence of Operators 90

Expressions 93
Definition 93
Type conversion in expressions 94
Type casting 96
Assignment statements 97
General form 98
Type conversion in assignments 100
Variable initialisations 101
Exercise 104

5 Control Statements **111**

The if Statement 113
General form Of if 113
Multipe Statements Within if 117
The if-else Statement 119
Nested if's 121
The if-else-if Ladder 122
A Word Of Caution 127
The ? As An Alternative To if 129
Summary Of if 130
switch 131
The Tips And Traps 135
Loop In C 140
The while Loop 141
Tips And Traps 144
The for Loop 147
Nesting Of Loops 153
Multiple Initialiation In The for Loop 154
The Odd Loop 155
do-while 156
The break statement 158
The continue Statement 160
The exit( ) Function 161
The goto Statement 162
Exercise 166

6 Console Input/Output **175**

Types Of I/O 176
Console I/O functions 178
Unformatted Console I/O Functions 179
getchar( ) And putchar( ) 179
gets( ) And puts( ) 180
Formatted Console I/O Functions 182
Conversion Specifications 183
Escape Sequences 187
The sprintf( ) Function 190
The scanf( ) Function 190
Exercise 192

7 Arrays **195**

Single Dimensional Arrays 196
A Simple Program Using Array 198
Array Declaration 199
Accessing Elemenys Of An Array 199
Entering Data Into An Array 199
Reading Data from An Array 200
More On Arrays 201
Array Initialisation 201
Array Elements In Memory 202
Bounds Checking 202
Strings 203
Two Dimensional Arrays 207
Initialising A 2 Dimensional Array 209
Memory Map Of A 2 Dimensional Array 210
Multi Dimensional Arrays 210
Exercise 213

8 Functions **217**

General form Of A Function 218
Why Use Functions 226

Functions With Arguments 226
Function Declaration And Prototypes 232
Call By Value And Call By Reference 235
An Introduction To Pointers 235
Back To Function Calls 240
Scope Rules Of Functions 244
Calling Functions With Arrays 245
Pointers And Arrays 248
Passing An Entire Array To A Function 253
The Real Thing 254
argc And argv - Arguments To main( ) 256
Recursion 257
Exercise 263

9 Pointers **269**

The & And * operators 271
Pointer Expressions 273
Pointer Assignments 273
Pointer Arithmetic 275
Pointer Comparison 279
Dynamic Memory Allocation 279
Pointers Versus Arrays 282
Pointers And 2 Dimensional Arrays 283
Arrays Of Pointers 286
Limitation Of Array Of Pointers To Strings 290
Pointers To Pointers 290
Pointers To Functions 292
Function Returning Pointers 295
Functions With Variable Number Of Arguments 297
Exercise 301

10 Structures, Unions and Enumerated Data Types **309**

Structures 310
Basics Of Structures 311
Declaring A Structure 313

Accessing Structure Elements 316
How Structure Elements Are Stored 317
Array Of Structure 319
Passing Structures Elements To Functions 321
Passing Entire Structure To Functions 322
Structure Pointers 324
Structures Within Structures 326
Uses Of Structures 327
Unions 328
Union Of Structures 334
Uses Of Unions 335
Enumerated Data Types 339
Uses Of Enumerated Data Type 341
typedef Statement 343
Exercise 345

11 File Handling In C **355**

Opening A File 359
Reading From A File 360
Trouble Opening The File 361
Closing The File 362
File Opening Modes 362
A Filecopy Program 364
Writing To a File 365
A Closer Look At fclose( ) 365
Using argc And argv 366
String (line) I/O Files 371
The Awkward Newline 373
A Brief Review 374
Formatted Disk I/O Functions 374
Binary Mode Versus Text Mode 377
Text Versus Binary Mode: Newlines 378
Text Versus Binary Mode: End Of File 379
Text Versus Binary Mode: Storage Of Numbers 380
Record I/O In Files 381
Making It All Make Sense 387

Detecting Errors In Reading/Writing 393
Exercise 395

12 The C Preprocessor **399**

Features Of C Preprocessor 400
#define Directive 402
Macros With Arguments 406
Macros Versus Functions 409
#include Directive 410
#undef Directive 412
Conditional Compilation Directives 412
#if And #elif Directives 415
Exercise 418

13 Header File And Standard Library Functions **423**

Header Files 425
stdio.h 425
ctype.h 425
string.h 426
math.h 426
stdlib.h 426
stdarg.h 427
time.h 427
Standard Library Functions 427
String Functions 427
Math Routines 429
Time And Date Routines 431
Variable Argument List Functions 431
Utility Functions 431
Standard I/O Functions 433
Character Class Test functions 435
Miscellaneous Functions 437

Appendix A - Summary Of C Language **439**
Appendix B - Chasing The Bugs **459**
Appendix C - Hexadecimal Numbering **469**
Appendix D - ASCII Chart **477**
Appendix E - DOEACC Solved Papers **481**

Index **511**

Before You Start

The basic aim of this book is to teach C programming language in as lucid a manner as possible, and to show how to write serious C programs. While writing this book I have in mind the thousands of newcomers to the big wide world of C, as will be clear from the gentle pace of the exposition. I therefore assume that you have only a few basic DOS/Unix skills with no prior experience of C or any other structured programming language. I also assume that you can perform such feats as putting on the computer, inserting diskettes the right way up, copying files and locating the shift, space bar and the enter key. However, those who are already familiar with a language are likely to derive more benefits from this book.

Starting from the most elementary concepts the book goes on to cover all the facets of C language. Flowcharting, a powerful aid for programming, is extensively used in initial chapters to demonstrate the logic of the solution procedure for a programming problem. The book uses simple-to-complex and easy-to-learn approach throughout. An attempt is made to make the material presented comprehensive, concise and practical. The emphasis is on the solution of practical problems. Several examples from real-life situations are used to demonstrate the various features of C language. Once you have imbibed the concepts you may test the skills acquired through carefully graded exercises at the end of each chapter. These exercises are designed to provide an insight into methods and applications of C language. A separate appendix titled 'Chasing the bugs' would help you avoid common errors that occur while programming in C. The material in this book has been organised as recommended by the Department of Electronics Accredition Of Computer Courses Committee (DOEACC) for 'A' and 'B' level examinations in C language.

By the end you should be able to approach any C program with the conviction that you know what you are doing. In my experience, knowing what you are doing before you start is always a good idea in any aspect of life. Finally, I hope this book puts you firmly on a path to obtain fluenC in C.

CHAPTER

1 An Overview Of Programming

Steps In Program Development
Programming Language Classification
Programming Techniques

Steps In Program Development

There is hardly a field left into which computers haven't made forays. We have reached a point where a problem, be it of scientific, commercial or of any other nature, can be solved by a computer. There are tonnes and tonnes of softwares available in every conceivable field. These softwares are nothing but a collection of programs. Irrespective of the application for which the program is meant, certain steps need to be followed while developing it. Developing any but the simplest of programs requires a systematic step by step approach. These steps are shown in Figure 1.1.

As indicated in the figure the program life cycle begins with the identification of the problem to be computerised. This phase begins as soon as someone - either the user or a member of the data processing department sees a problem or opportunity which suggests a programming solution. At such times the programmer analyst and the user meet to develop information in response to the following three questions:

(a) What is the problem perceived by the user
(b) What are the goals to be achieved by the solution

(c) What benefits will result from achieving the solution

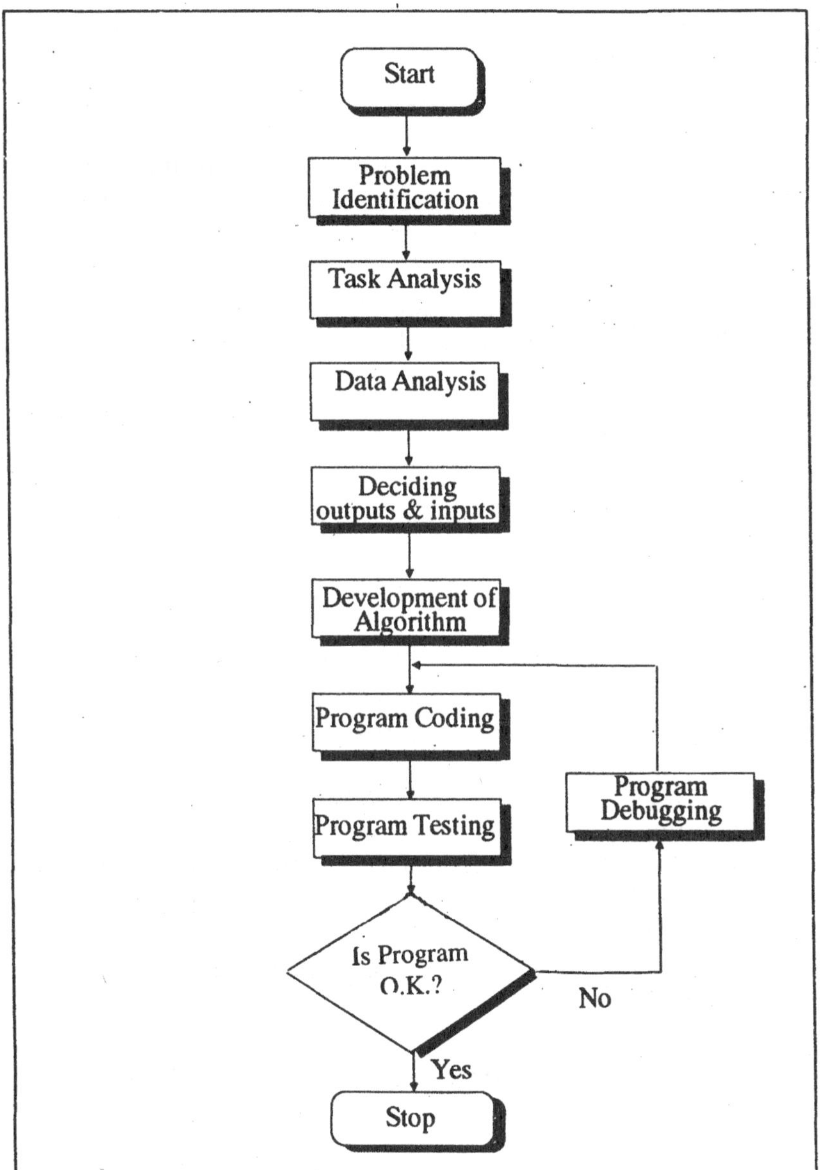

Figure 1.1

In the task analysis phase the problem is thoroughly analysed and a system solution is proposed taking into account all other alternative solutions possible. While arriving at the solution the known and unknown parameters are identified and the constraints under which the problem is to be solved are stated.

During the data analysis phase the data, information and documents relevant to the program are collected and the following details are chalked out:

(a) Outputs to be produced and its layout
(b) Inputs that must be received
(c) Data to be retained
(d) Operations to be performed to produce outputs and maintain files

In short the functional specifications are determined during this stage.

Once the problem and its inputs/outputs have been analysed next comes the all important step of developing a solution procedure (algorithm) for the problem. For this the sequence of operations to be performed in the process of solving the problem are identified and the program logic is planned, preferably using a program flowchart.

Once the algorithm is ready next comes the step of converting this algorithm into a program of instructions for the computer in a suitable language. Next the program written is keyed into the computer and tested thoroughly for different sets of data. Quite often there are errors (bugs) in the program. All these errors which may either be in writing the program or in the logic of the program are then removed.

Programming Language Classification

To communicate between two parties, whether they are machines or human beings, some common language or terminology is needed. Of course this language or terminology must be understood by both the parties. To communicate with a computer it has to be instructed to carry out various tasks like: what operations to perform, how to present results, when and how to make certain decisions, and so on. These set of instructions have to be communicated to the computer through a language called 'programming language'. The set of instructions written in a programming language is known as a 'program'.

There exist three levels of programming languages for communicating the instructions to the computer. They are:

(a) Machine languages (low level languages)
(b) Assembly languages
(c) Procedure oriented langauges (high level languages)
(d) Fourth Generation Languages (4GLs)

Let us now briefly discuss each of these languages.

Machine Langauage

Computers are made of two-state electronic components which can understand only pulse and no-pulse (or 1 and 0) conditions. Therefore, the instructions given to the computer and the data fed to it must be written using binary numbers 1 and 0. A computer's machine language consists of such strings of binary numbers.

Computers do not understand English, Hindi or any other such common language. They respond only to machine language. Added to this, computers are not identical in design. Therefore, each computer has its own machine langauge. However, the script, 1 and 0, is same for all computers. This poses several problems for the users.

It is very tedious to understand and remember the various combinations of 1's and 0's representing numerous data and instructions. In addition to remembering these codes, the programmer is also required to keep track of the storage locations of data and instructions. It takes several months to write programs. Also, writing error free instructions is a slow process. Checking instructions to locate errors is about as traumatic as writing them initially. And if a program has to be modified at a later date, the work involved may take weeks to finish. Thus machine language programs are difficult to write and maintain.

Also, since every computer has its own machine language, the programmer cannot communicate with other computers if he does not know its machine langauge.

Assembly Language

To ease the programmer's burden, mnemonic (pronounced ne-mon-ik) operation codes were developed in 1950s. One of the first steps in improving the program preparation process was to replace the numeric language operation codes with mnemonics.

Thus, an assembly language uses mnemonic codes (abbreviations) rather than numeric codes (as used in machine langauge). For example, ADD is used as a symbolic operation code to represent addition and SUB is used for subtraction. Memory locations containing data are given names such as TOTAL, MARKS, TIME etc. Thus, instead of referring a location using its number now it can be referred using the name given to it.

For example, the selling price of an item might be assigned to a location 0063 in memory by the programmer, and given the symbolic name SP. And the cost price may be assigned to a location 2047 and be given a name CP. Once this has been done the programmer would refer to the symbolic names CP and SP rather than to the location numbers when such items are to be processed. Thus an instruction SUB SP, CP would subtract the value of SP from CP.

As the computer understands only machine language instructions, a program written in assembly language must be translated into machine langauge before it can be executed. This translation is done by another program called 'assembler'. For example the instruction SUB SP, CP would be translated by the assembler into corresponding machine language instruction as,

011111	011111111111	000000111111
Mnemonic operation code	2047	0063
SUB	CP	SP

Assembly language has several advantages over machine language. First it saves programmer's time. Fewer errors are made, and those that are made are easier to find. Also assembly language programs are easier to modify than machine language programs. However, assembly language is again a machine oriented language and hence the program has to be different for different machines. The programmer should remember machine characteristics when he prepares a program.

Third Generation Languages

The earlier assembler programs produced only one machine language instruction for every assembly language instruction. To speed up program development new assemblers were developed which could produce several machine language instruction for one assembly language instruction. For example, the programmer might write READ FILE and the assebmler would then produce a detailed series of machine language instructions to read data from the file on the disk and store it in memory. Thus, the programmer was relieved of the task of writing an instruction for every machine operation performed. This development led to the development of Third generation languages (machine and assembly forming the first two generations). These languages consist of a set of words and symbols and one can write programs using these in conjunction with certain pre-specified rules of the language. These languages are oriented towards the problem to be solved or the procedures for the solution rather than mere computer instructions. These languages are more user-centered than machine-centered. These languages are also called high level languages. The commonly used high level languages are BASIC, FORTRAN, Pascal and COBOL.

The most important characteristic of a high level language is that it is machine independent and a program written in high level language can be run on computers of different makes with little or no modification. The programmer need not know the characteristics of that machine. However, such programs are to be translated into equivalent machine langauge instructions before actual execution.

A program written in high level language is known as a 'source program' and can be run on different machines using different translators. The translated program is called the 'object program'. The major disadvantage of high level languages is that they take extra time for conversion and thus are less efficient as compared to the machine language programs.

Fourth Generation Languages

A new set of languages are coming to the fore which allow even a non-technical user to interact with the computer in a simpler and more friendly manner. These are known as Fourth generation languages or simply, 4GLs. These languages are non-procedural, i.e. the users do not define the detailed procedure required to arrive at the final result. Examples of 4GLs are dBASE, FoxPro, PC/FOCUS etc.

Characteristics of 3GLs and 4GLs

A programming language is a notation with which people can communicate algorithms to computers and to one another. Hundreds of programming languages exist. They differ in their degree of closeness to natural or mathematical language on one hand and to machine language on the other. They differ also in the type of problem for which they are best suited. Some of the aspects of 3GLs and 4GLs which make them preferable to machine or assembly language are as follows.

(a) Ease of understanding

A 3GL or 4GL program is generally easier to read, write, and prove correct than is an assembly language program, because a high level language usually provides a more natural notation for describing algorithms than does assembly language. Even among high level languages, some are easier to use than others. Part of this has to do with the operators, data structures and flow of control features provided in a language.

(b) Naturalness

Much of the understandability of a 3GL or 4GL language comes from the ease with which one can express an algorithm in that language. Some languages are clearly more suitable than others in this regard for differing problem domains. FORTRAN was designed for numerical and mathematical calculations, COBOL for business applications and SNOBOL for string manipulation. One would not write a complex numerical calculation in COBOL or SNOBOL, even though, theoretically a program written in one of these languages can be simulated, with varying degrees of efficiency, by a program written in any of the other languages.

(c) Portability

Users must often be able to run their programs on a variety of machines. Languages such as FORTRAN or COBOL have relatively well defined 'standard versions', and programs confirming to the standard should run in any machine. There are pitfalls that come up unexpectedly, however. For example, a programmer using a huge constant on one machine may suddenly find that such a constant cannot be accomodated in the other machine.

(d) Efficiency of use

This area covers a number of aspects of both program and language design. One would like to be able to translate source programs into efficient object programs. One would also like the compilation process itself to be efficient. In both cases, the design of the language can affect how easily the computation can be done. But it is often more important that the programmer be able to implement programs in a way that makes efficient use of his time. To the latter end, a 3GL or a 4GL should have facilities for defining data structures, macros, subroutines and the like. The operating system and programming environment can also be as important as the language in reducing programming time.

Language Translators

Why do we need language translators? The answer to this question is obvious to anyone who has programmed in machine language. With machine language we must communicate directly with a computer in terms of bits, registers and very primitive machine operations. Since a machine language program is nothing more than a sequence of 0's and 1's, programming a complex algorithm in such a language is terribly tedious and fraught with opportunities for mistakes. Perhaps the most serious disadvantage of machine language coding is that all operations and operands must be specified in a numeric code. Not only is a machine language program cryptic, but it also may be impossible to modify it in a convenient manner.

Computers can understand instructions only when they are written in their own language - the machine langauge. Therefore, a program written in any other language should be translated into machine language. Special programs called language processors are available to do this job. These special programs accept the user programs and check each statement and, if it is grammatically correct, produce a corresponding set of machine language instructions. Language processors are also known as translators. There are two types of translators:

(a) Compilers
(b) Interpreters

A compiler checks the entire user-written program (known as the source program) and, if error free, produces a complete program in machine language (known as object program). The source program is retained for possible modifications and corrections and the object program is loaded into the computer's memory for execution.

An interpreter does a similar job but in a different style. The interpreter (as the name implies) translates one statement at a time and, if error-free, executes the instruction. This continues till the last statement in the program has been translated and executed. Thus, the interpreter translates and executes the first instruction before it goes to the second, while a compiler translates the whole program before execution can begin.

The major differences between them are:

(a) Error correction (called debugging) is much simpler in the case of an interpreter because it is done in stages. As against this the compiler produces an error list for the entire program before execution of even the first instruction can begin.

(b) Interpreters take more time for the execution of a program compared to compilers because a statement has to be translated every time the program is executed.

Since a compiler (or an interpreter) can translate only a particular language for which it is designed, one will need to use a separate compiler for each language.

Executing a program written in a high level programming language is basically a two step process. The source program must first be compiled, that is, translated into the object program. Then the resulting object program is loaded into memory and executed.

Programming Techniques

One caution in designing a program is to avoid 'clever' solutions that might save a little execution time but are difficult for humans to understand. Such programming contortions are usually hard to debug and even harder for someone else to maintain. Thus, though programming even today is largely considered to be an art, still some scientific methods have been developed to standardise the designing of a program with a view to write simple, efficient, easy-to-read and easy-to-maintain programs.

There are three programming techniques commonly used. These are:

(a) Top-down design
(b) Bottom-up Design
(c) Modular design

In the top-down design the overall task of the program is broken down into several smaller logics and then they are interlaced by calling these logics whenever necessary. As against this in Bottom-up design programming begins with the smallest of logics and from this the next bigger logic is built and so on further up till the entire problem is programmed.

Modular programming is a term used to describe dividing a program into areas of code or modules that perform specific tasks. Following are the important characteristics of modular programming.

(a) The programmer designs the program in levels, where a level consists of one or more modules. The first level is a complete main program and modules at successive levels consist of submodules referenced in the prior levels.

(b) A module is a set of program statements which, when acting together complete a specific task. In practice a module can be a function and the main program can consist of a sequence of calls to the functions that represent the modules at the next level down.

(c) The order in which the modules are executed by the computer is controlled by the main program. This describes fully the procedures required in the solution to a problem. The procedures being written in the order of machine execution.

(d) Modules should be structured within themselves by incorporating the constructs of sequencing, selection and repetition. Every program can and should be written using only these constructs.

Modular programming offers the following advantages over monolithic in line programming where the entire logic is packed together.

(a) By dividing the solution to a problem into many parts it is possible to obtain a better insight into the solution of the problem as a whole.

(b) It is often far easier and quicker to document specific tasks related to functions than document a complete unstructured program.

(c) Program maintenance (inserting new modules, amending code and deleting code from existing modules) is simpler for individual modules than for an entire program.

In 1976 Edsger Dijkstra wrote of the importance of using structured programming techniques. Structured programs use only three basic constructs:

(a) Sequential structure, with steps performed one after another in succession.

(b) Selection structure, such as implemented with an if-then-else or case statements.

(c) Repetition structure, such as implemented with a for, while or repeat loop.

Thus, the most important aspect of modular programming is the development of a solution in a modular fashion starting at the highest level with repeated refinement. It is impossible to keep all aspects of a complex program in mind. We can, however, design the major steps of the solution as modules. In turn, each of these steps can be further broken down into more manageable portions or submodules. Within a program the modules are usually realised as procedures or functions with the main program invoking subprograms at the highest level of design. It is best for each subprogram to perform only one major task and usually to have no more than say about 50 to 100 statements. Each of these modules can be tested and debugged independently.

Consider how much easier it would be to find an error in 100 lines of code of a module as opposed to 3000 lines in an entire program. In a modular design, only the offending module as opposed to the entire program, may need to be rewritten. Moreover, with such a design, if we find a better algorithm for performing a particular task - for example, a better method of alphabetizing names - we only need to substitute one module for another. We can also easily add new features to the program by inserting new modules

I hope the above discussion impresses upon readers that a proper methodology in designing of programs is necessary if program writing is to be kept as simple as possible and that programs which are written can be easily read, understood and hence maintained.

Exercise

[A] Pick the correct answer from the following.

(1) A machine language program consists of instructions written in

(a) Pnemonics
(b) 0's and 1's
(c) Keywords
(d) English like words

(2) An Assembly language program consists of instructions written in

(a) Pnemonics
(b) 0's and 1's
(c) Keywords
(d) English like words

(3) Pick the odd one out

(a) Interpreter
(b) Compiler
(c) Debugger
(d) Translator

(4) Pick the odd one out

(a) Bottom up design
(b) Parallel design
(c) Modular design
(d) Top down design

(5) Pick up the wrong sequence

(a) Problem identification, Task analysis, Data analysis
(b) Problem coding, Testing, Debugging
(c) Program coding, Debugging, Data analysis
(d) Problem analysis, Developement of algorithm, Coding

(6) Which language would offer a better portability?

(a) Machine language
(b) Assembly language
(c) C language
(d) None of the above

(7) Which of the following is a 4GL?

(a) Pascal
(b) COBOL
(c) C
(d) dBASE

(8) A 4GL program consists of

(a) Pnemonics
(b) 0's and 1's
(c) English like words
(d) None of the above

(9) Which of the following is not a usual feature of a 3GL or 4GL program?

(a) Naturalness
(b) Portability
(c) Ease of understanding
(d) Complex coding schemes

(10) Which of the following should not be present in a structured program?

(a) Decision control structure
(b) Repitition control structure
(c) Sequence control structure
(d) Unconditional jump control structure

(11) Structured programming concepts were first laid down by

(a) P. J. Plauger
(b) Edsger Dijkstra
(c) Dennis Ritchie
(d) Ken Thompson

[B] State true or false.

(a) Assembly languages are different for computer with different architectures.

(b) As far as portability is concerned High level languages are better than Machine or Assembly languages.

(c) Assembly language can use location names for referring the value stored at a particular location number.

(d) An interpreter first converts all instructions in machine language and then starts their execution.

(e) Error correction is simpler in interpreter because it is done in stages.

CHAPTER

2 An Overview Of C Language

History Of C Language
Structure Of A C Program

Before we can begin to write serious programs in C, it would be interesting to find out what really is C, how it came into existence and how does it compare with other computer languages. In this chapter we would briefly outline these issues and then move over to view the structure of a typical C program.

C is a programming language developed at AT & T's Bell Laboratories of USA in 1972. It was designed and written by a man named Dennis Ritchie. In the late seventies C began to replace the more familiar languages of that time like PL/I, ALGOL etc. No one pushed C. It wasn't made the 'official' Bell Labs language. Thus, without any advertisement C's reputation spread and its pool of users grew. Ritchie seems to have been rather surprised that so many programmers preferred C to older languages like FORTRAN or PL/I, or the newer ones like PASCAL and APL. But, that's what happened.

Possibly why C seems so popular is because it is reliable, simple and easy to use. Out of the dozens of languages available, the prize of purity is often given to PASCAL, C's pretty sister. C wasn't meant to win prizes; it was meant to be friendly, capable and reliable. Therefore, quite a few programmers who begin by falling in love with Pascal, end up happily married to C.

History Of C Language

By 1960 a hoarde of computer languages had come into existence, almost each for a specific purpose. For example, COBOL was being used for Commercial Applications, FORTRAN for Engineering and Scientific Applications and so on. At this stage people started thinking that instead of learning and using so many languages, each for a different purpose, why not use only one language which can program all possible applications. Therefore, an international committee was set up to develop such a language. This committee came out with a language called ALGOL 60. However, ALGOL 60 never really beacame popular because it seemed too abstract, too general. To reduce this abstractness and generality, a new language called Combined Programming Language (CPL) was developed at Cambridge University. CPL was an attempt to bring ALGOL 60 down to earth. However, CPL turned out to be so big, having so many features, that it was hard to learn and difficult to implement.

Basic Combined Programming Language (BCPL), developed by Martin Richards at Cambridge University aimed to solve this problem by bringing CPL down to its basic good features. But unfortunately it turned out to be too less powerful and too specific. Around same time a language called B was written by Ken Thompson at AT & T's Bell Labs, as a further simplification of CPL. But like BCPL, B too turned out to be very specific. Ritchie inherited the features of B and BCPL, added some of his own and developed C. Ritchie's main achievement is the restoration of the lost generality in BCPL and B, and still keeping it powerful.

C's compactness and coherence is mainly due to the fact that it's a one man language. Other examples of one man languages are LISP, PASCAL and APL. Counter examples include many headed monsters like PL/I, ALGOL 60 and ADA.

Figure 2.1 shows the various stages in evolution of C language.

Year	Language	Developed by	Remarks
1960	ALGOL	International Committee	Too general, too abstract
1963	CPL	Cambridge University	Hard to learn, difficult to implement
1967	BCPL	Martin Richards at Cambridge University	Too specific, could deal with only specific problems
1970	B	Ken Thompson at AT & T's Bell Labs.	Too specific, could deal with only specific problems
1972	C	Dennis Ritchie at AT & T's Bell Labs.	Lost generality of BCPL and B restored

Figure 2.1

Let us now see how does C compare with other programming languages. All the programming languages can be divided into two categories:

(a) Problem oriented languages or High level languages:
These languages have been designed to give a better programming efficiency, i.e. faster program development. Examples of languages falling in this category are FORTRAN, BASIC, PASCAl etc.

(b) Machine oriented languages or Low level languages:
These languages have been designed to give a better machine efficiency, i.e. faster program execution. Examples of languages falling in this category are Assembly language and Machine language.

C stands in between these two categories. That's why it is often called a Middle level language, since it was designed to have both: a relatively good progamming efficiency (as compared to Machine oriented languages) and a relatively good machine efficiency (as compared to Problem oriented languages).

Structure Of A C Program

Any C program consists of one or more distinct units called 'functions'. These functions consist of valid C statements and are linked together through 'function calls'. A 'function' is analogous to a subroutine or a procedure in other high level languages. Every 'function' in a program has a unique name and is designed to perform a specific task. The task to be accomplished by the function is defined by a group or block of instructions or statements. Each function with its block of statements is treated as one single unit in C language and can be placed anywhere in the program.

Each instruction in a function is written as a separate statement. These statements must appear in the same order in which we wish them to be executed; unless of course the logic of the problem demands a deliberate 'jump' or transfer of control to a statement which is out of sequence. However big a C program, the following rules are applicable to all statements present in it:

(a) Blank spaces may be inserted between two words to improve the readability of the statement. However, no blank spaces are allowed within a word.

(b) Usually all C statements are entered in small case letters.

(c) C has no specific rules about the position at which different parts of a statement are to be written. Not only can a C statement be written anywhere in a line, it can also be split over multiple lines. That is why it is many a times called a free form language.

(d) Any C statement always ends with a semicolon (;).

Figure 2.2 shows the skeleton of a typical C program which satisfies the afore-mentioned rules. Alongside a simple C program to calculate simple interest is also shown. At this stage you may not be able to understand this program. Don't worry, it has been given here just as a sample program.

```
main( )
{
    statement 1 ;
    statement 2 ;
}
function1( )
{
    variable declarations ;
    statement 1 ;
    statement 2 ;
}
```

Structure of C Program

```
/* Calculation of simple interest */
/* Author gekay    Date 12/01/94*/
main( )
{
    float p, n, r, si ;
    p = 1000 ;
    n = 3 ;
    r = 8.5 ;
    si = p * n * r / 100 ;
    printf ( "%f" , si ) ;
}
```

Sample C Program

Figure 2.2

Some conclusions can now be drawn from the program given in Figure 2.2

(a) A C program is nothing but a collection of one or more functions. A function name is always followed by a pair of parentheses, as in case of **main( )**.

(b) Every program must have a special function named **main( )**. The program execution starts from this function.

(c) The statements within a function are always enclosed within a pair of braces { }.

(d) The group of statements within **main( )** are executed sequentially. The closing brace of the **main( )** function signals the end of the program. When this brace is reached, the program execution stops and the control is handed over to the operating system.

(e) There should be a **main( )** function somewhere in the program so that the computer can determine where to start the execution.

(f) The **main( )** function can be located anywhere in the program, but the general practice is to place it as the first function for better readability.

How exactly does the simple interest program works? Well, for that you will have to wait for some more time. We will have to first understand the concepts of constants, variables and control instructions before we can grasp it. And this is what we intend to learn in the next few chapters.

Exercise

[A] Pick up the correct alternative for each of the following questions.

(1) C is a

(a) Middle level language
(b) High level language
(c) Low level language
(d) None of the above

(2) C can be used on

(a) Only MS DOS operating system
(b) Only UNIX operating system
(c) Only XENIX operating system
(d) All the above

(3) C programs are converted to the machine language with the help of

(a) An interpreter
(b) A compiler
(c) An assembler
(d) None of the above

(4) Which of the following statements is false

(a) Each new C instruction has to be written on a separate line
(b) Usually all C statements are entered in small case letters
(c) Blank spaces may be inserted between two words in a C statement
(d) C statement always ends with a semicolon

(5) C language has been developed by

(a) Ken Thompson
(b) Dennis Ritchie
(c) Peter Norton
(d) Martin Richards

(6) C language has been developed at

(a) Microsoft Corp., USA
(b) AT & T's Bell Labs, USA
(c) Borland International, USA
(d) Ashton Tate Corp., USA

(7) C language came into existence in the year

(a) 1971
(b) 1957
(c) 1972
(d) 1983

(8) A C program is a collection of

(a) Subroutines
(b) Functions
(c) Procedures
(d) None of the above

(9) Statements in a C program should begin

(a) In 1st column
(b) In 7th column
(c) In 10th column
(d) In any column

(10) Any C statement must end with a

(a) .
(b) ;
(c) !
(d) #

(11) The statements within a C function must always be enclosed within a pair of

(a) ( )
(b) [ ]
(c) { }
(d) < >

(12) Every C program must contain a

(a) printf( ) function
(b) scanf( ) function
(c) exit( ) function
(d) main( ) function

(13) A main( ) function in a C program should be located

(a) at the beginning of the program
(b) at the end of the program
(c) in the middle of the program
(d) anywhere in the program

CHAPTER

3 *Data Types, Variables And Constants*

The C Character Set
Data Types
Constants And Variables
C Constants
C Variables
C Keywords
The First C Program
Type Modifiers
Storage Class Specifiers

Communicating with a computer involves speaking the language the computer understands, which immediately rules out English as the language of communication with computer. However, there is a close analogy between learning English language and learning C language. The classical method of learning English is to first learn the alphabets or characters used in the language, then learn to combine these alphabets to form words, which in turn are combined to form sentences and sentences are combined to form paragraphs. Learning C is similar and much more easy.

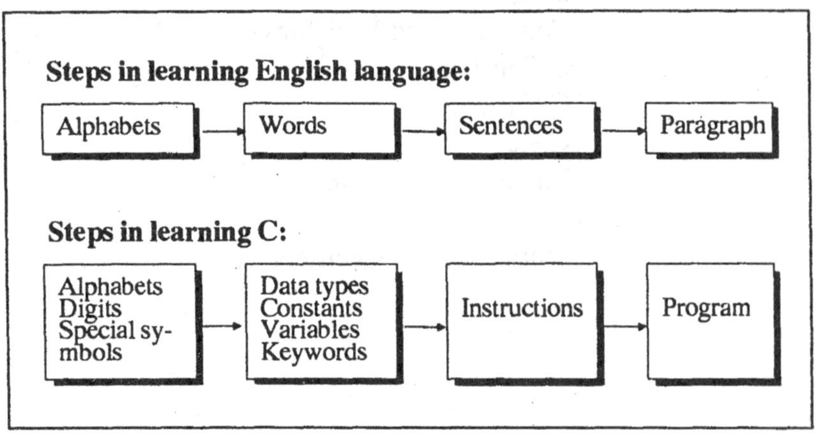

Figure 3.1

Therefore, instead of straight-away learning how to write programs, we must first know which alphabets, numbers and special symbols are used in C, then how using these data types, constants, variables and keywords are constructed, and finally how are these combined to form an instruction. A group of instructions would be combined later on to form a program. This is illustrated in Figure 3.1.

The C Character Set

A character denotes any alphabet, digit or special symbol used to represent information. Following table shows the valid alphabets, numbers and special symbols allowed in C:

<table>
<tr><td>Alphabets</td><td>A, B, ... , Y, Z
a, b, ... , y, z</td></tr>
<tr><td>Digits</td><td>0, 1, 2, 3, 4, 5, 6, 7, 8, 9</td></tr>
<tr><td>Special symbols</td><td>~ ‘ ! @ # % ^ & * ( ) _ - + =
| \ { } [ ] : ; " ’ < > , . ? /</td></tr>
</table>

Figure 3.2

Let us now see how these characters are combined to form data types, constants, variables and keywords.

Data Types

‘Data’ is possibly one word which has been used with gay abandon by programmers. It is almost impossible for a programmer to talk for two minutes about computing without saying 'data' in one context or the other. There are data types, data objects, data structures, data flow, data bases, data corruption, data validation, and so on - all of which are parts of data processing. Here however, we are concerned with only a part of the jargon - the 'data types'.

There are two fundamentally different types of data in C programming - integer and floating point. From these two we can derive two others - character and double precision. There also exists a data type called void, which isn't used as often as the other four. The bytes occupied by each of these data types as well as the name used to refer to them is shown in Figure 3.3

Data type	Meaning	Size (bytes)
char	a character	1
int	an integer	2
float	a single precision real number	4
double	a double precision real number	8
void	valueless	0

Figure 3.3

The data type **char** is used to store any character belonging to the C character set seen earlier. **int** type is used to store positive or negative integers. A **float** data type stores a single precision floating point (real) number. A **double** data type can store a floating point value with a greater exactness than a **float**. Hence it usually requires twice as much storage space as a **float** does. The use of **double** doesn't guarentee to double the number of significant digits in our results, but it improves the accuracy of the arithmetic and reduces the accumulation of rounding errors.

The data type **void** is used to specify an empty set of values. Its use can be appreciated in the chapters on Functions (Chapter 8) and Pointers (Chapter 9).

These data types put together are often known as 'Primary' data types. Several other data types can be derived from these Primary data types. Such data types are known as 'Secondary' data types or 'Derived' data types. The following figure shows these different data types.

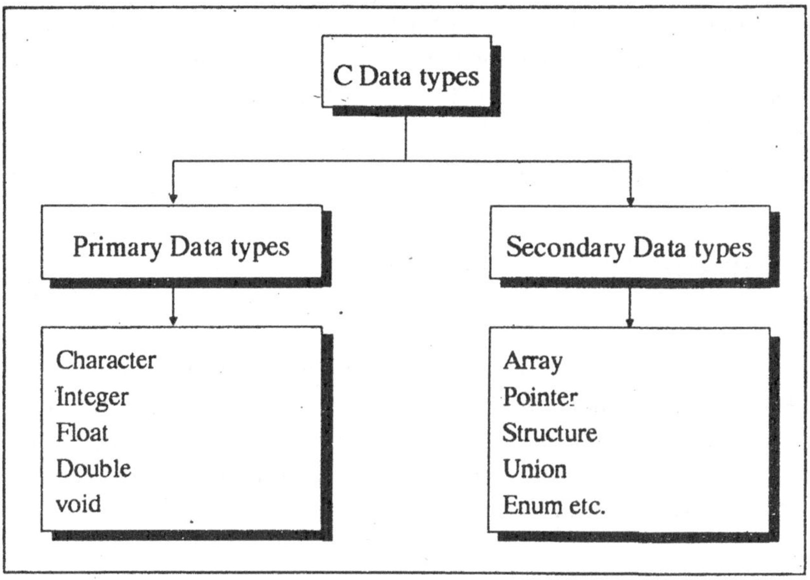

Figure 3.4

Constants And Variables

The alphabets, numbers and special symbols when properly combined form constants and variables. Let us see what are 'constants' and 'variables' in C. A 'constant' is a quantity that doesn't change. This quantity can be stored at a location in the memory of the computer. A variable can be considered as a name given to the location in memory where this constant is stored. Naturally the contents of the variable can change. For example in the equation

$$3X + Y = 20$$

since 3 and 20 cannot change, they are called constants, whereas the quantities X & Y can vary or change hence are called variables.

To be able to write error free programs, we will now take up a detailed discussion about, the different fundamental elements of C language, viz., constants, variables and keywords. Possibly, an absolutely clear understanding about the constants, variables and keywords and their interaction with one another is the single most important factor contributing towards writing error free programs.

C Constants

At this stage we would restrict our discussion to the more commonly used constants like character, integer, float, logical and string constants. Let us see the details of each of these constants. For constructing these different types of constants certain rules have been laid down. These rules are as under:

Rules For Constructing Integer Constants

(a) An integer constant must have at least one digit.
(b) It must not have a decimal point.
(c) It could be either positive or negative.
(d) If no sign precedes an integer constant it is assumed to be positive.
(e) No commas or blanks are allowed within an integer constant.
(f) The allowable range for integer constants is -32768 to +32767.

Integer constants must fall within this range because the IBM compatible microcomputers are usually 16 bit computers which cannot support a number falling outside the above mentioned range. For a 32 bit computer of course the range may be much larger.

Ex.: 426
+782
-8000
-7605

Rules For Constructing Real Constants

Real constants are often called Floating Point constants. The real constants could be written in two forms, Fractional form or Exponential form.

Following rules must be observed while constructing Real Constants expressed in Fractional form:

(a) A real constant must have atleast one digit.
(b) It must have a decimal point.
(c) It could be either positive or negative.
(d) Default sign is positive.
(e) No commas or blanks are allowed within a real constant.

Ex.: +325.34
426.0
-32.76
-48.5792

The exponential form of representation of real constants is usually used if the value of the constant is either too small or too large. It however dosen't restrict us in any way from using exponential form of representation for other real constants.

In exponential form of representation, the real constant is represented in two parts. The part appearing before 'e' is called mantissa, whereas the part following 'e' is called exponent. In place of a small case 'e' a capital 'E' can also be used.

Following rules must be observed while construction of Real Constants expressed in Exponential Form :

(a) The mantissa part and the exponent part should be separated by a letter e.
(b) The mantissa part may have a positive or a negative sign.
(c) Default sign of mantissa part is positive.
(d) The exponent must have at least one digit which must be a positive or a negative integer. Default sign is positive.
(e) Range of real constants expresed in exponential form is -3.4e38 to 3.4e38.

Ex.: +3.2e-5
4.1e8
-0.2e+3
-3.2e-5

Rules For Constructing Character Constants

(a) A character constant is either a single alphabet, a single digit or a single special symbol enclosed within a pair of single inverted commas. Both the inverted commas should point to the left. For Example, 'A' is a valid character constant whereas 'A' is not.
(b) The maximum length of a character constant can be 1 character.
Ex. 'A'
'I'
'5'
(c) The valid range of character constant is -128 to +127. It appears surprising that the character constant should have a numeric

range. But this fact can be appreciated once we understand that character and integer constants are often used interchangeably. For example, 'A' and 65 are one and the same thing, since when we say 'A' it is replaced by its ASCII value, which is 65.

The ranges of Integer, Float and Character constants are shown in Figure 3.5.

Logical Constants

A Logical constant can take either of two values: truth or falsity. In C a non-zero value is always treated as truth whereas a zero is treated as falsity. Hence values like 32, -45, 3.12 etc. are treated as logical constants having a truth value, whereas a 0 is treated as a logical constant with a false value. The logical constants are very useful in evaluating logical expressions and complex conditions as we would see in Chapters 4 and 5.

String Constants

A collection of characters enclosed within a pair of double inverted commas is treated as a string constant.

Ex.: "Hello"
"44-A, Gokulpeth, Nagpur"
"34.567"

In the above example though 34.567 appears to be a real constant, once it is enclosed within inverted commas there onwards it is treated as a string constant. Though not shown explicitly in the above examples each string constant always ends with a special character '\0'. This character acts as a string terminator. Using this fact we can find out where a string ends. The string of characters used in a string constant are always stored in adjacent memory locations. This arrangement is shown in Figure 3.6.

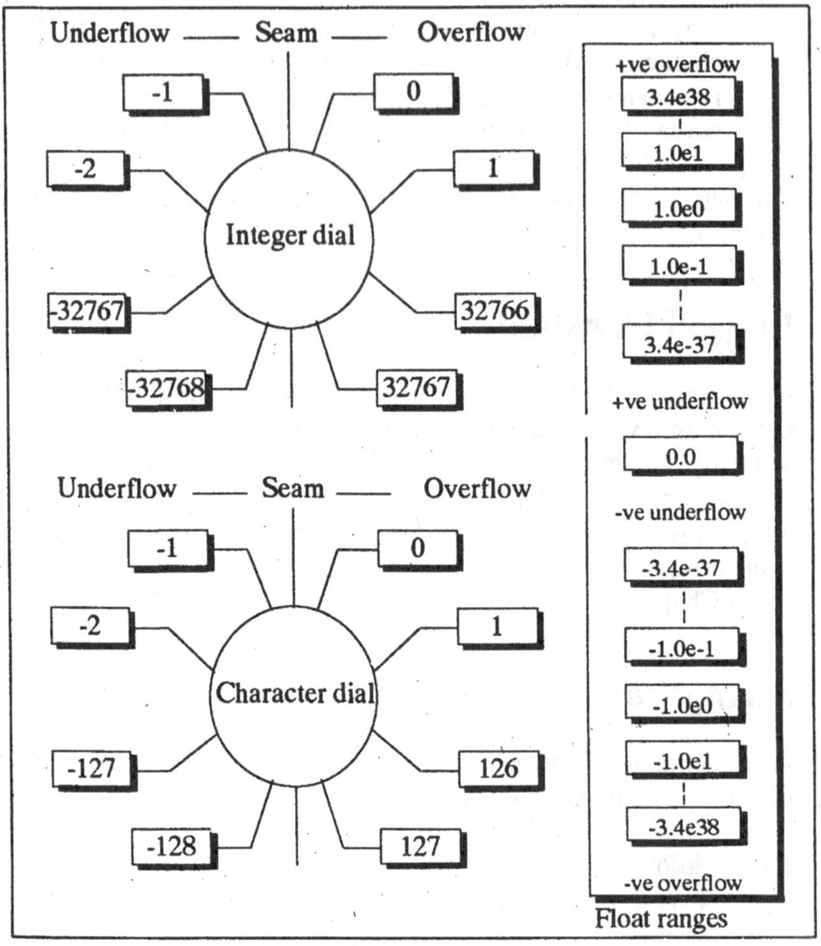

Figure 3.5 Integer, Character and Float ranges

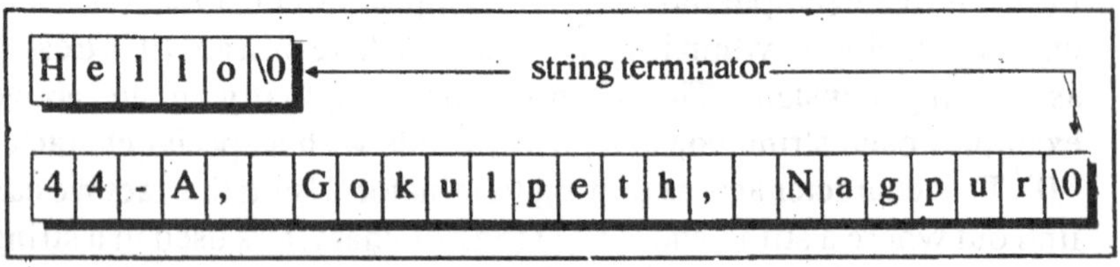

Figure 3.6

C Variables

In C, a quantity which may vary during program execution is called a variable. Variable names are names given to the locations in memory of a computer where different constants are stored. These locations can contain character, integer, real, or any such constants. In any language, the types of variables that it can support depends on the types of constants that it can handle. This is because a constant stored in a location with a particular type of variable name can hold only that type of constant. For example, a constant stored in a memory location with an integer variable name must be an integer constant, one stored in a location with a real variable name must be a real constant and the one stored in a location with a character variable name must be a character constant and so on.

The rules for constructing different type of constants are different. However for constructing variable names of all types the same set of rules apply. These rules are given below.

Rules For Constructing Variable Names

(a) A variable name is any combination of 1 to 8 alphabets, digits or underscores. Some compilers allow variables names whose length could be upto 40 characters. Still, it would be safer to stick to the rule of 8 characters.

(b) The first character in the variable name must be an alphabet.

(c) No commas or blanks are allowed within a variable name.

(d) No special symbol other than an underscore (as in **gross_sal**) can be used in a variable name.

Ex.:
```
si_int
m_hra
bassal
pop_e_89
```

Variable Declaration

The rules for constructing variables remain same for all types of variables: integer variables, real variables, character variables, string variables etc. For that matter, even all the secondary variables (of which, we have not talked much as yet) are constructed using the same rules mentioned above. Naturally, the question follows... How is C able to differentiate between these variables? This is a rather simple matter. C compiler is able to distinguish between the variable names, by making it compulsory for you to declare the type of any variable name which you wish to use in a program. This type declaration is done at the beginning of the program. Following are the examples of type declaration statements:

Ex.:
```
int si, m_hra ;
float bassal ;
char code ;
```

Since the maximum length of a variable name is 8 characters, an enormous number of variable names can be constructed using the afore- mentioned rules. It is a good practice to exploit this enormous choice in naming variables by using meaningful variable names.

Thus, if we want to calculate simple interest, it is always advisable to construct meaningful variable names like **prin, roi, noy** to represent Principle, Rate of interest and Number of years rather than using the variables **a, b, c**.

Scope Of Variables: Local & Global

Scope of variable means where the variable is available within the program. All variables may not necessarily be available to all statements in a program. Variables can have two types of scopes - local and global. A variable with a global scope is accessible to all the statements in the program, whereas the one with local scope is available only to certain selected statements in the program. Global variables are declared outside all functions whereas the local variables are defined inside a function. The details of these declaration we would postpone till the end of the chapter. Before that let us first look at another important component of a C program - 'keywords'.

C Keywords

Keywords are the words whose meaning has already been explained to the C compiler (or in a broad sense to the computer). The keywords **cannot** be used as variable names because if we do so we are trying to assign a new meaning to the keyword, which is not allowed by the computer. Some C compilers allow you to construct variable names which exactly resemble the keywords. However, it would be safer not to mix up the variable names and the keywords. The keywords are also known as 'Resreved words'.

There are only 32 keywords available in C. Figure 3.7 shows a list of these keywords, given here for your ready reference. A detailed discussion of each of these keywords would be taken up in later chapters wherever their use is relevant.

auto	double	int	struct
break	else	long	switch
case	enum	register	typedef
char	extern	return	union
const	float	short	unsigned
continue	for	signed	void
default	goto	sizeof	volatile
do	if	static	while

Figure 3.7

The First C Program

Armed with the knowledge about the types of variables, constants & keywords, and the hierarchy of operations, we would now try to write down our first C program. To keep things simple we would begin with the most elementary one. The one which will find out the average of three numbers. Here it is...

```
/* Calculation of average of three numbers */
main( )
{
    int a, b, c, avg ;

    a = 100 ;
    b = 120 ;
    c = 180 ;

    avg = ( a + b + c ) / 3 ;
    printf ( "%d", avg ) ;
}
```

Now a few useful tips about the program...

- Comment about the program should be enclosed within /* */. For example, the first statement in our program is a comment.

- Any number of comments can be given at any place in the program.

- Comments cannot be nested. For example,

  ```
  /* Cal of SI /* Author Sam date 01/01/90 */ */
  ```

  is invalid.

- A comment can be split over more than one line, as in,

```
/* This is
   a jazzy
   comment */
```

- Although a lot of comments are probably not necessary in this program, it is usually the case that programmers tend to use too few comments rather than too many. Comments should be used at any place where there is possibility of confusion. We will refrain from repeating the standard lecture on how adequate number of comments can save hours of misery and suffering when you later try to figure out what the program does.

- Any C program is nothing but a combination of functions. **main( )** is one such function. Empty parentheses after **main** are necessary.

- The set of statements belonging to a function are enclosed within a pair of braces.

  For example,

```
main( )
{
    statement 1 ;
    statement 2 ;
    statement 3 ;
}
```

Any variable used in the program must be declared before using it.

Ex.: `int a, b, c ;`

Any C statement always ends with a ;

Ex.:
```
int a, b, c ;
c = 180 ;
```

In the statement,

```
avg = ( a + b + c ) / 3 ;
```

* and / are the arithmetic operators. The arithmetic operators available in C are **+**, **-**, ***** and **/**. C is very rich in operators. There are about 45 operators available in C. Surprisingly, there is no operator for exponentiation... a slip, which can be forgiven considering the fact that C has been developed by one man rather than a team.

printf( ) is a function which is used to print the value contained in a variable on the screen.

The general form of **printf** statement is ,

```
printf ("<format string"> , <list of variables> ) ;
```

<format string> could be:

%c for printing character values
%d for printing integer values
%f for printing float values
%lf for printing double values

Following are some examples of usage of **printf( )** statement:

```
printf ( "%f", si ) ;
printf ( "%f %f %f %f", p, n, r, si ) ;
printf ( "Simple interest = Rs. %f", si ) ;
printf ( "Average = %d \nSum = %d", avg, sum ) ;
```

The output of the last statement would look like this...

```
Average = 100
Sum = 300
```

What is '\n' doing in this statement ? It is called a 'newline' and it takes the cursor to the next line. Therefore, you get the output split over two lines. '\n' is one of the several 'escape sequences' available in C. These are discussed in detail in Chapter 6. Right now, all that we can say is '\n' comes in handy when we want to format the output properly on separate lines.

In the above progam we assumed the values of **a**, **b** and **c** to be 100, 120, and 180. If we want to make a provision for supplying the values of **a**, **b** and **c** through the keyboard, a statement called **scanf** should be used. This is illustrated in the program given below:

```
main( )
{
    int a, b, c, avg ;

    printf ( "Enter values of a, b, c" ) ;
    scanf ( "%d %d %d", &p, &n, &r ) ;
    avg = ( a + b + c ) / 3 ;
    printf ( "%d", avg ) ;
}
```

The first **printf( )** statement outputs the message 'Enter values of a, b, c' on the screen. Here we have not used any variables in **printf( )** which means that using variables in **printf( )** is optional. Note that using the ampersand (&) before the variables in the **scanf** statement is a must. & is a pointer operator. The meaning and working of this pointer operator would be taken up later during the discussion on pointers. Also note that the values for **a**, **b** and **c** to be supplied through the keyboard, must be seperated by a blank, a tab or a newline.

Ex.: The three values separated by blank.

```
110 275 140
```

Ex.: The three values separated by tab.

```
110	275	140
```

Ex.: The three values separated by newline.

```
110
275
140
```

So much for the tips. How about another program to give you a feel of the things...

```
/* Just for fun.   Author: Bozo */
main( )
{
    int num ;

    printf ( "Enter a number " ) ;
    scanf ( "%d", &num ) ;

    printf ( "Now I am letting you on a secret..." ) ;
    printf ( "You have just entered the number %d", num ) ;
}
```

Type Modifiers

As seen earlier the primary data types could be of five varieties: **character, integer, float, double** and **void.** It may seem odd to many, how C programmers manage with such a tiny set of data types. Fact is, the C programmers aren't really deprived. They can derive any number of data types from these five types. In fact, the number of data types that can be derived in C, is in principle, unlimited. A C programmer can always invent whatever data type he needs.

Not only this, the primary data types themselves could be of several types. For example, a **char** could be an **unsigned char** or a **signed char**. Or an **int** could be a **short int** or a **long int**. Sufficiently confusing? Well, let us take a closer look at these variations of primary data types.

Integers, Long & Short

We had seen earlier that an integer constant is any number in the range -32768 to +32767. This is because an integer constant always occupies two bytes in memory and in two bytes we cannot store a number bigger than +32767 or smaller than -32768.

Remember that out of the two bytes used to store an integer, the highest bit (sixteenth bit) is used to store the sign of the integer. This bit is 1 if the number is negative, and 0 if the number is positive. Most of the times C programs can be managed within this generous range, but bigger ranges are available should you need them. C offers a variation of the integer data type that will provide what are called **long** integer values. **long** integers require twice the space in memory than ordinary **ints** do. Thus, **long** integers would occupy four bytes of memory. **long** variables which hold **long** integers are declared using the keyword **long**, as in,

```
long int i ;
long int abc ;
```

long integers cause the program to run a bit slower, but the range of values that we can use is expanded tremendously. The value of a **long** integer can vary from -2147483648 to +2147483647. More than this you should not need unless you are taking a world census.

If there are such things as **longs**, symmetry requires **shorts** as well... integers which need less space in memory and thus help speed up program execution. **short** integer variables are declared as,

```
short int j ;
short int height ;
```

In fact, a **short int** is nothing but our ordinary **int**, which we were using all the time without knowing that it was a **short int**. C allows the abbreviation of **short int** to **int** and of **long int** to **long**. So the declarations made above can be written as,

```
long i ;
long abc ;
int j ;
int height ;
```

Naturally, most C programmers prefer this short-cut.

Sometimes we come across situations where the constant is small enough to be an **int**, but still we want to give it as much storage as a **long**. In such cases we add the suffix 'L' or 'l' at the end of the number. Thus 23 is an integer and would occupy two bytes, whereas 23L is a long integer and hence would occupy four bytes.

Integers, Signed & Unsigned

Sometimes, we know in advance that the value stored in a given integer variable will always be positive - when it is being used to only count things, for example. In such a case we can declare the variable to be **unsigned**, as in,

```
unsigned int num_students ;
```

With such a declaration, the range of permissible integer values will shift from the range -32768 to +32767 to the range 0 to 65535. Thus, declaring the integers as **unsigned** almost doubles the size of the largest possible value that it can otherwise take. This so happens because on declaring the integer as **unsigned**, the sixteenth bit is now free and is not used to store the sign of the number. Note that an **unsigned** integer still occupies two bytes.

In fact the **unsigned int** is nothing but a **short unsigned int**. Thus, all the following declarations are same:

```
short unsigned int i ;
unsigned int i ;
unsigned i ;
```

The way there exists a **short unsigned int**, there also exists a **long unsigned int** which has a range of 0 to 4294967295 and occupies four bytes of memory.

By default a **short int** is a **signed short int** and a **long int** is a **signed long int**.

Chars, Signed & Unsigned

The way there are **signed** and **unsigned ints** (either **short** or **long**), similarly there are **signed** and **unsigned chars**, both occupying one byte each, but having different ranges. A **signed char** is same as our ordinary **char** and has a range from -128 to +127; whereas an **unsigned char** has a range from 0 to 255. Let us now see a program that illustrates this range:

```
main( )
{
    char ch = 291 ;
    printf ( "%d %c\n", ch, ch ) ;
}
```

What output do you expect from this program? Possibly, 291 and the character corresponding to it. Well, not really. Surprised? The reason is that **ch** has been defined as a **char**, and a **char** cannot take a value bigger than +128. Hence when value of **ch** exceeds +127, an appropriate value from the other side of the range is picked up and stored in **ch**. This value in our case happens to be 35, hence 35 and its corresponding character, #, gets printed out.

Let us now write a program which puts to use all the data types that we have learnt in this chapter. Go through the following program carefully, which shows how to use these different data types. Note the format specifiers used to input and output these data types.

```
main( )
{
    char c ;
    unsigned char d ;
    int i ;
    unsigned int j ;
    long int k ;
    unsigned long int m ;
    float x ;
    double y ;

    scanf ( "%c %c", &c, &d ) ;
    printf ( "%c %c", c, d ) ;
    scanf ( "%d %u", &i, &j ) ;
    printf ( "%d %u", i, j ) ;
    scanf ( "%ld %lu", &k, &m ) ;
    printf ( "%ld %lu", k, m ) ;
    scanf ( "%f %lf", &x, &y ) ;
    printf ( "%f %lf", x, y ) ;
}
```

Let us capture the essence of all the data types that we have learnt so far in a figure.

Data Type	Range	Bytes	Format
signed char	-128 to + 127	1	%c
unsigned char	0 to 255	1	%c
short signed int	-32768 to +32767	2	%d
short unsigned int	0 to 65535	2	%u
long signed int	-2147483648 to +2147483647	4	%ld
long unsigned int	0 to 4294967295	4	%lu
float	-3.4e38 to +3.4e38	4	%f
double	-1.7e308 to +1.7e308	8	%lf
long double	-1.7e4932 to 1.7e4932	10	%Lf

Figure 3.8 Datatypes in C

Storage Class Specifiers

We have already said all that needs to be said about constants, but we are not finished with variables. To fully define a variable one needs to mention not only its 'type' but also its 'storage class'. In other words, not only do all variables have a data type, they also have a 'storage class'.

We have not mentioned storage classes yet, though we have written a program in C. We were able to get away with this because storage classes have defaults. If we don't specify the storage class of a variable in its declaration, the compiler will assume a storage class dependent on the context in which the variable is used. Thus, C has got certain default storages classes.

From C compiler's point of view, a variable name identifies some physical location within the computer where the string of bits representing the variable's value is stored. There are basically two kinds of locations in a computer where such a value may be kept: Memory and CPU registers. It is the variable's storage class which determines in which of these two locations the value is stored.

Moreover, a variable's storage class tells us:

(a) Where the variable would be stored.
(b) What will be the initial value of the variable, if the initial value is not specifically assigned. (i.e. the default initial value).
(c) What is the scope of the variable; i.e. in which functions the value of the variable would be available.
(d) What is the life of the variable; i.e. how long would the variable exist.

There are four storage classes in C :

(a) Automatic storage class
(b) Register storage class
(c) Static storage class
(d) External storage class

Let us examine these storage classes one by one.

Automatic Storage Class

The features of a variable defined to have an automatic storage class are as under:

Storage	- Memory.
Default initial value	- An unpredictable value, which is often called a garbage value.
Scope	- Local to the block in which the variable is defined.
Life	- Till the control remains within the block in which it is defined.

Following program shows how an automatic storage class is declared, and the fact that if the variable is not initialised it contains a garbage value.

```
main( )
{
    auto int i, j ;
    printf ( "%d\n%d", i, j ) ;
}
```

The output of the above program could be...

```
1211
221
```

where, 1211 and 221 are garbage values of **i** and **j**. When you run this program you may get different values, since garbage values could be absolutely any values. So always make it a point that you initialise the automatic variables properly, otherwise you are likely to get unexpected results. Note that the keyword for this storage class is **auto** and not automatic.

Scope and life of an automatic variable is illustrated in the following program.

```
main( )
{
    auto int i = 1 ;
    {
        {
            {
                printf ( "%d\n", i ) ;
            }
            printf ( "%d\n", i ) ;
        }
        printf ( "%d\n", i ) ;
    }
}
```

```
}
```

The output of the above program is:

```
1
1
1
```

This is because, all **printf( )** statements occur within the outermost block (a block is all statements enclosed within a pair of braces) in which i has been defined. It means the scope of i is local to the block in which it is defined.

The moment the control comes out of the block in which the variable is defined, the variable and its value is irretrievably lost. To catch my point, go through the following program.

```
main( )
{
	auto int i = 1 ;
	{
		auto int i = 2 ;
		{
			auto int i = 3 ;
			printf ( "%d\n", i ) ;
		}
		printf ( "%d\n", i ) ;
	}
	printf ( "%d\n", i ) ;
}
```

The output of the above program would be:

```
3
2
1
```

Note that the Compiler treats the three **i**'s as totally different variables, since they are defined in different blocks. Once the control comes out of the innermost block the variable **i** with value 3 is lost, and hence the **i** in the second **printf( )** refers to **i** with value 2. Similarly when the control comes out of the next innermost block, the third **printf( )** refers to the **i** with value 1.

Understand the concept of life and scope of an automatic storage class variable thoroughly before proceeding with the next storage class.

Register Storage Class

The features of a variable defined to be of **register** type are as under:

Storage	- CPU registers.
Default initial value	- garbage value.
Scope	- Local to the block in which it is defined.
Life	- Till the control remains within the block in which it is deifned.

Value stored in a CPU register can always be accessed faster than the one which is stored in memory. Therefore, if a variable is used at many places in a program it is better to declare its storage class as **register**. A good example of frequently used variables are loop counters. We can name their storage class as **register**.

```
main( )
{
    register int i ;

    /* this is a for loop in C */
    for ( i = 1 ; i <= 10 ; i++ )
        printf ( "%d", i ) ;
}
```

Here, even though we have declared the storage class of **i** as **register**, we cannot say for sure that the value of **i** would be stored in a CPU register. Why? Because the number of CPU registers are limited (14 in case of a microcomputer), and they may be busy doing some other task. What happens in such an event... the variable works as if its storage class is **auto**.

We cannot use **register** storage class for all types of variables. For example, the following declarations are wrong:

```
register float q ;
register double a ;
register long c ;
```

This is because the CPU registers in a microcomputer are usually 16 bit registers and therefore cannot hold a **float** value or a **double** value, which require 4 and 8 bytes respectively for storing a value. However, if you use the above declarations you won't get any error messages. All that would happen is the compiler would print the variables to be of **auto** storage class.

Static Storage Class

The features of a variable defined to have a **static** storage class are as under:

Storage	- Memory.
Default initial value	- Zero.
Scope	- Local to the block in which it is defined.
Life	- Value of the variable persists between different function calls.

Compare the two programs and their output given in Figure 3.9 to understand the difference between the storage classes **automatic** and **static**.

```
main( )                              main( )
{                                    {
    increment( ) ;                       increment( ) ;
    increment( ) ;                       increment( ) ;
    increment( ) ;                       increment( ) ;
}                                    }

increment( )                         increment( )
{                                    {
    auto int i = 1 ;                     static int i = 1 ;
    printf ( "%d\n", i ) ;               printf ( "%d\n", i ) ;
    i = i + 1 ;                          i = i + 1 ;
}                                    }

The output of the above programs would be:

1                                    1
1                                    2
1                                    3
```

Figure 3.9

We haven't done function calls as yet. The programs above consist of two functions **main( )** and **increment( )**. The function **increment( )** increments the value of **i** and prints it. The function **increment( )** gets called from **main( )** thrice. Whenever a function is called, the control is transferred to this function, all statements within it are executed and then the control is returned to the next statement after the place from where the function call was made. The only difference in the two programs is that one uses an **auto** storage class for variable **i**, whereas the other uses **static** storage class.

Like **auto** variables, **static** variables are also local to the block in which they are declared. The difference between them is that **static** variables don't disappear when the function is no longer active. Their values persist. If the control comes back to the same function again the **static** variables have the same values they had last time around.

In the above example, when variable **i** is **auto**, each time **increment( )** is called it is re-initialised to one. When the function terminates, **i** vanishes and its new value of 2 is lost. The result: no matter how many times we call **increment( )**, **i** is initialised to 1 every time.

On the other hand, if **i** is **static**, it is initialised to 1 only once. It is never initialised again. During the first call to **increment( )**, **i** is incremented to 2. Because **i** is static, this value persists. The next time **increment( )** is called, **i** is not re-initialised to 1; on the contrary its old value 2 is still available. This current value of **i** (i.e. 2) gets printed and then **i = i + 1** adds 1 to **i** to get a value of 3. The third time **increment( )** is called, the current value of **i** (i.e. 3) gets printed and once again **i** is incremented. In short if the storage class is **static** then the statement **static int i = 1** is executed only once, irrespective of how many times the same function is called.

All this having been said, a word of advice: avoid using static variables unless you really need them. Because their values are kept in memory when the variables are not active, which means they take up space in memory that could otherwise be used by other variables.

External Storage Class

The features of a variable whose storage class has been defined as extern are as follows:

Storage	- Memory
Default initial value	- Zero
Scope	- Global
Life	- As long as the program's execution doesn't come to an end.

External variables differ from those we have already discussed in that their scope is global, not local. External variables are declared outside all functions, yet are available to all functions that care to use them. Here is an example to illustrate this fact.

```
int i ;
main( )
{
     printf ( "i = ", i ) ;
     increment( ) ;  /* function call */
     increment( ) ;
     decrement( ) ;  /* function call */
     decrement( ) ;
}
increment( )
{
     i = i + 1 ;
     printf ( "on incrementing i = %d\n", i ) ;
}
decrement( )
{
     i = i - 1 ;
     printf ( "on decrementing i = %d\n", i ) ;
}
```

The output would be:

```
i = 0
on incrementing i = 1
on incrementing i = 2
on decrementing i = 1
on decrementing i = 0
```

As is obivous from the above output, the value of **i** is available to the functions **increment( )** and **decrement( )** since **i** has been declared outside all functions.

Strictly speaking the function that uses an external variable should declare that variable external via the keyword **extern**, as shown below.

```
int x = 21 ;
main( )
{
    extern int x ;
    printf ( "%d", x ) ;
}
```

Then how come the previous program worked without using the keyword **extern** in **increment( )** or **decrement( )**. This is because use of **extern** inside a function is optional as long as as we declare it outside and above that function in the same source code file.

Another small issue. What will be the output of the following program?

```
int x = 10 ;
main( )
{
    int x = 20 ;
    printf ( "%d\n", x ) ;
    display( ) ;
}
display( )
{
    printf ( "%d", x ) ;
}
```

Here **x** is defined at two places, once outside **main( )** and once inside it. When the control reaches the **printf( )** in **main( )** which **x** gets printed? Whenever such a conflict arises it's the local variable which gets preference over the global variable. Hence the **printf( )** outputs 20. When **display( )**is called and control reaches the **printf( )** there is no such conflict. Hence this time the value of the global **x**, i.e. 10 gets printed.

Which To Use When

Dennis Ritchie has made available to the C programmer a number of storage classes with varying features, believing that the programmer is in a best position to decide which one of these storage classes is to be used when. We can make a few ground rules for usage of different storage classes in different programming situations with a view to :

(a) economise the memory space consumed by the variables
(b) improve the speed of execution of the program

The rules are as under:

- Use **static** storage class only if you want the value of a variable to persist between different function calls. A typical application of this storage class is recursive functions which are discussed at length in Chapter 8.

- Use **register** storage class for only those variables which are being used very often in the program. Reason is, there are very few CPU registers at our disposal and many of them might be busy doing something else. Make careful utilisation of the scarce resources. A typical application of **reigster** storage class is loop counters, which get used a number of times in a program.

- Use **extern** storage class for only those variables which are being used by almost all the functions in the program. This would avoid unnecessary passing of these variables as arguments when making a function call. Declaring all the variables as **extern** would amount to a lot of wastage of memory space because these variables remain active throughout the life of the program.

If you don't have any of the express needs mentioned above, then use the **auto** storage class. In fact most of the times we end up using the **auto** variables, because often it so happens that once we have used the variables in a function we don't mind loosing them.

Exercise

[A] What will be the output of the following programs:

(1)
```
main( )
{
    /* sizeof operator gives size of a data type in bytes */
    char ch ;
    int a ;
    float b ;
    printf ( "bytes occupied by ch = %d\n", sizeof ( ch ) ) ;
    printf ( "bytes occupied by a = %d\n", sizeof ( a ) ) ;
    printf ( "bytes occupied by b = %d\n", sizeof ( b ) ) ;
}
```

(2)
```
main( )
{
    int a, b ;
    a = -3 - -3 ;
    b = -3 - -(-3) ;
    printf ( "a = %d b = %d", a, b ) ;
}
```

(3)
```
main( )
{
    register float r = 3.14 ;
    register double y = 3.4 ;
    printf ( "r = %f y = %lf", r, y ) ;
}
```

(4)
```
main( )
{
    auto int i = 100 ;
    printf ( "i = %d\n", i ) ;
    {
```

```
        int i = 1 ;
        printf ( "i = %d\n", i ) ;
        {
            i = i + 1 ;
            printf ( "i = %d\n", i ) ;
        }
        printf ( "i = %d\n", i ) ;
    }
    printf ( "i = %d\n", i ) ;
}
```

(5)
```
main( )
{
    int fh, cent ;

    printf ( "\nEnter temperature in farenheit " ) ;
    scanf ( "%d", &fh ) ;
    cent = ( fh - 32 ) * 5 / 9 ;
    printf ( "\nTemperature in centegrades is : %d", cent ) ;
}
```

(6)
```
main( )
{
    int a = 32768, b = -1 ;

    printf ( "\na = %d", a ) ;
    printf ( "\nb = %d", b ) ;
}
```

(7)
```
main( )
{
    float f = 3.14 ;
    int a = 10 ;
    printf ( "\nf = %d a = %d b = %d", f, a, b ) ;
    printf ( "\na = %d b = %d f = %d", a, b, f ) ;
}
```

(8)
```
int m ;
main( )
{
    auto int i ;
    register int j ;
    static int k ;
    printf ( "%d.%d %d %d", i, j, k, m ) ;
}
```

(9)
```
int i = 100 ;
int j = 200 ;
int k = 300 ;
main( )
{
    auto int i = 10 ;
    register int j = 20 ;
    static int k = 30 ;
    printf ( "%d %d %d", i, j, k ) ;
}
```

(10)
```
main( )
{
    int i = 10 ;
    char ch = 'A' ;
    float a = 3.14 ;
    printf ( "%d %c %f\n", i, ch, a ) ;
    printf ( "%d %f %f\n", i, ch, a ) ;
    printf ( "%f %c %f\n", i, ch, a ) ;
}
```

(11)
```
main( )
{
    int i = 10, j = 20 ;
    float a, b, c ;
    a = i / j ;
    b = 1.0 * i / j ;
```

```
    c = i / j * 1.0 ;
    printf ( "%f %f %f", a, b, c ) ;
}
```

(12)
```
main( )
{
    char ch = 300 ;
    int j = 300 ;
    printf ( "%d %c", ch, i ) ;
    printf ( "%c %d", ch, i ) ;

    ch = 40000 ;
    i = 40000 ;
    printf ( "%c %d", ch, i ) ;
    printf ( "%c %d", ch, i ) ;
}
```

[B] Two variables **a** and **b** contain values 10 and 20. Write a program to interchange the contents of **a** and **b** without using a third variable.

CHAPTER

4 Operators, Expressions And Assignment Statements

Operators
Expressions
Assignment Statements

Operators

Operators are C's forte. It is extremely rich in operators. It has as many as 45 different operators. We are going to discuss most of these operators and their interaction with one another in this chapter. Depending on the function performed the operators can be classified as:

- Arithmetic
- Increment and Decrement
- Modulo division
- Relational
- Logical
- Bitwise
- Conditional
- Assignment

In addition to this classification operators can also be designated as 'unary', 'binary' or 'ternary' depending on whether they operate on one, two or three operands respectively.

Arithmetic Operators

What is an operator? It is a symbol which represents a particular operation that can be performed on some data. The data itself (which can be either a variable or a constant) is called the 'operand'. The operator thus operates on an operand. It's much simple to imagine these through an example. In the expression,

```
4 + 2 - 3
```

the symbols + and - are operators and the constants 4, 2 and 3 are operands. Quite simple, you would agree. The operators + and - symbolize the operations of addition and subtraction, and they are used in a C program just as in everyday arithmetic. So the above expression, assuming it's a C expression, tells the compiler to add or subtract these constants.

In addition to + and - C has two more arithmetic operators: * for multiplication and / for division. All these operators are 'binary' operators since they operate on two operands at a time. Each of these operators can work with **ints, floats** or **chars**.

Increment And Decrement Operators

C offers two special operators **++** and **--** called increment and decrement operators, respectively. These are 'unary' operators since they operate on only one operand. The operand has to be a variable and not a constant. Thus, the expression **a++** is valid whereas **6++** is invalid. The use of these operators results in incrementing or decrementing the value of the variable by 1. So the expression **a++** increments value in **a** by 1, and the expression **a--** decrements it by 1. These operators can be used either before or after their operand (i.e. in either 'prefix' or 'postfix' position), so we can have **a++** (postfix) as well as **++a** (prefix), and **a--** as well as **--a**. Prefix and postfix operators have same effect if they are used in an isolated C statement. For example, the effect of the following two statements would be same.

```
a++ ;
++a ;
```

However, prefix and postfix operators have different effects when used in association with some other operator in a C statement. For example, if we assume the value of the variable **a** to be 5, then execution of the statement

```
b = ++a ;
```

will first increase the value of **a** to 6 and then assign that new value to **b**. The effect is exactly same as if the following two statements have been executed:

```
a = a + 1 ;
b = a ;
```

On the other hand, execution of the statement

```
b = a++ ;
```

will first set the value of **b** to 5 and then increase the value of **a** to 6. The effect now is same as if the following two statements had been executed:

```
b = a ;
a = a + 1 ;
```

The decrement operators are used in a similar way, except, of course, the values of **a** and **b** are decreased. First the prefix decrement:

```
b = --a ;
```

which is same as

```
a = a - 1 ;
b = a ;
```

Now the postfix decrement:

```
b = a-- ;
```

which is same as

```
b = a ;
a = a - 1 ;
```

Note that the increment and decrement operators can not only be used in association with an assignment (=) operator, but also with any other operator and even with **printf( )**. This is shown in the following program.

```
main( )
{
    int a = 10, b = 10 ;

    printf ( "%d", a++ ) ;
    printf ( "%d", ++b ) ;
}
```

In the first **printf( )** firstly value of **a**(10) is printed and then incremented to 11. As against this in the second **printf( )** firstly **b** is incremented to 11 and then printed out.

Modulo Division Operator

C provides one more binary arithmetic operator % called Modulo Division operator. This operator is a supplement to the division operator. We use it for division. But unlike division where we get the quotient on division, here we get the remainder. For example, what is the result of the expression **5 / 3**? The reuslt is 1 since the remainder is simply thrown away when in C an integer is divided by another integer. But what if we are interested in the remainder and not the quotient? You guessed it right. That's the time when the modulo division operator is to be used, as in, **5 % 3**.

Note that **5 % 3** yields 2 whereas **3 % 5** yields 3. Similarly **6 % 3** or **3 % 3** or **9 % 3** all yield 0. Got it? Be careful, though. The modulo division operator works only on **ints** and **chars** and not on **floats** or **doubles**.

If you think you have grasped the concept, then try your hand at the following program. Can you guess its ouput?

```
main( )
{
    printf ( "%d", 4 % 3 ) ;
    printf ( "%d", 4 % -3 ) ;
    printf ( "%d", -4 % 3 ) ;
    printf ( "%d", -4 % -3 ) ;
}
```

The output of the first two **printf( )**s is 1 whereas that of the next two **printf( )**s is -1. This is because the sign of the output is always same as the sign of the numerator irrespective of the sign of the denominator.

Relational Operators

These operators are used to compare two operands to see whether they are equal to each other, unequal, or whether one is greater than the other. The operands can be variables, constants or expressions that ultimately get evaluated to a numerical value. Since characters are also represented internally as integers (by their ascii code), elements to be compared can be characters as well. C has six relational operators. The following figure shows these operators alongwith their meanings.

Operator	Meaning
<	less than
>	greater than
<=	less than equal to
>=	greater than equal to
==	equal to
!=	not equal to

Figure 4.1

Each relational operator needs two operands for comparison of their values. Hence, these operators come under the category of 'binary operators'. Following examples show the expressions involving the relational operators.

```
a < b
a == b + 3
d >= 5.66
alphabet != 't'
( p + q ) <= ( t + r - 5 )
```

The expression **a < b** means "is a less than b?". The result of comparing **a** with **b** may be either 'true' or 'false'. If it is false, the value of the expression is treated as 0, and if true as 1. The following program confirms this fact.

```
main( )
{
    int a = 10, b = 20, c = 30, d, e ;

    d = a > b ;
    e = b <= c ;
    printf ( "%d %d", d, e ) ;
```

```
}
```

Here since the first expression evaluates to false, 0 gets assigned to **d**. On the other hand, since the second expression evaluates to truth, 1 gets assigned to **e**.

The results of comparisons using relational operators are used in programs to decide the sequence of execution of instructions in a program. If the expression evaluates to true, a certain set of instructions are executed; otherwise another set is executed. Such programs are discussed in the next chapter.

Before we switch onto the next section one last issue. The expressions **a == b** and **a = b** are different. The first one tests whether the value of **a** is equal to that of **b**, whereas the second simply assigns the value of **b** to the variable **a**. If by mistake the second expression is used, and if the value of **b** is non-zero then the second expression would always be considered as true. This is becuase in C any non-zero value is treated as truth value whereas a zero value is treated as falsity. Moreover, if = is used in place of == the compiler will not give any error message.

Logical Operators

As we saw in the last section, an expression evaluates to either true (non-zero value) or false (0). In a number of situations it may become necessary to combine the results of evaluation of such expressions. For this purpose C provides three operators **&&**, **||** and **!**, standing for 'logical and', 'logical or' and 'logical not'.

The **&&** operator is usually used in situations where a set of statements are to be executed if two expression are true. In such cases the two expressions can be connected as shown below:

```
( expression 1 ) && ( expression 2 )
```

If it is enough for either of them to be true then 'logical' or could be made use of:

```
( expression 1 ) || ( expression 2 )
```

The compound expressions formed by using relational and logical operators again evaluate to either true or false. The following table shows the result of the combined expressions depending on the value of the expressions.

Operands		**Results**	
exp 1	**exp 2**	**expl && exp2**	**expl || exp2**
0	0	0	0
0	non-zero	0	1
non-zero	0	0	1
non-zero	non-zero	1	1

Figure 4.2

So far we have used only the logical operators **&&** and **||**. The third logical operator is the not operator, written as !. This operator reverses the value of the expression it operates on; it makes a true expression false and a false expression true. Here is an example of the not operator applied to a relational expression.

```
! ( y < 10 )
```

This means "not **y** less than 10". In other words, if **y** is less than 10, the expression will be false, since (**y < 10**) is true. We could express the same condition as (**y >= 10**).

The not operator is often used to reverse the logical value of a single variable, as in the expression

```
if ( ! flag )
```

this is another way of saying

```
if ( flag == 0 )
```

Does the NOT operator sound confusing? Avoid it if you find it confusing, since the same thing can always be said without using the not operator.

Bitwise Operators

So far we have dealt with characters, integers, floats and their variations. The smallest element in memory on which we are able to operate as yet is a byte; and we operated on it by making use of the data type **char**. However, we haven't attempted to look within these data types to see how they are constructed out of individual bits, and how these bits can be manipulated. Being able to operate on a bit level, can be very important in programming, especially when a program must interact directly with the hardware. This is because, the programming languages are byte oriented, whereas hardware tends to be bit oriented. Let us now delve inside the byte and see how it is contructed and how it can be manipulated effectively. So let us take apart the byte... bit by bit.

One of C's powerful features is a set of bit manipulation operators. These permit the programmer to access and manipulate individual bits within a piece of data. The various Bitwise Operators available in C are shown in Figure 4.3.

Operator	Meaning
~	one's complement
>>	right shift
<<	left shift
&	Bitwise AND
|	Bitwise OR
^	Bitwise XOR (Exclusive OR)

Figure 4.3

These operators can operate upon **ints** and **chars** but not on **floats** and **doubles**. Before moving on to the details of the operators, let us first take a look at the bit numbering scheme in integers and characters. Bits are numbered from zero onwards, increasing from right to left as shown below:

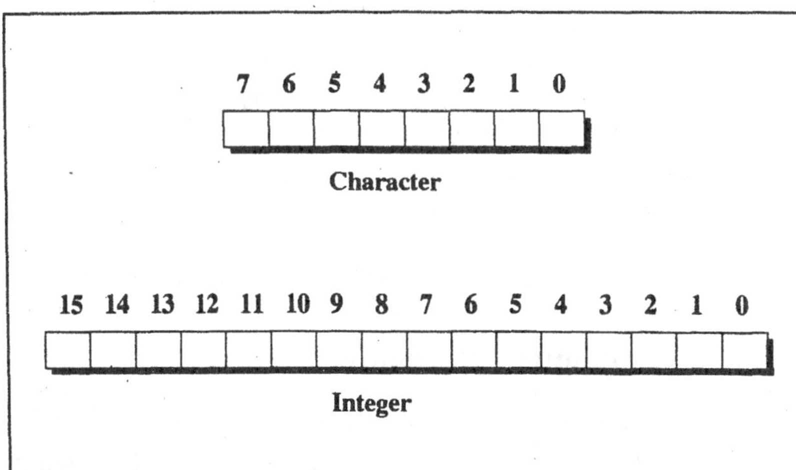

Figure 4.4

Throughout this discussion of bitwise operators we are going to use a function called **showbits( )**, but we are not going to show you the details of the function. The task of **showbits( )** is to display the binary representation of any integer or character value.

We begin with a plain-jane example with **showbits( )** in action.

```
/* Print binary equivalent of integers using showbits( ) function */
main( )
{
    int j ;

    for ( j = 0 ; j <= 5 ; j++ )
    {
        printf ( "\nDecimal %d is same as binary ", j ) ;
        showbits ( j ) ;
    }
}
```

And here is the output...

```
Decimal 0 is same as binary 0000000000000000
Decimal 1 is same as binary 0000000000000001
Decimal 2 is same as binary 0000000000000010
Decimal 3 is same as binary 0000000000000011
Decimal 4 is same as binary 0000000000000100
Decimal 5 is same as binary 0000000000000101
```

Let us now explore the various bitwise operators one by one.

One's Complement Operator

On taking one's complement of a number, all 1's present in the number are changed to 0's and all 0's are changed to 1's. For example one's complement of 1010 is 0101. Similarly one's complement of 1111 is 0000. Note that here when we talk of a number we are talking of binary equivalent of the number. Thus, one's complement of 65 means one's complement of 0000 0000 0100 0001, which is binary equivalent of 65. One's complement of 65 therefore would be, 1111 1111 1011 1110. One's complement operator is represented by the symbol ~. Following program shows one's complement operator in action.

```
main( )
{
    int j, k ;

    for ( j = 0 ; j <= 3 ; j++ )
    {
        printf ( "\nDecimal %d is same as binary ", j ) ;
        showbits ( j ) ;

        k = ~j ;
        printf ( "\nOnes complement of %d is ", j ) ;
        showbits ( k ) ;
    }
}
```

And here is the output of the above program...

```
Decimal 0 is same as binary 0000000000000000
Ones complement of 0 is 1111111111111111
Decimal 1 is same as binary 0000000000000001
Ones complement of 1 is 1111111111111110
Decimal 2 is same as binary 0000000000000010
Ones complement of 2 is 1111111111111101
Decimal 3 is same as binary 0000000000000011
Ones complement of 3 is 1111111111111100
```

In real-world situations where could the one's complement operator be useful? Since it changes the original number beyond recognition, one potential place where it can be effectively used is in developement of file encryption utilities.

Right Shift Operator

Like one's complement operator 'right shift operator' too operates on a single variable. It is represented by >> and it shifts each bit in the operand to the right. The number of places the bits are shifted depends on the number following the operand.

Thus, **ch >> 3** would shift all bits three places to the right. Similarly, **ch >> 5** would shift all bits 5 places to the right.

For example, if the variable **ch** contains the bit pattern 11010111, then, **ch >> 1** gives, 01101011 and, **ch >> 2** gives, 00110101.

Note that as the bits are shifted to the right, blanks are created on the left. These blanks must be filled somehow. They are always filled with zeros. The following program demonstrates the effect of right shift operator.

```
main( )
{
    int i = 5225, j, k ;

    printf ( "Decimal %d is same as binary ", i ) ;
    showbits ( i ) ;

    for ( j = 0 ; j <= 5 ; j++ )
    {
        k = i >> j ;
        printf ( "%d right shift %d gives ", i, j ) ;
        showbits ( k ) ;
    }
}
```

The output of the above program would be...

```
Decimal 5225 is same as binary 0001010001101001
5225 right shift 0 gives 0001010001101001
```

```
5225 right shift 1 gives 0000101000110100
5225 right shift 2 gives 0000010100011010
5225 right shift 3 gives 0000001010001101
5225 right shift 4 gives 0000000101000110
5225 right shift 5 gives 0000000010100011
```

Note that if the operand is a multiple of 2 then shifting the operand one bit to right is same as dividing it by 2. Thus,

```
64 >> 1 gives 32
64 >> 2 gives 16
128 >> 2 gives 32
```

but,

```
27 >> 1 is 13
49 >> 1 is 24
```

Left Shift Operator

This is similar to the right shift operator, the only difference being that the bits are shifted to the left, and for each bit shifted, a 0 is added to the right of the number. The following program should clarify my point.

```
main( )
{
    int i = 5225, j, k ;

    printf ( "Decimal %d is same as ", i ) ;
    showbits ( i ) ;

    for ( j = 0 ; j <= 5 ; j++ )
    {
        k = i << j ;
        printf ( "%d left shift %d gives  ", i, j ) ;
```

```
        showbits ( k ) ;
    }
}
```

The output of the above program would be...

```
Decimal 5225 is same as binary 0001010001101001
5225 left shift 0 gives 0001010001101001
5225 left shift 1 gives 0010100011010010
5225 left shift 2 gives 0101000110100100
5225 left shift 3 gives 1010001101001000
5225 left shift 4 gives 0100011010010000
5225 left shift 5 gives 1000110100100000
```

Bitwise AND Operator

This operator is represented as **&**. Remember it is different than the **&&**, the logical AND operator. Unlike one's complement, left shift and right shift operators the **&** operator operates on two operands. While operating upon these two operands they are compared on a bit-by-bit basis. Hence both the operands must be of the same type (either **char** or **int**). The second operand is often called an AND mask. The **&** operator operates on a pair of bits to yield a resultant bit. The rules that decide the value of the resultant bit are shown below:

first bit	second bit	first bit & second bit
0	0	0
0	1	0
1	0	0
1	1	1

Figure 4.5

This can be represented in a more understandable form as a 'Truth Table' as shown below.

&	0	1
0	0	0
1	0	1

Figure 4.6

The example below shows more clearly what happens while ANDing one operand with another. The rules given in the above table are applied to each pair of bits one by one.

7	6	5	4	3	2	1	0	
1	0	1	0	1	0	1	0	This operand when ANDed bitwise

7	6	5	4	3	2	1	0	
1	1	0	0	0	0	1	1	with this operand yields

7	6	5	4	3	2	1	0	
1	0	0	0	0	0	1	0	this result.

Figure 4.7

Work through the Truth Table and confirm that the result obtained is really correct.

Thus, it must be clear that the operation is being performed on individual bits, and the operation performed on one pair of bits is completely independent of the operation performed on the other pairs.

Probably, the best use of the AND operator is to check whether a particular bit of an operand is ON/OFF. This is explained in the following example.

Suppose, from the bit pattern 10101101 of an operand, we want to check whether bit number 3 is ON (1) or OFF (0). Since we want to check the bit number 3, the second operand for the AND operation we choose is, $1 * 2^3$, which is equal to 8. This operand can be represented bitwise as 00001000.

Then the ANDing operation would be,

```
10101101        original bit pattern
00001000        AND mask
--------------
00001000        resulting bit pattern
```

The resulting value we get in this case is 8, i.e the value of the second operand. The result turned out to be 8 since the third bit of the first operand was ON. Had it been OFF, the bit number 3 in the resulting bit pattern would have evaluated to 0 and the complete bit pattern would have been 00000000.

Thus, depending upon the bit number to be checked in the first operand we decide the second operand, and on ANDing these two operands the result decides whether the bit was ON or OFF. If the bit is ON (1), the resulting value turns out to be a non-zero value which is equal to the value of second operand, and if the bit is OFF (0) the result is zero as seen above.

The second, and equally important use of the AND operator is in changing the status of the bit, or more precisely to switch OFF a particular bit.

If the first operand happens to be 00000111, then to switch OFF bit number 1, our AND mask bit pattern should be 11111101. On applying this mask, we get,

```
0000 0111    original bit pattern
1111 1101    AND mask
-------------
0000 0101    resulting  bit pattern
```

Thus, here in the AND mask we keep the value of all other bits as 1 except the one which is to be switched OFF (which is purposefully kept as 0). Therefore, irrespective of whether the first bit is ON or OFF previously, it is switched OFF. At the same time the value 1 provided in all the other bits of the AND mask (second operand) keeps the bit values of the other bits in the first operand unaltered.

Bitwise OR operator

Another important Bitwise operator is the OR operator which is represented as |. The rules that govern the value of the resulting bit obtained after ORing of two bits is shown in the following truth table.

|	0	1
0	0	1
1	1	1

Figure 4.8

Using the Truth table confirm the result obtained on ORing the two operands as shown below.

```
1101 0000    original bit pattern
0000 0111    OR mask
--------------
1101 0111    resulting bit pattern
```

Bitwise OR operator is usually used to put ON a particular bit in a number.

Let us consider the bit pattern 11000011. If we want to put on bit number 3, then the OR mask to be used would be 00001000. Note that all the other bits in the mask are set to 0 and only the bit which we want to set ON in the resulting value is set to 1.

Bitwise XOR operator

The XOR operator is represented as ^ and is also called an Exclusive OR Operator. The OR operator returns 1, when any one of the two bits or both the bits are 1 , whereas XOR returns 1 only if one of the two bits is 1. The truth table for the XOR operator is given below.

^	0	1
0	0	1
1	1	0

Figure 4.9

XOR operator is used to toggle a bit ON or OFF. A number XORed with another number twice gives the original number. This is shown in the following program.

```
main( )
{
    int b = 50 ;

    b = b ^ 12 ;
    printf ( "%d\n", b ) ; /* this will print 62 */

    b = b ^ 12 ;
    printf ( "%d\n", b ) ; /* this will print 50 */
}
```

Conditional Operators

The conditional operators **?** and **:** are sometimes called ternary operators since they take three operands. Their general form is

```
expression 1 ? expression 2 : expression 3
```

What this form says is: "if expression 1 is true (that is, if its value is non zero), then the value returned will be expression 2 otherwise the value returned will be expression 3". Here are a few practical examples of conditional operators.

Example:

```
int x, y ;
scanf ( "%d", &x ) ;
y = ( x > 5 ? 3 : 4 ) ;
```

This statement will store 3 in **y** if **x** is greater than 5, otherwise it will store 4 in **y**.

Example:

```
char a ;
int y ;
```

```
scanf ( "%c", &a ) ;
y = ( a >= 65 && a <= 90 ? 1 : 0 ) ;
```

The following points should be noted about the conditional operators.

(a) It's not necessary that the conditional operators should be used only in arithmetic statements. This is illustrated in the following examples:

Example:

```
int i ;
scanf ( "%d", &i ) ;
( i == 1 ? printf ( "Amit" ) : printf ( "All and sundry" ) ) ;
```

Example:

```
char a = 'z' ;
printf ( "%c" , ( a = ='a' ? a : '!' ) ) ;
```

(b) The conditional operators can be nested, as shown in the following example.

```
int big, a, b, c ;
big = ( a > b ? ( a > c ? 3 : 4 ) : ( b > c ? 6 : 8 ) ) ;
```

(c) The limitation of the conditional operators is that after the **?** or after the **:** only one C statement can occur. Now in practise rarely is this the requirement. Therefore, in serious C programming conditional operators aren't used very frequently.

The Comma Operator

The comma operator (,) permits two different expressions to appear in situations where only one expression would ordinarily be used.

The expressions are separated by the comma operator. The following program illustrates the use of comma operator.

```
main( )
{
    int a, b, c ;

    c = ( a = 10, b = 20, a + b ) ;
    printf ( "%d", c ) ;
}
```

Here firstly value 10 is asssigned to **a**, followed by this 20 is assigned to **b** and then the result of **a + b** is assigned to **c**.

The comma operator is often used while exchanging values of two variables. This is shown in the following program.

```
main( )
{
    int x = 10, y = 20, t ;

    t = x, x = y, y = t ;
    printf ( "%d %d", x, y ) ;
}
```

The comma operator is often used in conjunction with a control statement called **for**. This is discussed in Chapter 5.

sizeof Operator

The **sizeof** operator returns the number of bytes the operand occupies in memory. The operand may be a variable, a constant or a data type qualifier. Consider the following program.

```
main( )
{
```

```
        int sum ;

        printf ( "%d", sizeof ( float ) ) ;
        printf ( "%d", sizeof ( sum ) ) ;
        printf ( "%d", sizeof ( 234L ) ) ;
        printf ( "%d", sizeof ( 'A' ) ) ;
}
```

Here the first **printf( )** would print out 4 since a **float** is always 4 bytes long. With the similar reasoning the next three **printf( )**s would output 2 , 4 and 1.

The **sizeof** operator is generally used to determine the lengths of entities called arrays and structures when their sizes are not known to the programmer. It is also used to allocate memory space dynamically during execution of the program.

Precedence Of Operators

While executing an arithmetic statement which has two or more operators, we may have some problems about how exactly does it get executed. For example, does the expression 2 * x - 3 * y correspond to (2x)-(3y) or to 2(x-3y)? Similarly, does A / B * C correspond to A / (B * C) or to (A / B) * C?

To answer these questions satisfactorily one has to understand the precedence of operators. The order or priority in which the operations are performed in an expression is called precedence. The precedence of all operators available in C is shown in Figure 4.10. Form this figure you can observe that the function expression operator has the highest priority, whereas the comma operator has the lowest priority. Operators between horizontal lines have the same precedence. Some of the operators shown in Figure 4.10 have not been covered yet and would be dealt with in later chapters.

Description	**Operator**	**Associativity**
Function expression	()	Left to right
Array expression	[ ]	Left to right
Structure operator	->	Left to right
Structure operator	.	Left to right
Unary minus	-	Right to left
Increment/Decrement	++ --	Right to left
One's complement	~	Right to left
Negation	!	Right to left
Address of	&	Right to left
Value at address	*	Right to left
Type cast	(type)	Right to left
Size in bytes	sizeof	Right to left
Multiplication	*	Left to right
Division	/	Left to right
Modulus	%	Left to right
Addition	+	Left to right
Subtraction	-	Left to right
Left shift	<<	Left to right
Right shift	>>	Left to right
Less than	<	Left to right
Less than or equal to	<=	Left to right
Greater than	>	Left to right
Greater than or equal to	>=	Left to right
Equal to	==	Le fFft to right
Not equal to	!=	Left to right
Bitwise AND	&	Left to right
Bitwise exclusive OR	^	Left to right

Figure 4.10 (continued on next page)

<table>
<tr><th>Description</th><th>Operator</th><th>Associativity</th></tr>
<tr><td>Bitwise inclusive OR</td><td>|</td><td>Left to right</td></tr>
<tr><td>Logical AND</td><td>&&</td><td>Left to right</td></tr>
<tr><td>Logical OR</td><td>||</td><td>Left to right</td></tr>
<tr><td>Conditional</td><td>? :</td><td>Right to left</td></tr>
<tr><td>Assignment</td><td>=</td><td>Right to left</td></tr>
<tr><td></td><td>*= /= %=</td><td>Right to left</td></tr>
<tr><td></td><td>+= -= &=</td><td>Right to left</td></tr>
<tr><td></td><td>^= |=</td><td>Right to left</td></tr>
<tr><td></td><td><<= >>==</td><td>Right to left</td></tr>
<tr><td>Comma</td><td></td><td>Right to left</td></tr>
</table>

Figure 4.10 (continued)

Now a few tips about usage of the operators in general.

(a) In case of a tie between operators of same priority preference is given to the operator which occurs first.

For example, consider the statement ,

```
z = a * b + c / d ;
```

Here, **a * b** will be performed before **c / d** even though * and / has same priority. This is because * occurs prior to the / operator.

(b) Within a pair of parentheses, the same hierarchy as mentioned in the above table is operative. Also, if there are more than one set of parentheses, the operations within the innermost parentheses will be performed first, followed by the operations within the second innermost pair and so on.

Examples: Determine the hierarchy of operations in the following expressions.

```
imb * 3 / 4 + k / 4 + 8 - imb + 5 / 8
j / 2 * 4 + 3 / 8 + j
-3 - -3
-3 + 4 - 7 * 8 / 5 % 10
4 % 5 - 6 % 8
4 / 4 % 4 * 4 + 4 - 4
3 + 3 * 3 - 4 + 4 * 4
```

All operators in C are ranked according to their precedence. And mind you there are as many as 45 odd operators in C, and these can affect the evaluation of an expression in subtle and unexpected ways if we aren't careful. Unfortunately, there are no simple rules that one can follow, such as "BODMAS" that tells algebra students in which order does an expression evaluate. It is almost impossible to remember the precedence of all the operators. Figure 4.10 showing precedence of operators may sound daunting to begin with, but when its contents are absorbed in small bites, it becomes more palatable.

Expressions

Knowingly or unknowingly we have used several 'expressions' in the earlier section, as well as in the programs that we wrote in the previous chapter. Well, let us now define it formally.

Definition

An expression is a combination of variables, constants and operators arranged as per the syntax (grammar) of the language. C can handle any complex expression with ease. Some of the examples of C expressions are shown in Figure 4.11.

Algebric Expression	C Expression
$a \times b - c \times d$	a * b - c * d
$(m + n)(a + b)$	(m + n) * (a + b)
$3x^2 + 2x + 5$	3 * x * x + 2 * x + 5
$\frac{a + b + c}{d + e}$	(a + b + c) / (d + e)

Figure 4.11

Type Conversion In Expressions

In order to effectively develop C programs, it will be necessary for you to understand the rules that are used for the implicit conversion of operands. For example, if an expression contains an operation between an **int** and a **float**, the **int** would be automatically promoted to a **float** before carrying out the operation. The other conversion rules are shown in the following figure. Note them carefully.

oper. 1	oper. 2	Result
char	char	char
char	int	int
char	long int	long int
char	float	float
char	double	double

oper. 1	oper. 2	Result
int	char	int
int	int	int
int	long int	long int
int	float	float
int	double	double

Figure 4.12 (continued on next page)

oper. 1	oper. 2	Result
long int	char	long int
long int	int	long int
long int	long int	long int
long int	float	float
long int	double	double

ope. 1	oper. 2	Result
float	char	float
float	int	float
float	long int	float
float	float	float
float	double	double

oper. 1	oper. 2	Result
double	char	double
double	int	double
double	long int	double
double	float	double
double	double	double

Figure 4.12 (continued)

And I think a few practical examples shown in the following figure would put the issue beyond doubt.

Operation	Result	Operation	Result
5 / 2	2	2 / 5	0
5.0 / 2	2.5	2.0 / 5	0.4
5 / 2.0	2.5	2 / 5.0	0.4
5.0 / 2.0	2.5	2.0 / 5.0	0.4

Figure 4.13

Type Casting

Sometimes we are needed to force the compiler to explicitly convert the value of an expression to a particular data type. This would be clear from the following example:

```
main( )
{
    float a ;
    int x = 6, y = 4 ;

    a = x / y ;
    printf ( "Value of a = %f", a ) ;
}
```

And here is the output...

```
Value of a = 1.000000
```

The answer turns out to be 1.000000 and not 1.5. This is because, 6 and 4 are both integers and hence **6 / 4** yields an integer, 1. This 1 when stored in **a** is converted to 1.000000 . But what if we don't want the quotient to be truncated. One solution is to make either **x** or **y** as **float**. Let us say that other requirements of the program does not permit us to do this. In such a case what do we do? Use typecasting. The following program illustrates this.

```
main( )
{
    float a ;
    int x = 6, y = 4 ;
    a = ( float ) x / y ;
    printf ( "Value of a = %f", a ) ;
}
```

And here is the output...

```
Value of a = 1.500000
```

This program uses 'typecasting'. This consists of putting a pair of parentheses around the name of the data type.

In this program we said,

```
a = ( float ) x / y ;
```

The expression (**float**) causes the variable **x** to be converted from type **int** to type **float** before being used in the division operation.

Here is another example of typecasting:

```
main( )
{
    float a = 6.35 ;
    printf ( "Value of a on typecasting = %d", ( int ) a ) ;
    printf ( "Value of a = %f", a ) ;
}
```

And here is the output...

```
Value of a = 6
Value of a = 6.350000
```

Note that the value of **a** doesn't get permanently changed as a result of typecasting. Rather it is the value of the expression that undergoes type conversion whenever the cast appears.

Assignment Statements

These are possibly the most commonly used statements in C programming. These are written using the assignment operator **=**. These statements are used to assign the value to a variable. We would have a lot of things to say about the assignment statement in this section. Let us first begin with the general form of this statement.

General Form

The general form of an assignment statement is:

```
variable = expression ;
```

The expression as we said in the earlier section comprises of operands linked together by various operators.

Following are a few examples of assignment statement:

```
a = q * 4 / d - 12 / 12 + 12 / 3 * 16 / d ;
x = ( a != 10 ) && ( b == 50 ) ;
i = 400 * 400 / 400 ;
y = !x && !(!z) ;
z = ( c > 1 ? d > 1 || e > 1 ? 100 : 200 : 300 ) ;
a = ++x && ++y || --z ;
d = a & b | c ;
```

You should not be surprised if you encounter an assignment statement like **a = a + 1**. You must note that here = doesn't stand for equality in the usual arithmetic sense, and hence it doesn't mean that value of left hand side is equal to that of right hand side. All that it means is evaluate the expression on right hand side and assign its value to the variable on left hand side. There is a more compact way of writing the same statement:

```
a += 1 ;
```

+= is a compound assignment operator. It first adds 1 to the current value of **a** and then assigns this new value to **a**. There are several other compound assignment operators available in C. These are:

+=, -=, *=, /=, %=, <=, >=, |=, &= and ^=.

The following figure shown the meaning of these operators.

the expression	is same as
a = a + 1	a += 1
a = a - 4	a -= 4
b = b * (c + d)	b *= (c + d)
b = b / (n + 1)	b /= (n + 1)
b = b % 10	b %= 10

Figure 4.14

A few tips for writing statements using the assignment operator are in order...

(a) C allows only one variable on left hand side of '='. That is the expression **z = k * l** is legal, whereas **k * l = z** is illegal.

(b) Arithmetic operations can be performed **chars, ints, floats** and **doubles.**

Thus the statements,

```
char x, y ;
int z ;
x = 'a' ;
y = 'b' ;
z = x + y ;
```

are perfectly valid, since the addition is performed on the ASCII values of the characters and not the characters themselves. The ASCII values of 'a' and 'b' are 97 and 98 (refer the

ASCII Table in Appendix D), and hence can definitely be added.

(c) No operator is assumed to be present. It must be written explicitly. In the following example, the multiplication operator after **b** must be explicitly written.

```
b = c.d.b(xy)              usual arithmetic statement
b = c * d * b * (x * y)    C statement
```

(e) Unlike other high level languages, there is no operator for performing exponentiation operation. Thus following statements are invalid.

```
a = 3 ** 2 ;
b = 3 ^ 2 ;
```

Type Conversion In Assignments

It may so happen that the type of the expression and the type of the variable on the left hand side of the assignment operator may not be same. In such a case the value of the expression is promoted or demoted depending on the type of the variable on left hand side of =.

For example, consider the following assignment statements.

```
int i ;
float b ;
i = 3.5 ;
b = 30 ;
```

Here in the first assignment statement though the expression's value is a **float** (3.5) it cannot be stored in **i** since it is an **int**. In such a case the **float** is demoted to an **int** and then its value is stored. Hence what gets stored in **i** is 3. Exactly opposite happens in the next statement.

Here, 30 is promoted to 30.000000 and then stored in **b**, since **b** being a **float** variable cannot hold anything except a **float** value.

Thus while storing the value the expression always takes the type of the variable into which its value is being stored.

Instead of the simple expression used in the above examples if a complex expression occurs still the same rules apply. For example, consider the following program fragment.

```
float a, b, c ;
int s ;
s = a * b * c / 100 + 32 / 4 - 3 * 1.1 ;
```

Here, in the assignment statement some operands are **ints** whereas others are **floats**. As we know during evaluation of the expression the **ints** would be promoted to **floats** and the result of the expression would be a **float**. But when this **float** value is assigned to s it is again demoted to an **int** and then stored in s.

Note that when in an expression contains operands of different types the exprssion is called a 'mixed mode' expression.

Variable Initialisation

There are several ways in which a variable can be initialised. This is done using the assignment operator. The simplest way to initialise say a variable **i** to a value 10 would be,

```
int i ;
i = 10 ;
```

If we so desire we can combine the two statements together and initialise the variable at the same place where we declare it. For example,

```
int i = 10 ;
```

If we want to initialise several variables in a program, we can either do so in separate statements or in one statement. For example,

```
int i = 10 ;
int j = 20 ;
```

can be combined in one statement,

```
int i = 10, j = 20 ;
```

A programming situation may arise where several variables are to be initialised to the same value. For example,

```
int i = 10, j = 10, k = 10, l = 10, m = 10 ;
```

Instead of this we can as well use the following form.

```
int i, j, k, l, m ;
i = j = k = l = m = 10 ;
```

This statement evaluates from right to left assigning the value 10 to each variable in succession.

However, the following statement is invalid.

```
int i = j = k = l = m = 10 ;
```

This is because a variable can be initialised to another variable's value only if this another variable has been defined earlier. In the above statement we are attempting to initialise **i** to value of **j**. But at the point in time when this initialisation is carried out **j** has not been declared. Hence the error. Do you think the following statements would work?

```
int j = 10 ;
```

```
int i = j ;
int k = i ;
int l = k ;
int m = k ;
```

These statements are perfectly acceptable since when **i** is initialised to value of **j**, **j** is already known to the compiler. Similarly, when **k** is initialised to value of **i**, **i** is already known to the compiler, and so on.

Exercise

[A] What will be the output of the following programs:

(1)
```
main( )
{
    int x ;

    x = 3 * 4 % 5 ;
    printf ( "x = %d", x ) ;
}
```

(2)
```
main( )
{
    int x ;

    x = 3 + 4 - 7 * 8 / 5 % 10 ;
    printf ( "x = %d", x ) ;
}
```

(3)
```
main( )
{
    int x ;
    x = -3 + 4 - 7 * 8 / 5 % 10 ;
    printf ( "x = %d", x ) ;
}
```

(4)
```
main( )
{
    int x ;

    x = 4 % 5 + 6 % 5 ;
    printf ( "x = %d", x ) ;
}
```

(5)
```
main( )
{
    int x ;

    x = -3 * -4 % -6 / -5 ;
    printf ( "x = %d", x ) ;
}
```

(6)
```
main( )
{
    float a = 1.5 ;
    int b = 3 ;

    a = b / 2 + b * 8 / b - b + a / 3 ;
    printf ( "a = %f", a ) ;
}
```

(7)
```
main( )
{
    int a, b ;

    a = 5.999999 ;
    b = 5.000001 ;

    printf ( "a = %d b = %d", a, b ) ;
}
```

(8)
```
main( )
{
    int x = 10, y = 5, p, q ;

    p = x > 9 ;
    q = x > 3 && y != 3 ;

    printf ( "p = %d q = %d", p, q ) ;
}
```

(9)
```
main( )
{
    int a = 30, b = 40, x ;

    x = ( a != 10 ) && ( b = 50 ) ;
    printf ( "x = %d", x ) ;
}
```

(10)
```
main( )
{
    int x = 11, y = 6, z ;

    z = x == 5 || y != 4 ;
    printf ( "z = %d", z ) ;
}
```

(11)
```
main( )
{
    int i = -4, j, num = 10 ;

    j = i % -3 ;
    j = ( j ? 0 : num * num ) ;

    printf ( "j = %d", j ) ;
}
```

(12)
```
main( )
{
    int x = 3 ;

    x *= x + 4 ;
    printf ( "x = %d", x ) ;
}
```

(13)
```
main( )
{
```

```
    int x = 3, y, z ;

    z = y = x ;
    z *= y = x * x ;

    printf ( "x = %d y = %d z = %d", x, y, z ) ;
}
```

(14)
```
main( )
{
    int x = 3, z ;

    z = x++ + 10 ;
    printf ( "x = %d z = %d", x, z ) ;
}
```

(15)
```
main( )
{
    int x = 3, z ;

    z = x---111 ;
    printf ( "x = %d z = %d", x, z ) ;
}
```

(16)
```
main( )
{
    int x = 3, z ;

    z = x++ + ++x ;
    printf ( "x = %d z = %d", x, z ) ;
}
```

(17)
```
main( )
{
    int i = 3, j ;
```

```
        j = ++i * ++i * ++i ;
        printf ( "%d", j ) ;
    }
```

(18)
```
main( )
{
    int x = 10, y, z ;

    z = y = x ;
    y -= x-- ;
    z -= --x ;
    x -= --x - x-- ;

    printf ( "y = %d z = %d x = %d", y, z, x ) ;
}
```

(19)
```
main( )
{
    int x, y, z ;

    x = y = z = 1 ;
    z = ++x && ++y && ++z ;
    printf ( "x = %d y = %d z = %d\n", x, y, z ) ;
}
```

(20)
```
main( )
{
    int x, y, z ;

    x = y = z = -1 ;
    z = ++x && ++y || ++z ;

    printf ( "x = %d y = %d z = %d\n", x, y, z ) ;
}
```

(21)
```
main( )
```

```
{
    int i = 32, j = 65, k ;

    k = j ^ 32 ;
    printf ( "k = %d\n", k ) ;

    k = j << 2 ;
    printf ( "k = %d\n", k ) ;

    k = i >> 5 ;
    printf ( "k = %d\n", k ) ;
}
```

(22)
```
main( )
{
    int a = 0xff ;
    ( a << 4 >> 12 ) ? printf ( "Leftist" ) : printf ( "Rightist" ) ;
}
```

(23)
```
main( )
{
    int a = 10 ;
    ( a & 8 == 8 ? printf ( "Bit no. 3 is on" ) : printf ( "3 rd bit is off" ) ) ;
}
```

(24)
```
main( )
{
    int a = b = c = d = 30 ;
    printf ( "%d %d %d %d", a, b, c, d ) ;
}
```

(25)
```
main( )
{
    float a, b ;
    int i, j ;
```

```
        a = ( i = sizeof ( i ), j = sizeof ( b ), i + j ) ;
}
```

[B] Attempt the following:

(1) Any integer is input through the keyboard. Write a program to find out whether it is an odd number or an even number.

(2) A number is entered through the keyboard. The number may contain 1, 2, 3, or 5 digits. Write a program to find the number of digits in the number.

(3) Any year is input through keyboard. Using conditional operators, determine whether the year is leap or not.

[C] State true or false:

(1) Binary equivalent of -32768 and 32768 is same.

(2) Logical operators enjoy a higher priority as compared to the relational operators.

(3) Bitwise operators can manipulate individual bits of a **float**.

(4) ~ and ! both are unary operators.

(5) Left Shift operator rotates the bits on the left and places them to the right.

CHAPTER

5 Control Statements

The if Statement
Nested if's
switch
Loops In C
The while Loop
The for Loop
The do-while Loop
The break Statement
The continue Statement
The exit( ) Function
The goto statement

As the name suggests the 'control statements' enable us to specify the order in which the various instructions in a program are to be executed by the computer. In other words the control statements determine the 'flow of control' in a program. There are four types of control statements in C. They are:

(a) Sequence control statement
(b) Selection or Decision control statement
(c) Case control statement
(d) Repitition or Loop control statement

The sequence control statement ensures that the instructions in the program are executed in the same order in which they appear in the program. Decision and Case control statements allow the computer to take a decision as to which statement is to be executed next. The Loop control statement helps computer to execute a group of statements repeatedly till a condition is satisfied. In this chapter we are going to learn these statements in detail. Let us begin with the decision control statement.

The if Statement

In the programs written in the previous chapters we have used sequence control statement in which the various steps in the program are executed sequentially, i.e. in the same order in which they appear in the program. In fact to execute the instructions sequentially, we don't have to do anything at all. By default the instructions in a program are executed sequentially. However, in serious programming situations, seldom do we want the instructions to be executed sequentially. Many a times, we want one set of instructions to be executed in one situation, and an entirely different set of instructions in another situation. This kind of situation is dealt in C programs using a decision control statement. Before we begin with this control statement let us first see its real life anology.

We all need to alter our actions in the face of changing circumstances. If the weather is fine, then I will go for a stroll. If the highway is busy I would take a diversion. If she says no, I would look elsewhere. If you like this book, I would write the next one on viruses. Note that all these decisions depend on a certain condition being met.

Computer language too must be able to perform different sets of actions depending on the circumstances. In fact that is what makes it worth its salt. C has three major decision making instructions: the **if** statement, the **if-else** statement, and the **switch** statement. A fourth, somewhat less important structure is the conditional operator. Let us now explore these ways in which a C program can react to changing circumstances. We would begin with the **if** statement.

General Form Of if

The general form of **if** statement looks like this:

```
if ( this condition is true )
    execute this statement ;
```

The keyword **if** tells the compiler that what follows, is a decision control instruction. The condition following the keyword **if** is always enclosed within a pair of parentheses. If the condition, whatever it is, is true, then the statement is executed. If the condition is not true then the statement is not executed; instead the program skips past it. But how do we express the condition itself in C? And how do we evaluate its truth or falsity? As a general rule, we express a condition using C's Relational operators. The relational operators allow us to compare two values to see whether they are equal to each other, unequal, or whether one is greater than the other. Here's how they look and how they are evaluated in C.

this expression	**is true if**
x == y	x is equal to y
x != y	x is not equal to y
x < y	x is less than y
x > y	x is greater than y
x <= y	x is less than or equal to y
x >= y	x is greater than or equal to y

Figure 5.1

These symbols should be familiar to you except for the equality symbol == and the inequality symbol !=. Note that = is used for assignment, whereas == is used for comparison of two quantities. Here is a simple program which demonstrates the use of **if** and the relational operators.

```
main( )
{
    int num ;
    printf ( "Enter a number greater than 5" ) ;
    scanf ( "%d", &num ) ;
```

```
        if ( num > 5 )
            printf ( "What an obedient servant you are !" ) ;
}
```

On execution of this program, if you type a number greater than 5, you get a message on the screen through **printf ()**. If you type some other number the program doesn't do anything. To make you comfortable with the decision control statement one more example has been given below; study it carefully before reading further. To help you understand it easily, the program is accompanied by an appropriate flowchart.

Example: While purchasing certain items, a discount of 10% is offered if the quantity purchased is more than 1000. If quantity and price per item are input through the keyboard, write a program to calculate the total expenses.

```
/* Calculation of total expenses */
main( )
{
    int qty, dis = 0 ;
    float rate, tot ;

    printf ( "Enter quantity and rate" ) ;
    scanf ( "%d %f", &qty, &rate ) ;

    if ( qty > 1000 )
        dis = 10 ;

    tot = ( qty * rate ) - ( qty * rate * dis / 100 ) ;
    printf ( " \nTotal expenses = Rs. %f", tot ) ;
}
```

Here is some sample interaction with the program.

```
Enter quantity and rate 1200 15.50
Total expenses = Rs. 16740.000000
```

```
Enter quantity and rate 200 15.50
Total expenses = Rs. 3100.000000
```

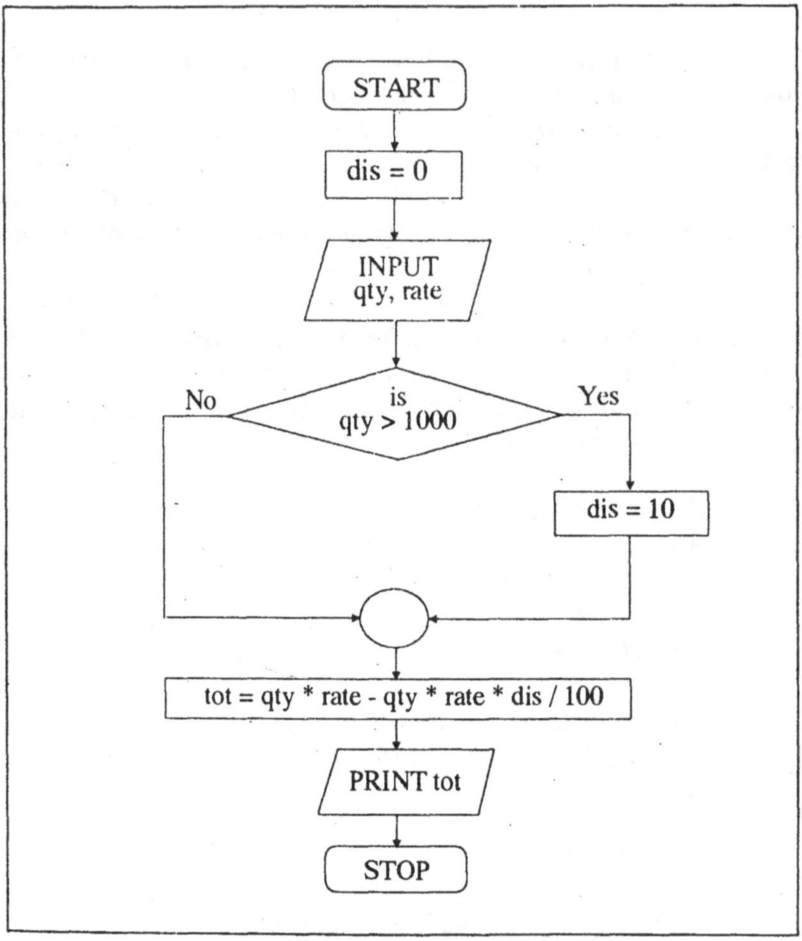

Figure 5.2

In the first run of the program, the condition evaluates to true, since 1200 (value of **qty**) is greater than 1000. Therefore, the variable **dis** which was earlier set to 0, now gets a new value 10. And using this new value total expenses are calculated and printed.

In the second run the condition evaluates to false, since 200 (the value of qty) isn't greater than 1000. Thus, **dis** which is earlier set to 0, remains 0, and hence the expression after the minus sign evaluates to zero, and hence no discount is offered.

Is the statement **dis = 0** necessary? The answer is yes, since in C, a variable if not specifically initialised contains some unpredictable value (garbage value).

Multiple Statements Within if

It may so happen that in a program we want more than one statement to be executed if the condition following **if** is satisfied. If such multiple statements are to be executed then they must be placed within a pair of braces, as illustrated in the following example.

Example: The current year and year in which the employee joined the organisation are entered through the keyboard. If the number of years for which the employee has served the organisation is greater than 3 then a bonus of Rs.2500/- is given to the employee. If the years of service in not greater than 3, then the program should not do anything.

```
main( )
{
    int bonus, cy, yoj, yr_of_ser ;

    printf ( "Enter current year and year of joining" ) ;
    scanf ( "%d %d", &cy, &yoj ) ;
    yr_of_ser = cy - yoj ;
    if ( yr_of_ser > 3 )
    {
        bonus = 2500 ;
        printf ( "Bonus = Rs. %d", bonus ) ;
    }
}
```

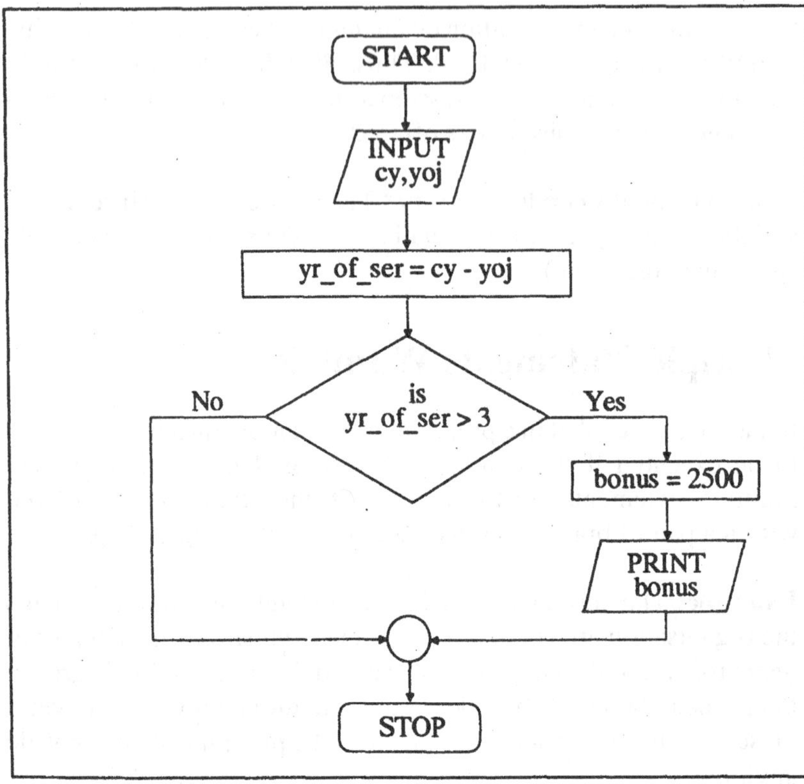

Figure 5.3

Observe that here the two statements to be executed on satisfaction of the condition have been enclosed within a pair of braces. If a pair of braces is not used then the C compiler assumes that the programmer wants only the immediately next statement after the **if** to be executed on satisfaction of the condition. In other words the default scope of the **if** statement is the immediately next statement after it.

The if-else Statement

The **if** statement by itself will execute a single statement, or a group of statements, when the condition following **if** is true. It does nothing when it is false. Can we execute one group of statements if the condition is true and another group of statements if the condition is false? Of course. This is what is the purpose of the **else** statement, which is demonstrated in the following example.

Example: In a company an employee is paid as under:

If his basic salary is less than Rs. 1500, then HRA = 10% of basic salary and DA = 25% of basic. If his salary is either equal to or above Rs. 1500, then HRA = Rs. 500 and DA = 50% of basic. If the employee's salary is input through the keyboard write a program to find his gross salary.

```
/* Calculation of Gross salary */
main( )
{
    float bs, gs, da, hra ;

    printf ( "Enter basic salary" ) ;
    scanf ( "%f", &bs ) ;

    if ( bs >= 1500 )
    {
        hra = 500 ;
        da = bs * 50 / 100 ;
    }
    else
    {
        hra = bs * 10 / 100 ;
        da = bs * 25 / 100 ;
    }
    gs = bs + hra + da ;
```

```
        printf ( "gross salary = Rs. %f", gs ) ;
}
```

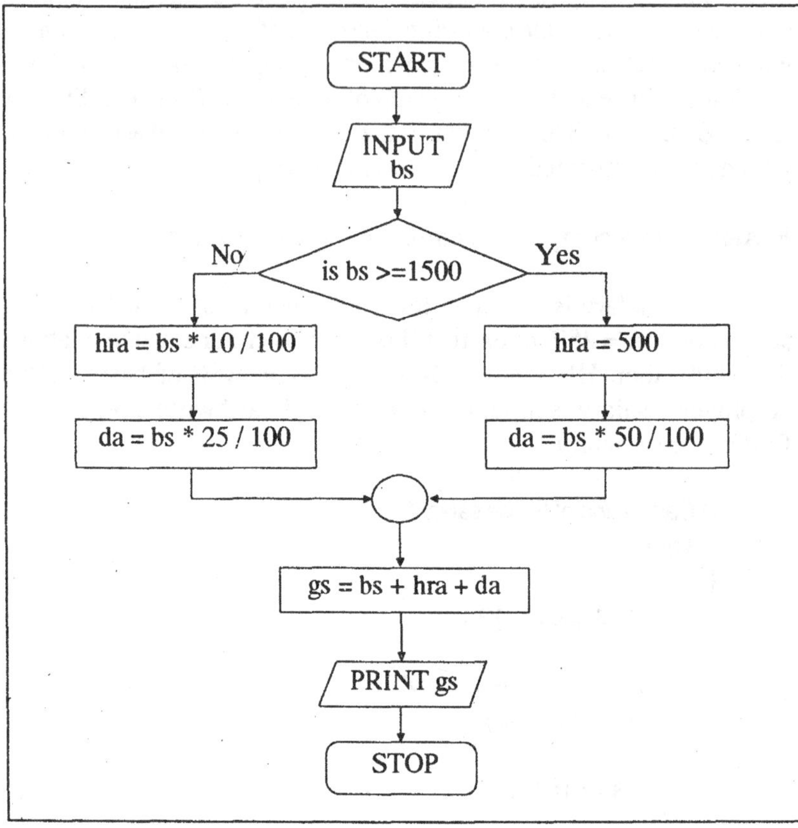

Figure 5.4

A few points worth noting...

(a) The group of statements after the **if** upto and not including the **else** is known as an if block. Similarly, the statements after the else forms the else block.

(b) Notice that the **else** is written exactly below the **if**. The statements in the if block and those in the else block have been indented to the right. This formatting convention is followed throughout the book, to enable you to understand the working of the program better.

(c) Had there been only one statement to be executed in the if block and only one statement in the else block we could have dropped the pair of braces.

(d) As with the **if** statement, the default scope of **else** is also the statement immediately after the **else**. To override this default scope a pair of braces as shown in the above example must be used.

Nested if's

It is perfectly possible to write an entire **if** - **else** construct within either the body of the **if** statement or the body of an **else** statement. This is called 'nesting' of if's. This is shown in the following program.

```
/* A quick demo of nested if else's */
main( )
{
    int i ;

    printf ( "Enter either 1 or 2" ) ;
    scanf ( "%d", &i ) ;

    if ( i == 1 )
        printf ( "You would go to heaven !" ) ;
    else
    {
        if ( i == 2 )
            printf ( "Hell was created with you in mind" ) ;
        else
            printf ( "How about mother earth !" ) ;
    }
}
```

Note that the second **if-else** construction is nested in the first **else** statement. If the condition in the first **if** statement is false, then the condition in the second **if** statement is checked. If it is false as well, the final **else** statement is executed.

You can see in the program how each time a structure is nested within another structure, it is also indented for clarity. Inculcate this habit of indentation, otherwise you would end up writing programs which nobody (you included) can understand easily at a later date.

In the above program an **if-else** occurs within the **else** block of the first **if** statement. Similarly in some other program an **if-else** may occur in the **if** block as well. There is no limit on how deeply the **ifs** and the **elses** can be nested.

The if-else-if Ladder

Consider the following problem.

Example: The marks obtained by a student in 5 different subjects are input through the keyboard. The student gets a division as per the following rules:

Percentage above or equal to 60 - First division
Percentage between 50 and 59 - Second division
Percentage between 40 and 49 - Third division
Percentage less than 40 - Fail

Write a program to calculate the division obtained by the student.

Here is the program...

```
/* Determine the division obtained by a student */
main( )
{
    int m1, m2, m3, m4, m5 ;
```

```
        float per ;

        printf ( "Enter marks in five subjects" ) ;
        scanf ( "%d %d %d %d %d", &m1, &m2, &m3, &m4, &m5 ) ;

        per = ( m1 + m2 + m3 + m4 + m5 ) / 5 ;

        if ( per >= 60 )
            printf ( "First division" ) ;
        else
        {
            if ( per >= 50 )
                printf ( "Second division" ) ;
            else
            {
                if ( per >= 40 )
                    printf ( "Third division" ) ;
                else
                    printf ( "Fail" ) ;
            }
        }
    }
```

Observe that this program uses nested **if-else**'s. This leads to three disadvantages:

(a) As the number of conditions go on increasing the level of indentation also goes on increasing. As a result the whole program creeps to the right.

(b) Care needs to be exercised to match the corresponding **ifs** and **elses**.

(c) Care needs to be exercised to match the corresponding pair of braces.

All these three problems can be eliminated by usage of 'Logical operators' that we studied in the last chapter. The following program illustrates this.

```
/* Determine the division obtained by a student */
main( )
{
    int m1, m2, m3, m4, m5 ;
    float per ;

    printf ( "Enter marks in five subjects" ) ;
    scanf ( "%d %d %d %d %d", &m1, &m2, &m3, &m4, &m5 ) ;

    per = ( m1 + m2 + m3 + m4 + m5 ) / 5 ;

    if ( per >= 60 )
        printf ( "First division" ) ;

    if ( ( per >= 50 ) && ( per < 60 ) )
        printf ( "Second division" ) ;

    if ( ( per >= 40 ) && ( per < 50 ) )
        printf ( "Third division" ) ;

    if ( per < 40 )
        printf ( "Fail division" ) ;
}
```

Two distinct advantages can be cited in favour of this program:

(a) The matching (or do I say mismatching) of the **ifs** with their corresponding **elses** gets avoided, since there are no **elses** in this program.

(b) In the earlier program the statements go on creeping to the right. The effect becomes more pronounced as the number of conditions go on increasing. This would make the task of matching the **ifs** with their corresponding **elses** and matching of opening and closing braces that much more difficult.

Another place where logical operators are useful is when we want to write down programs for complicated logics which ultimately boil down to only two answers. For example, consider the following problem:

Example: A company insures its drivers in the following cases:

- If the driver is married.
- If the driver is unmarried, male & above 30 years of age.
- If the driver is unmarried, female & above 25 years of age.

In all other cases the driver is not insured. If the marital status, sex and age of the driver are the inputs, write a program to determine whether the driver is to be insured or not.

Now, we would write down programs for the above problem in 2 ways:

(a) Without using **&&** and **||** operators
(b) Using **&&** and **||** operators

Method (a)

```
main( )
{
    char sex, ms ;
    int age ;

    printf ( "Enter age, sex, marital status" ) ;
    scanf ( "%d %c %c", &age, &sex, &ms ) ;

    if ( ms == 'M' )
        printf ( "Driver is insured" ) ;
    else
    {
        if ( sex == 'M' )
        {
            if ( age > 30 )
                printf ( "Driver is insured" ) ;
```

```
                else
                    printf ( "Driver is not insured" ) ;
            }
            else
            {
                if ( age > 25 )
                    printf ( "Driver is insured" ) ;
                else
                    printf ( "Driver is not insured" ) ;
            }
        }
    }
```

Method (b)

As mentioned above, in this example we expect the answer to be either 'Driver is insured' or 'Driver is not insured'. If we list down all those cases in which the driver is insured, then they would be:

(a) Driver is married.
(b) Driver is an unmarried male above 30 years of age.
(c) Driver is an unmarried female above 25 years of age.

Since all these cases lead to the driver being insured, they can be combined together using **&&** and **||** as shown in the program below:

```
/* Insurance of driver using logical operators */
main( )
{
    char sex, ms ;
    int age ;

    printf ( "Enter age, sex, marital status" ) ;
    scanf ( "%d %c %c" &age, &sex, &ms ) ;

    if( ( ms =='M') || ( ms == 'U' && sex =='M' && age > 30 ) ||
                ( ms == 'U' && sex =='F' && age > 25 ) )
```

```
        printf ( "Driver is insured" ) ;
    else
        printf ( "Driver is not insured" ) ;
}
```

In this program it is important to note that:

- The driver will be insured only if one of the conditions enclosed in parentheses evaluates to true.

- For the second pair of parentheses to evaluate to true, each condition in the parentheses separated by **&&** must evaluate to true.

- Even if one of the conditions in the second parentheses evaluates to false, then the whole of the second parentheses evaluates to false.

- The last two of the above arguments apply to third pair of parentheses as well.

Thus we can conclude that the **&&** and **||** are useful in following programming situations:

(a) When it is to be tested whether a value falls within a particular range or not.
(b) When after testing several conditions the outcome is only one of the two answers.

A Word Of Caution

What will be the output of the following program:

```
main( )
{
    int i ;
```

```
        printf ( "Enter value of i" ) ;
        scanf ( "%d", &i ) ;

        if ( i = 5 )
            printf ( " \n You entered 5" ) ;
        else
            printf ( " \n You entered something other than 5" ) ;
    }
```

And here is the output of two runs of this program...

```
Enter value of i 200
You entered 5

Enter value of i 9999
You entered 5
```

Surprising? You have entered 200 and 9999, and still you find in either case the output as 'You entered 5'. This is because we have written the condition wrongly. We have used the assignment operator (=) instead of the relational operator (==). As a result of this, the condition gets reduced to **if (5)**, irrespective of what you supply as the value of **i**. And remember that in C truth is always non-zero, whereas falsity is always zero. Therefore, **if (5)** always evaluates to true and hence the result.

Another common mistake while using the **if** statement is to write a semicolon (;) after the condition, as shown below:

```
main( )
{
    int i ;

    printf ( "Enter value of i" ) ;
    scanf ( "%d", &i ) ;
```

```
    if ( i == 5 ) ;
        printf ( "You entered 5" ) ;
}
```

The ; makes the compiler to interpret the statement as if you have written it in following manner:

```
if ( i == 5 )
    ;
printf ( "You entered 5" ) ;
```

Therefore, irrespective of whether the condition evaluates to true or false the **printf( )** is bound to get executed. Remember that the compiler would not point out this as an error, since as far as the syntax is concerned nothing has gone wrong, but the logic has certainly gone awry. Moral is, be aware of these pitfalls.

The ? As An Alternative To if

Consider the following program:

```
main( )
{
    int i = 5 ;
    if ( i >= 10 )
        printf ( "Hello" ) ;
    else
        printf ( "Hi" ) ;
}
```

The same program can be written using the conditional operators as shown below.

```
main( )
{
```

```
    int i = 5 ;
    ( ( i >= 10 ) ? printf ( "Hello" ) : printf ( "Hi" ) ) ;
}
```

You would agree that this program is more compact than the earlier one. If it is so can we not use conditional operators at all places where we use the **if-else**? No. Because while using the conditional operators after the **?** and after the **:** only one C statement can occur. In practise rarely is this the requirement. Therefore, in serious C programming conditional operators aren't as frequently used as the **if-else**.

Summary Of if

The **if** statement can take any of the following forms:

(a)
```
if ( condition )
    do this ;
```

(b)
```
if ( condition )
{
    do this ;
    and this ;
}
```

(c)
```
if ( condition )
    do this ;
else
    do this ;
```

(d)
```
if ( condition )
{
    do this
    and this ;
}
else
{
```

```
        do this ;
        and this ;
    }
```

(e)
```
    if ( condition )
        do this ;
    else
    {
        if ( condition )
            do this ;
        else
        {
            do this ;
            and this ;
        }
    }
```

(f)
```
    if ( condition )
    {
        if ( condition )
            do this ;
        else
        {
            do this ;
            and this ;
        }
    }
    else
        do this ;
```

switch

In real life we are often faced with situations where we are required to make a choice between a number of alternatives rather than only one or two. For example, which school to join or which hotel to visit or still harder which girl to marry (you almost always end up making a wrong decision is a different matter altogether!). Serious C programming is same; the choice we are asked to make is more complicated than merely selecting between two alternatives. C provides a special control statement that allows us to handle such cases effectively; rather than using a series of **if** statements.

The control statement which allows us to make a decision from the number of choices is called a **switch**, or more correctly a **switch-case-default**, since these three keywords go together to make up the control statement. They most often appear as follows:

```
switch ( integer expression )
{
    case constant 1:
        do this ;
    case constant 2:
        do this ;
    case constant 3:
        do this ;
    default:
        do this ;
}
```

The integer expression following the keyword **switch** is any C expression that will yield an integer value. It could be an integer constant like 1, 2 or 3, or an expression that evaluates to an integer.

The keyword **case** is followed by an integer or a character constant. Each constant in each **case** must be different from all the others. The "do this" lines in the above form of **switch** represent any valid C statement.

What happens when we run a program containing a **switch**? First, the integer expression following the keyword **switch** is evaluated. The value it gives is then matched, one by one, against the constant values that follow the **case** statements. When a match is found, the program executes the statements following that **case**, and all subsequent **case** and **default** statements as well. If no match is found with any of the **case** statements, only the statements following the **default** are executed. A few examples will show how this control structure works.

Consider the following program:

```
main( )
{
    int i = 2 ;
    switch ( i )
    {
        case 1 :
            printf ( "I am in case 1 \n" ) ;
        case 2 :
            printf ( "I am in case 2 \n" ) ;
        case 3 :
            printf ( "I am in case 3 \n" ) ;
        default :
            printf ( "I am in default \n" ) ;
    }
}
```

The output of this program would be:

```
I am in case 2
I am in case 3
I am in default
```

Definitely not what we expected. We didn't expect the second and third line in the above output. The program prints cases 2 and 3 and the default case. Well, yes. We said the **switch** executes the case where a match is found and all the subsequent **cases** and the **default** as well.

If you think that only case 2 should be executed, it is upto you to get out of the control structure then and there by using a **break** statement.

The following example shows how this is done. Note that there is no need for a **break** statement after the **default**, since the control comes to the end anyway.

```
main( )
{
	int i = 2 ;
	switch ( i )
	{
		case 1 :
			printf ( "I am in case 1 \n" ) ;
			break ;
		case 2 :
			printf ( "I am in case 2 \n" ) ;
			break ;
		case 3 :
			printf ( "I am in case 3 \n" ) ;
			break ;
		default :
			printf ( "I am in default \n" ) ;
	}
}
```

The output of this program would be:

```
I am in case 2
```

The operation of **switch** is shown below in the form of a flowchart for a better understanding.

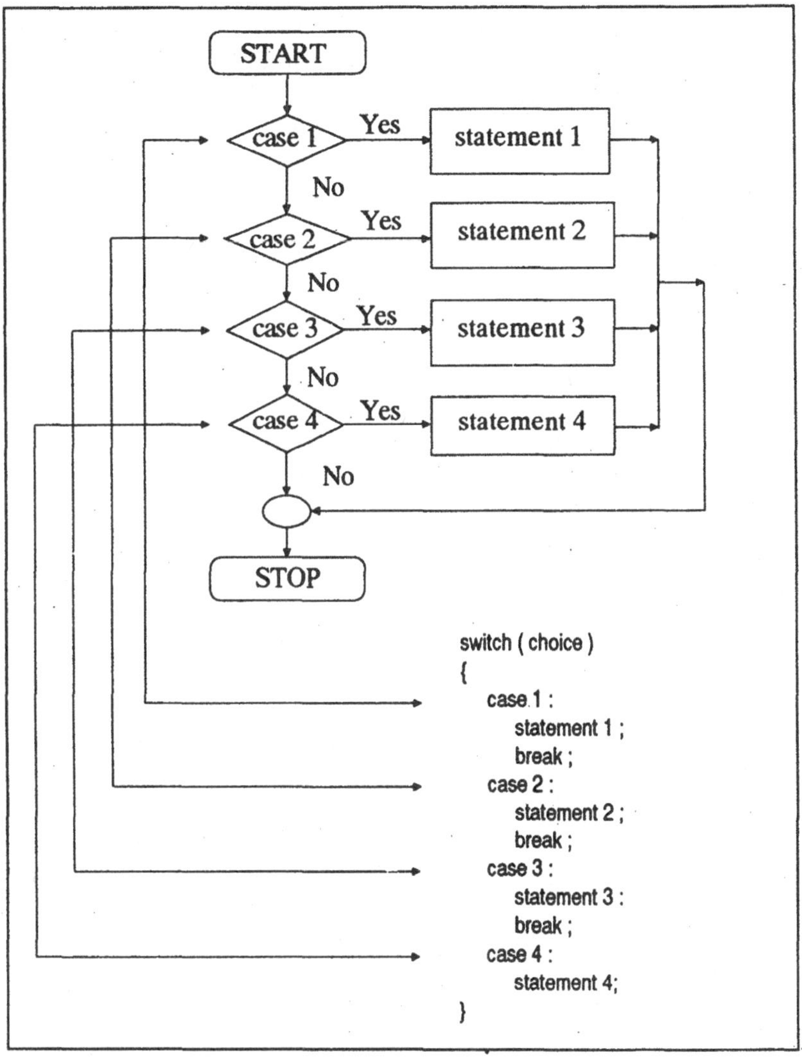

Figure 5.5

The Tips And Traps

A few useful tips about the usage of **switch**and a few pitfalls to be avoided:

(a) The earlier program which used **switch** may give you the wrong impression that you can use only cases arranged in ascending order, 1, 2, 3 and default. You can in fact put the cases in any order you please. Here is an example of scrambled case order:

```
main( )
{
    int i = 22 ;

    switch ( i )
    {
        case 121 :
            printf ( "I am in case 121 \n" ) ;
            break ;
        case 22 :
            printf ( "I am in case 22 \n" ) ;
            break ;
        case 7 :
            printf ( "I am in case 7 \n" ) ;
            break ;
        default :
            printf ( "I am in default \n" ) ;
    }
}
```

The output of this program would be:

```
I am in case 22
```

(b) You are also allowed to use **char** values in **case** and **switch** as shown in the following program:

```
main( )
{
    char c = 'x' ;
```

```
    switch ( c )
    {
        case 'v' :
            printf ( "I am in case v \n" ) ;
            break ;
        case 'a' :
            printf ( "I am in case a \n" ) ;
            break ;
        case 'x' :
            printf ( "I am in case x \n" ) ;
            break ;
        default :
            printf ( "I am in default \n" ) ;
    }
}
```

The output of this program would be:

```
I am in case x
```

(c) We can mix integer and character constants in different **cases** of a **switch**.

```
main( )
{
    int c = 3 ;

    switch ( c )
    {
        case 'v' :
            printf ( "I am in case v \n" ) ;
            break ;
        case 3 :
            printf ( "I am in case 3 \n" ) ;
            break ;
        case 12 :
            printf ( "I am in case 12 \n" ) ;
```

```
                break ;
            default :
                printf ( "I am in default \n" ) ;
        }
}
```

(d) Sometimes there may not be any statement in some of the **cases** in **switch**, but still they might turn out to be useful. This is shown below with an example.

```
main( )
{
    char ch ;

    printf ( "Enter any of the alphabet a, b, or c" ) ;
    scanf ( "%c", &ch ) ;

    switch ( ch )
    {
        case 'a' :
        case 'A' :
            printf ( "a as in ashar" ) ;
            break ;
        case 'b' :
        case 'B' :
            printf ( "b as in brain" ) ;
            break ;
        case 'c' :
        case 'C' :
            printf ( "c as in cookie" ) ;
            break ;
        default :
            printf ( "wish you knew what are alphabets" ) ;
    }
}
```

Here, we are making use of the fact that once a **case** is satisfied the control simply falls through the **case** till it doesn't encounter a **break** statement. That is why if an alphabet **a** is entered the **case 'a'** is satisfied and since there are no statements to be executed in this **case** the control automatically reaches the next **case** i.e. **case 'A'** and executes all the statements in this **case.**

Note that here the order in which the cases are written is important.

(e) Even if there are multiple statements to be executed in each **case** there is no need to enclose these within a pair of braces (unlike **if**, and **else**).

(f) If we have no **default** case, then the program simply falls through the entire switch and continues with the next instruction (if any) that follows the control structure.

(g) Is **switch** a replacement for **if**? Yes and no. Yes, because it offers a better way of writing programs as compared to **if**, and no because in certain situations we are left with no choice but to use **if**.The disadvantage of **switch** is that one cannot have a case in a **switch** which looks like...

```
case i <= 20 :
```

All that we can have after the case is an **int** constant or a **char** constant. Even a **float** is not allowed.

The advantage of **switch** over **if** is that it leads to a more structured program and the level of indentation is manageable, more so if there are multiple statements within each **case** of a **switch**.

(h) The **break** statement when used in a **switch** takes the control outside the **switch**. However, use of **continue** will not take the control to the beginning of **switch** as one is likely to believe.

(i) In principle, a **switch** may occur within another, but in practise it is rarely done. Such statements would be called nested **switch** statements.

Loops In C

The programs that we have developed so far used either a sequential or a decision control statement. In the first one, the calculations were carried out in a fixed order, while in the second, an appropriate set of instructions was carried out depending upon the outcome of a condition being tested (or a logical decision being taken).

These programs were of limited nature, because when executed, they always performed the same series of actions, in the same way, exactly once. Almost always, if something is worth doing, it's worth doing more than once. You can probably think of several examples of this from real life, such as eating a good dinner or going for a movie. Programming is the same; we frequently need to perform an action over and over, often with variations in the details each time. The mechanism which meets this need is the 'loop', and loops is what we are going to study now.

The versatility of the computer lies in its ability to perform a set of instructions repeatedly. This involves repeating some portion of the program either a specified number of times or until a particular condition is being satisfied. This repetitive operation is done through a loop control statement.

There are three methods by way of which we can repeat a part of a program. They are:

(a) Using a **while** statement.
(b) Using a **for** statement.
(c) Using a **do-while** statement.

Let us first begin with the **while** loop.

The while Loop

It is often the case in programming that you want to do something a fixed number of times. Perhaps you want to calculate gross salaries of ten different persons, or you want to convert temperatures from centigrade to farenheit for 15 different cities. The **while** loop is ideally suited for such cases. Let us look at a simple example which uses a **while** loop. The flowchart shown in Figure 5.6 would help you to understand the operation of the **while** loop.

```
/* Calculation of simple interest for 3 sets of p, n and r */
main( )
{
	int p, n, count ;
	float r, si ;

	count = 1 ;
	while ( count <= 3 )
	{
		printf ( "\nEnter values of p, n and r " ) ;
		scanf ( "%d %d %f", &p, &n, &r ) ;

		si = p * n * r / 100 ;
		printf ( "Simple interest = Rs. %f\n", si ) ;

		count = count + 1 ;
	}
}
```

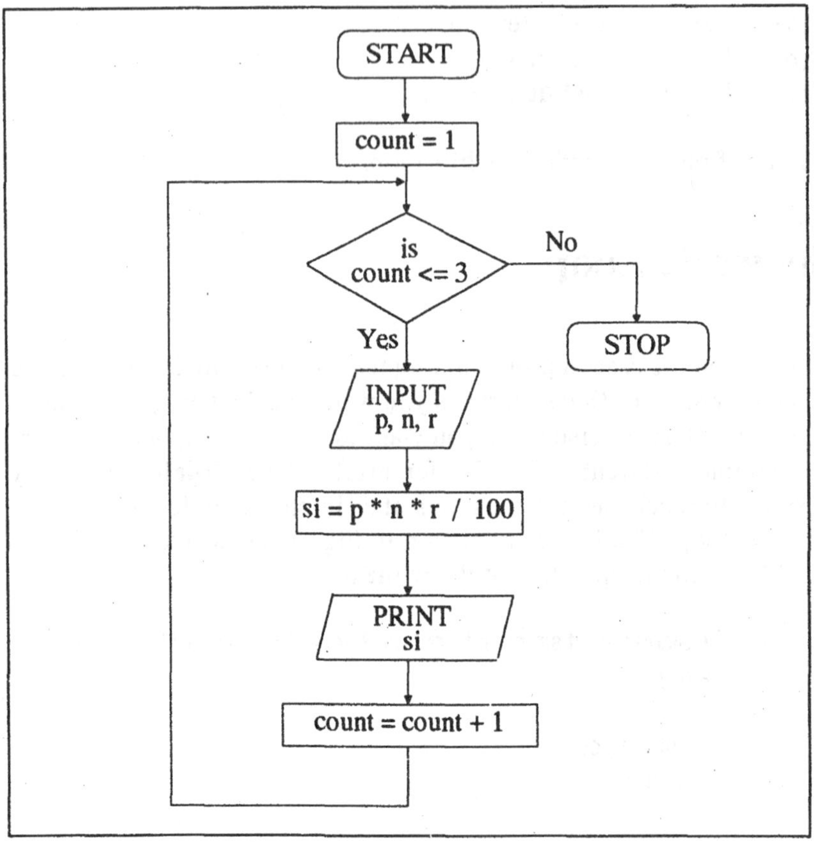

Figure 5.6

And here's is the sample run:

```
Enter values of p, n and r 1000 5 13.5
Simple interest = Rs. 675.000000
Enter values of p, n and r 2000 5 13.5
Simple interest = Rs. 1350.000000
Enter values of p, n and r 3500 5 3.5
Simple interest = Rs. 612.500000
```

The program executes all statements after the **while** 3 times. The logic for calculating the simple interest is written within a pair of braces immediately after the **while** keyword. These statements form what is called the 'body' of the **while** loop. The parentheses after the **while** contains a condition. So long as this condition remains true all statements within the body of **while** loop keep getting executed repeatedly. To begin with the variable **count** is initialised to 1 and everytime the simple interest logic is executed the value of **count** is incremented by one. The variable **count** is many a times called either a 'loop counter' or an 'index variable'.

Finally, what for are we using the '\n' in the **printf( )**? Just to ensure that every time, after printing out the value of simple interest, the cursor should go to the next line, so that the message 'Enter values of p, n and r' appears on a new line. As seen in the first chapter '\n' is called newline and is an escape sequence. More about escape sequences later in the chapter on Input / Output. The operation of the **while** loop is illustrated in the following figure.

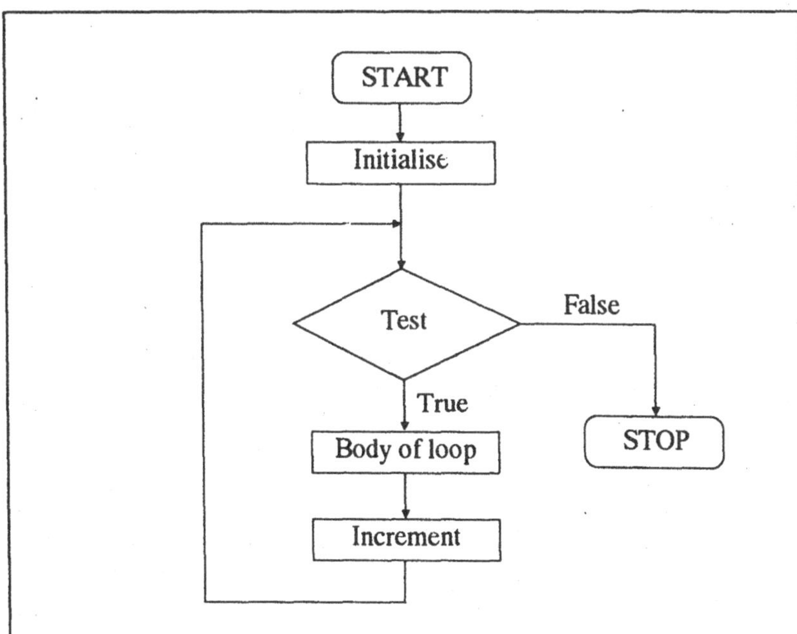

Figure 5.7

Tips And Traps

The general form of **while** is as shown below:

```
initialise loop counter ;
while ( test loop counter using a condition )
{
    do this ;
    and this ;
    increment loop counter ;
}
```

Note the following points about **while**...

- The statements within the **while** loop would keep on getting executed till the condition being tested remains true. When the condition becomes false, the control passes to the first statement that follows the body of the **while** loop.

- The condition being tested may use relational or logical operators, as shown in the following examples.

```
while ( i <= 10 )
while ( i <= 10 && j < 15 )
while ( j > 10 && ( b < 15 || c < 20 )
```

- The statements within the loop may be a single statement or a block of statements. In the first case the parentheses are optional. For example,

```
while ( i <= 10 )
    i = i + 1 ;
```

is same as

```
while ( i <= 10 )
```

```
{
    i = i + 1 ;
}
```

As a rule the **while** must test a condition that will eventually become false, otherwise the loop would be executed forever, indefinitely.

```
main( )
{
    int i = 1 ;
    while ( i <= 10 )
        printf ( "%d", i ) ;
}
```

This is an indefinite loop, since **i** remains equal to 1 forever. The correct form would be as under:

```
main( )
{
    int i = 1 ;
    while ( i <= 10 )
    {
        printf ( "%d", i ) ;
        i = i + 1 ;
    }
}
```

Instead of incrementing a loop counter, we can even decrement the loop counter and still manage to get the body of the loop executed repeatedly. This is shown below:

```
main( )
{
    int i = 5 ;
    while ( i >= 1 )
    {
```

```
        printf ( "Make the computer literate!\n " ) ;
        i = i - 1 ;
    }
}
```

It is not necessary that a loop counter must only be an **int**. It can even be a **float**.

```
main( )
{
    float a = 10.0 ;
    while ( a <= 10.5 )
    {
        printf ( "Raindrops on roses...\n" ) ;
        printf ( "..and whiskers on kittens\n" ) ;
        a = a + 0.1 ;
    }
}
```

Even floating point loop counters can be decremented. Once again the increment and decrement could be by any value, not necessarily 1.

What do you think will be the output of the following program

```
main( )
{
    int i = 1 ;
    while ( i <= 32767 )
    {
        printf ( "%d", i ) ;
        i = i + 1 ;
    }
}
```

No, it doesn't print numbers from 1 to 32767. It's an indefinite loop. To begin with, it prints out numbers from 1 to 32767, after that value of **i** is incremented by 1, therefore it tries to become 32768, which falls outside the valid integer range, so it goes to other side and becomes -32767 which would certainly satisfy the condition in the **while**. This process goes on indefinitely.

What will be the output of the following program segment?

```
main( )
{
    int i = 1 ;
    while ( i <= 10 ) ;
    {
        printf ( "%d", i ) ;
        i = i + 1 ;
    }
}
```

It is another indefinite loop, and it doesn't give any output at all.The reason is, we have carelessly given a ; after the **while**. This would make the loop look like this...

```
while ( i <= 10 )
{
    ;
}
```

Since the value of **i** is not getting incremented the control would keep rotating within the loop, eternally.

The for Loop

Perhaps one reason why few programmers use **while** is that they are too busy using **for**, which is probably the most popular looping control statement. The **for** allows us to specify three things about a loop in a single line:

(a) setting a loop counter to an initial value.
(b) testing the loop counter to determine whether its value has reached the number of repetitions desired.
(c) increasing the value of loop counter each time the program segment within the loop has been executed.

The general form of **for** statement is as under:

```
for ( initialise counter ; test counter ; increment counter )
{
    do this ;
    and this ;
}
```

Let us write down the 'simple interest' program using **for.** Compare this program with the one which we wrote using **while**. The flowchart is shown in Figure 5.8 for clarity.

```
/* Calculation of simple interest for 3 sets of p,n,r*/
main( )
{
    int p, n, count ;
    float r, si ;

    for ( count = 1 ; count <= 3 ; count = count + 1 )
    {
        printf ( "Enter values of p, n and r " ) ;
        scanf ( "%d %d %f", &p, &n, &r ) ;

        si = p * n * r / 100 ;
        printf ( "Simple Interest = Rs. %f \n", si ) ;
    }
}
```

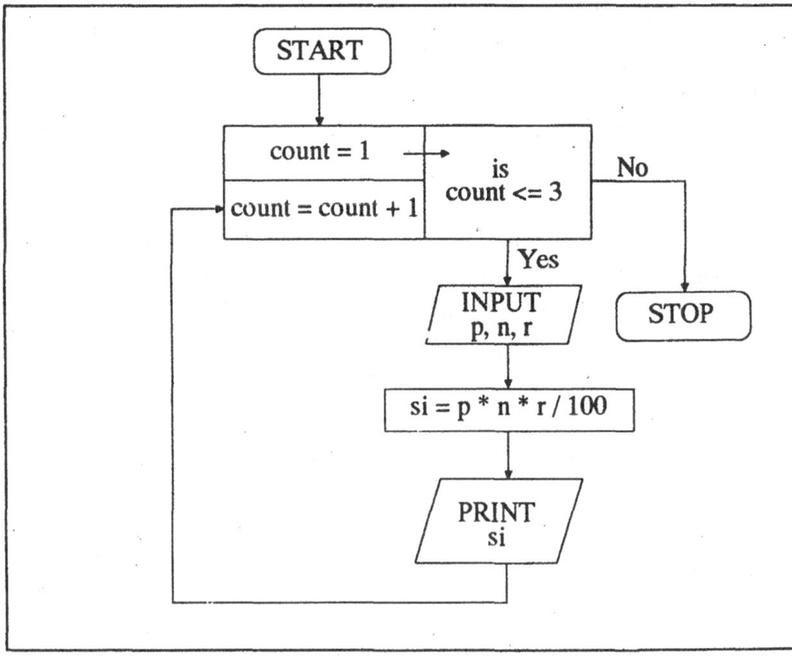

Figure 5.8

If this program is compared with the one written using **while**, it can be seen that the three steps initialisation, testing & incrementation required for the loop construct have all been incorporated in the **for** statement.

Let us now examine how the **for** statement gets executed:

- When the **for** statement is executed for the first time, the value of **count** is set to the initial value 1.

- Upon reaching the closing brace of **for**, the control comes back to the **for** statement, where value of **count** gets incremented by 1.

- Now, the **for** statement tests whether the new value of **count** exceeds the final value of **count** i.e. 3.

- If the value of **count** is still within the range 1 to 3, the statements within the braces of **for** are executed again.

- The body of the **for** loop will continue to get executed till **count** doesn't exceed the final value 3.

- When **count** reaches the value 4 the control will exit from the loop and will be transferred to the statement (if any) immediately after the body of **for**.

The following figure would help to make the concept of execution of the **for** loop still clearer.

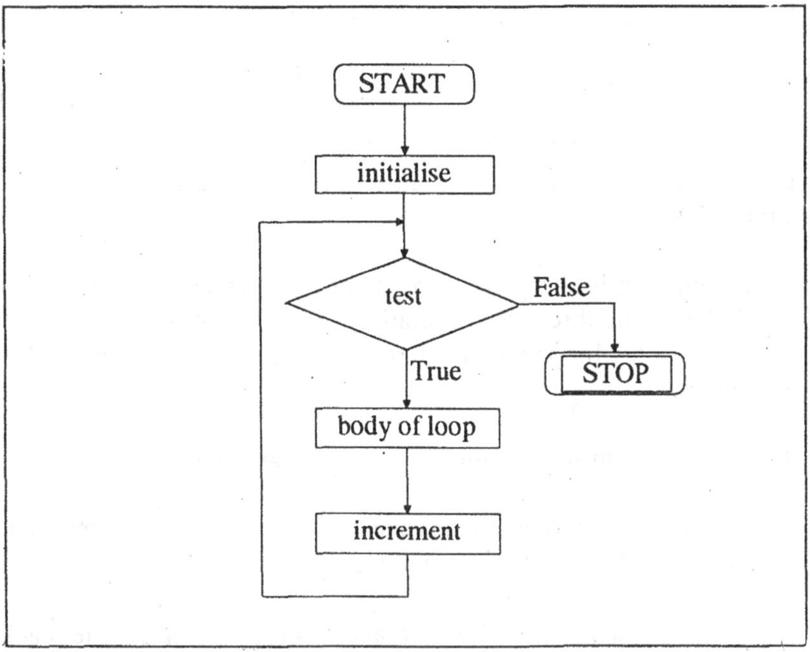

Figure 5.9

Let us now write down the program to print numbers from 1 to 10 using **for** in different ways:

(a)
```
main( )
{
    int i ;
    for ( i = 1 ; i <= 10 ; i = i + 1 )
        printf ( "%d", i ) ;
}
```

Note that the initialisation, testing and incrementation of loop counter is done in **for** statement itself.

Instead of **i = i + 1**, the statements **i++** or **i += 1** can also be used.

Since there is only one statement in the body of the **for** loop, the pair of braces have been dropped. As with the **while**, the default scope of **for** is the immediately next statement after **for**.

(b)
```
main( )
{
    int i ;
    for ( i = 1 ; i <= 10 ; )
    {
        printf ( "%d", i ) ;
        i = i + 1 ;
    }
}
```

Here, the incrementation is done within the body of the **for** loop and not in the **for** statement. Note that inspite of this ';' after the condition is necessary.

(c)
```
main( )
{
    int i = 1 ;
    for ( ; i <= 10 ; i = i + 1 )
        printf ( "%d", i ) ;
```

```
}
```

Here the initialisation is done in the declaration statement itself, but still the ; before the condition is necessary.

(d)
```
main( )
{
    int i =1 ;
    for ( ; i <= 10 ; )
    {
        printf ( "%d", i ) ;
        i = i + 1 ;
    }
}
```

Here, neither the initialisation, nor the incrementation is done in the **for** statement, but still the two semicolons are necessary.

(e)
```
main( )
{
    int i ;
    for ( i = 0 ; i++ < 10 ; )
        printf ( "%d", i ) ;
}
```

Here, the comparison and incrementation is done through the same statement **i++ < 10**. Firstly comparison is done, followed by incrementation. Note that it is necssary to initialise **i** to a value 0.

(f)
```
main( )
{
    int i ;
    for ( i = 0 ; ++i <= 10 ; )
        printf ( "%d", i ) ;
}
```

Here, the comparison and incrementation is done through the same statement **++i <= 10**. Firstly incrementation is done, followed by comparison. Note that it is necssary to initialise **i** to a value 0.

Nesting Of Loops

The way **if** statements can be nested, similarly even **while**'s and **for**'s can be nested. To understand how nested loops work, look at the program given below:

```
/* Demonstration of nested loops */
main( )
{
    int r, c, sum ;

    for ( r = 1 ; r <= 3 ; r++ ) /* outer loop */
    {
        for ( c = 1 ; c <= 2 ; c++ ) /* inner loop */
        {
            sum = r + c ;
            printf ( "r = %d c = %d sum = %d\n", r, c, sum ) ;
        }
    }
}
```

When you run this program you will get the following output:

```
r = 1 c = 1 sum = 2
r = 1 c = 2 sum = 3
r = 2 c = 1 sum = 3
r = 2 c = 2 sum = 4
r = 3 c = 1 sum = 4
r = 3 c = 2 sum = 5
```

Here, for each value of **r** the inner loop is cycled through twice, with the variable **c** taking values from 1 to 2. The inner loop terminates when the value of **c** exceeds 2, and the outer loop terminates when the value of **r** exceeds 3. Having printed each line of output, the cursor is sent to the next line using '\n' in **printf( )**.

As you can see, the body of the outer **for** loop is indented, and the body of the inner **for** loop is further indented. These multiple indentations make the program easier to understand. Instead of using two statements one to calculate **sum** and another to print it out, we can compact this into one single statement by saying:

```
printf ( "r = %d c = %d  sum = %d\n", r, c, r + c ) ;
```

The way **for** loops have been nested here, similarly, two **while** loops can also be nested. Not only this, a **for** loop can occur even within a **while** loop, or a **while** within a **for**.

Multiple Initialisations In The for Loop

The initialisation expression of the **for** loop can contain more than one statement separated by a comma. For example,

```
for ( i = 1 , j = 2 ; j <= 10 ; j++ )
```

Multiple statements can also be used in the incrementation expression of **for** loop; i. e., you can increment (or decrement) two or more variables at the same time. However only one expression is allowed in the test expression, since a single condition must determine when the loop terminates.

Use of multiple statements in the initialisation expression also demonstrates why semicolons are used to separate the three expressions in the **for** loop. If commas had been used, they could not also have been used to separate multiple statements in the initialisation expression, without confusing the compiler.

The Odd Loop

The loops that we have used so far executed the statements within them a finite number of times. However, in real life programming one comes across a situation when it is not known beforehand how many times the statements in the loop are to be executed. This situation can be programmed as shown below:

```
main( )
{
    char another = 'y' ;
    int num ;

    while ( another == 'y' )
    {
        printf ( "Enter a number " ) ;
        scanf ( "%d", &num ) ;

        printf ( "\n Its square = %d\n", num * num ) ;
        printf ( "Want to enter another number y/n " ) ;
        scanf ( "%c", &another ) ;
    }
}
```

And here is the sample output...

```
Enter a number 5
Its square is 25
Want to enter another number y/n y
Enter a number 7
Its square is 49
Want to enter another number y/n n
```

In this program the **while** loop would keep getting executed till the user continues to answer y. The moment he answers n, the loop terminates, since the condition (**another == 'y'**) fails.

The do-while Loop

The **do - while** loop looks like this:

```
do
{
    this ;
    and this ;
    and this ;
} while ( this condition is true ) ;
```

There is a minor difference between the working of **while** and **do-while** loops. The difference between them is the place where the condition is tested. The **while** tests the condition before executing any of the statements within the **while** loop. As against this the **do-while** tests the condition after having executed the statements within the loop.

This means that **do-while** would execute its statements at least once, even if the condition fails for the first time itself. The **while**, on the other hand will not execute its statements if the condition fails for the first time. This difference is illustrated by the following program.

```
main( )
{
    while ( 4 < 1 )
    {
        printf ( "Hello there \n" ) ;
    }
}
```

Since in the above program the condition fails for the first time itself the **printf( )** will not get executed at all.

```
main( )
{
    do
    {
        printf ( "Hello there \n" ) ;
    } while ( 4 < 1 ) ;
}
```

In this program the **printf** statement would be executed once, since first the body of the loop is executed and then the condition is tested.

Apart from this peculiarity of the **do-while**, the **while** and **do-while** behave exactly identically. **do-while** loops are rarely used in C programs, since there are comparatively fewer occasions when we want to execute a loop at least once no matter what. The following figure would clarify the execution of **do-while** loop still further.

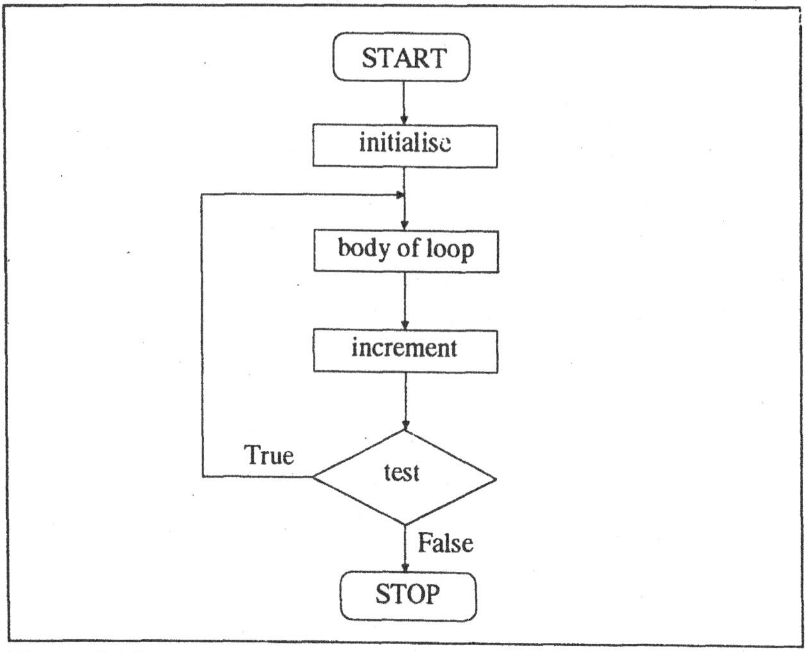

Figure 5.10

The break Statement

We often come across situations where we want to jump out of a loop instantly, without waiting to get back to the conditional test. The keyword **break** allows us to do this. When **break** is encountered inside any C loop, control automatically passes to the first statement after the loop.

A **break** is usually associated with an **if**. As an example, let's consider the following problem.

Example: Write a program to determine whether a number is prime or not. A prime number is one which is divisible only by 1 or itself.

All we have to do to test whether a number is prime or not, is to divide it successively by all numbers from 2 to one less than itself. If remainder of any of these divisions is zero, the number is not a prime.

Following is the program to do this...

```
main( )
{
    int num, i ;

    printf ( "Enter a number" ) ;
    scanf ( "%d", &num ) ;

    i = 2 ;
    while ( i <= num-1 )
    {
        if ( num % i == 0 )
        {
            printf ( "Not a prime number" ) ;
            break ;
        }
```

```
        }
        if ( i == num )
            printf ( "Prime number" ) ;
    }
```

In the above program the moment **num % i** turns out to be zero, (i.e. **num** is exactly divisible by **i**) the message "Not a prime number" is printed and the control breaks out of the **while** loop.

Why does the program require the **if** statement after the **while** loop at all? Well, there are two ways the control could have reached outside the **while** loop:

(a) It jumped out because the number proved to be not a prime.
(b) The loop came to an end because the value of **i** became equal to **num**.

In the second case it means that there was no number between 2 and **num - 1** that could exactly divide **num**. That is, **num** is indeed a prime. If this is true, the program should print out the message "Prime number".

The keyword **break**, breaks the control only from the **while** in which it is placed. Consider the following program which illustrates this fact.

```
main( )
{
    int i = 1 , j = 1 ;

    while ( i++ <= 100 )
    {
        while ( j++ <= 200 )
        {
            if ( j == 150 )
                break ;
            else
```

```
                printf ( "%d %d \n", i, j ) ;
            }
        }
    }
```

In this program, when **j** equals 150 **break** takes the control outside the inner **while** only, since it is placed inside the inner **while.**

The continue Statement

In some programming situations we want to take the control to the beginning of the loop, bypassing the statements inside the loop which have not yet been executed. The keyword **continue** allows us to do this. When the keyword **continue** is encountered inside any loop, control automatically passes to the beginning of the loop.

A **continue** is usually associated with an **if**. As an example, let's consider the following program.

```
main( )
{
    int i, j ;

    for ( i = 1 ; i <=  2 ; i++ )
    {
        for ( j = 1 ; j <=  2; j++ )
        {
            if ( i == j )
                continue ;
            else
                printf ( "%d %d\n", i, j ) ;
        }
    }
}
```

The output of the above program would be...

```
12
21
```

Note that when the value of **i** equals that of **j**, the **continue** statement takes the control to the **for** loop (inner) bypassing rest of the statements pending execution in the **for** loop (inner).

The exit( ) Function

exit( ) is a standard library function that comes ready-made with the C compiler. Its purpose is to terminate the execution of the program. Very often it is confused with the **break** statement, though its work is quite different than that of **break**. **break** just terminates the execution of loop (or **switch**) in which it is written, whereas **exit( )** terminates the execution of the program itself. The following program would make this point clear.

```
main( )
{
    int i ;

    for ( i = 1 ; i <= 100 ; i++ )
    {
        if ( i == 3 )
            break ;
    }
    printf ( "Out of loop" ) ;
}
```

In this program the statements within the loop continue to get executed till **i** is less than 3. The moment **i** gets a value 3 the condition in **if** gets satisfied. As a result the break forces the abrupt termination of the loop and takes the control to the first statement after the loop.

Since this statement is **printf( )**, 'Out of loop' gets printed. Suppose in place of **break** the function **exit( )** is used, the moment the condition is satisfied **exit( )** would terminate the execution of the program without executing the **printf( )**.

The goto Statement

Avoid **goto** statements! They make a C programmer's life miserable. There is seldom a legitimate reason for using **goto**, and its use is one of the reasons that programs become unreliable, unreadable, and hard to debug. And yet many programmers (especially those using BASIC) find **goto** seductive.

In a difficult programming situation it seems so easy to use a **goto** to take the control where you want to. However, almost always, there is a more elegant way of writing the same program using **if**, **for**, **while** and **switch**. These constructs are far more logical and easy to understand.

A **goto** statement can cause program control to end up almost anywhere in the program, for reasons that are often hard to unravel. Trust me, with good programming skills, **goto** can always be avoided. This is the first and last time that we are going to use **goto** in this book.

For sake of completeness of the book, here is how the **goto** is used. Consider the following program.

```
main( )
{
    int goals ;

    printf ( "Enter the number of goals scored against India" ) ;
    scanf ( "%d", &goals ) ;
```

```
    if ( goals <= 5 )
        goto sos ;
    else
    {
        printf ( "About time soccer players learnt C\n" ) ;
        printf ( "and said goodbye! adieu! to soccer" ) ;
        exit( ) ;  /* terminates program execution */
    }

    sos:
        printf ( "To err is human!" ) ;
}
```

And here are two sample runs of the program...

```
Enter the number of goals scored against India 3
To err is human!
Enter the number of goals scored against India 7
About time soccer players learnt C
and said goodbye! adieu! to soccer
```

A few remarks about the program would make the things clearer.

- If the condition is satisfied the **goto** statement transfers control to the label 'sos', causing **printf( )** following **sos** to be executed.

- The label can be on a separate line or on the same line as the statement following it, as in,

  ```
  sos: printf ( "To err is human!" ) ;
  ```

  Any number of **goto**'s can take the control to the same label.

The **exit( )** function is a standard library function which terminates the execution of the program. It is necessary to use this function since we don't want the statement

```
printf ( "To err is human!" ) ;
```

to get executed after execution of the **else** block.

The big problem with **goto**'s is that when we do use them we can never be sure how we got to a certain point in our code. They obscure the flow of control. So as far as possible skip them. You can always get the job done without them.

The only programing situation in favour of using **goto** is when we want to take the control out of the loop which is contained in several other loops. The following program illustrates this.

```
main( )
{
    int i, j, k ;

    for ( i = 1 ; i <= 3 ; i++ )
    {
        for ( j = 1 ; j <= 3 ; j++ )
        {
            for ( k = 1 ; k <= 3 ; k++ )
            {
                if ( i == 3 && j == 3 && k == 3 )
                    goto out ;
                else
                    printf ( "%d %d %d\n", i, j, k ) ;
            }
        }
    }
    out:
        printf ( "Out of the loop at last!" ) ;
```

```
}
```

Go through the program carefully and find out how it works. Also write down the same program without using **goto**.

Exercise

[A] What will be the output of the following programs:

(1)
```
main( )
{
    int a = 500, b = 100, c ;

    if ( ! a >= 400 )
        b = 300 ;
    c = 200 ;
    printf ( "b = %d c = %d", b, c ) ;
}
```

(2)
```
main( )
{
    if ( ! 3.14 )
        printf ( "I have robbed and killed..." ) ;
    else
        printf ( "Until my evil purse was filled" ) ;
}
```

(3)
```
main( )
{
    float a = 12.25, b = 13.65 ;

    if ( a = b )
        printf ( "a and b are equal" ) ;
    else
        printf ( "a and b are not equal" ) ;
}
```

(4)
```
main( )
{
    int i = 10, j = 40 ;
```

```
        if ( ( j - i ) % 10 )
            printf ( "man sees your actions.." ) ;
        else
            printf ( "god sees your motives.." ) ;
    }
```

(5)
```
    main( )
    {
        float a = 0.7 ;

        if ( a < 0.7 )
            printf ( "Stoned" ) ;
        else
            printf ( "Avenged" ) ;
    }
```

(6)
```
    main( )
    {
        int x = 10, y = 20 ;

        if ( ! ( !x ) && x )
            printf ( "x = %d", x ) ;
        else
            printf ( "y = %d", y ) ;
    }
```

(7)
```
    main( )
    {
        float a = 0.5, b = 0.9 ;

        if ( a && b > 0.9 )
            printf ( "Idleness is a virtue.." ) ;
        else
            printf ( "..so is stupidity!" ) ;
    }
```

(8)
```
main( )
{
    int x = 100 ;

    if ( !!x )
        printf ( "x = %d", !x ) ;
    else
        printf ( "x = %d", x ) ;
}
```

(9)
```
main( )
{
    int i ;

    printf ( "Enter any number " ) ;
    scanf ( "%d", &i ) ;

    switch ( i )
    {
        case 1 :
            printf ( "Do" ) ;
        case 2 :
            printf ( "Re" ) ;
        case 3 :
            printf ( "Me" ) ;
        case default :
            printf ( "Fa So La Ti Do" ) ;
    }
}
```

(10)
```
main( )
{
    int k = -2, j = 4 ;

    switch ( k /= j / k )
    {
```

```
        default :
            printf ( "All are same!\n" ) ;
        case 0 :
            printf ( "Happy birthday\n" ) ;
        case 1 :
            printf ( "A punch on the mouth\n" ) ;
        case 2 :
            printf ( "A kick in the back\n" ) ;
    }
}
```

(11)
```
main( )
{
    char ch = 'E' ;

    switch ( ch )
    {
        case ( ch >= 65 && ch <= 90 ) :
            printf ( "Capital Letter" ) ;
            break ;
        case ( ch >= 97 && ch <= 122 ) :
            printf ( "Small case Letter" ) ;
            break ;
        case ( ch >= 48 && ch <= 57 ) :
            printf ( "Digit" ) ;
            break ;
        default :
            printf ( "Any other character" ) ;
    }
}
```

(12)
```
main( )
{
    int i, j ;

    for ( j = 1 ; j <= 10 ; j++ )
    {
```

```
            for ( i = 1 ; i <= 10 ; i++ )
            {
                if ( j < 10 )
                    goto out ;
            }
            printf ( "Murphy's first law\n" ) ;
            printf ( "If the price of the PC is a dream...\n" ) ;
            printf ( "then the service would be a nightmare" ) ;
        }
        out :
            printf ( "Dream about a nightmare" ) ;
    }
```

(13)
```
    main( )
    {
        int i, j, k ;

        for ( j = 1 ; j <= 4 ; j++ )
        {
            if ( j * j == 16 )
                goto secretplace ;
        }

        for ( i = 1 ; i <= 5 ; i++ )
        {
            k = i * i ;
            j = k + 2 ;

            secretplace :
                printf ( "Murphy's second law\n" ) ;
                printf ( "Good computers are always priced...\n" ) ;
                printf ( "just beyond your budget\n" ) ;
        }
    }
```

(14)
```
    main( )
    {
```

```
    char j = 1 ;
    while ( j <= 255 )
    {
        printf ( "%d\n", j ) ;
        j = j + 1 ;
    }
}
```

(15)
```
main( )
{
    int j = 1 ;
    while ( j <= 255 )
        printf ( "%d\n", ++j )
}
```

(16)
```
main( )
{
    int a ;
    for ( a = 1 ; a <= 32767 ; a++ )
        printf ( "%d ", a ) ;
}
```

(17)
```
main( )
{
    int i ;
    for ( i = 1 ; i++ <= 5 ; printf ( "%d ", i ) ) ;
}
```

(18)
```
main( )
{
    int i = 1 ;
    for ( ; i++ ; )
        printf ( "%d ", i ) ;
}
```

(19)
```
main( )
```

```
{
    int a = 5 ;

    do
    {
        printf ( "%d\n", a ) ;
        a =- 1 ;
    } while ( a > 0 ) ;
}
```

[B] Attempt the following:

(1) Here is an ecological simulation of wolf and rabbit populations. Rabbits eat grass. Wolves eat rabbits. There is plenty of grass, so wolves are the only obstacle to the rabbit population increase. The wolf population increases with the population of rabbits. The day-by-day changes in the rabbit population R and the wolf population W can be expressed by the following formulae:

R(tomorrow) = (1 + a).R(today) - c.R(today).W(today)

W(tomorrow) = (1 - b).W(today) + c.d.R(today).W(today)

a = 0.01 = fractional increase in rabbit population without threat from wolves (0.01 means 1 % increase)

b = 0.005 = fractional decrease in wolf population without rabbit to eat

c = 0.00001 = likelihood that a wolf will encounter and eat a rabbit

d = 0.01 = fractional increase in wolf population attributed to a devoured rabbit.

Assume that initially there are 10,000 rabbits and 1000 wolves. Write a program to calculate populations of rabbits and wolves over a 1000-day period. Have the program print the populations every 25 days. See what happens when you start with 500 wolves instead of 1000. Try starting with 2000 wolves too.

(2) Super-Duper Micros currently sells 100 Super-Dupers per month at a profit of Rs. 500/- per Super-Duper. They have a fixed operating cost of Rs 10,000/- that does not depend on the volume of sales. They currently spend Rs 1000/- per month on advertising. A marketing consultant advised them that if they double the amount spent on advertising, sales will increase by 20 %. Write a program that begins with the company's current status, and successively doubles the amount spent on advertising until the net profit begins to decline. Have the program print the number of Super-Duper sales, the advertising budget, and the net profit just before the profit begins to decline.

(3) The equation $x^2 + y^2 = r^2$ represents a circle with centre at origin and radius **r**. Write a program that reads **r** from the keyboard and prints the number of points with integer coordinates that lie within the circle.

(4) Write a program that, for all positive integers **i, j, k,** and **l** from 1 through 1000, finds and prints all combinations of **i, j, k,** and **l** such that **i + j + k = l** and **i < j < k < l**.

(5) Write a program which finds four digit perfect squares where the number represented by the first two digits and the number represented by the last two digits are also perfect squares.

(6) Write a program which finds a four digit number AABB which is a perfect square. A and B represent different digits.

(7) If a number 972 is entered through the keyboard, your program should print "Nine Seven Two". Write the program such that it does this for any positive integer.

(8) A positive integer is entered through the keyboard. Alongwith it the base of the numbering system in which you want to convert this number is entered. Write a program to display the number entered, the base, and the converted number.

For example, if the input is 64 2 then the output should be 64 2 1000000. Similarly, if the input is 64 16, then the output should be 64 16 40.

CHAPTER

6 Console Input/Output

Types Of I/O
Console I/O Functions
Unformatted Console I/O Functions
Formatted Console I/O Functions

As mentioned in the first chapter, Dennis Ritchie wanted C to remain compact. In keeping with this intention he deliberately omitted everthing related with Input/Output (I/O) from his definition of the langauge. Thus, C simply has no provision for receiving data from any of the input devices (like say keyboard, floppy etc.), nor for sending data to the output devices (like say VDU, floppy etc.). Then how do we manage I/O, and how is it that we were we able to use **printf( )** and **scanf( )** if C has nothing to offer for I/O. This is what we intend to explore in this chapter.

Types of I/O

Though C has no provision for I/O, it of course has to dealt with at some point or the other. There is not much use writing a program that spends all it's time telling itself a secret. Each Operating System has it's own facility for inputting and outputting data from and to the files and devices. It's a simple matter for a system programmer to write a few small programs that would link the C compiler for particular Operating system's I/O facilities.

The developers of C Compilers do just that. They write series of standard I/O functions and put them in libraries. Though these functions are not part of C's formal definiton, they have become a standard feature of C langauge, and have been imitated more or less faithfully by every designer of a DOS based or a UNIX based C compiler. Whatever version of C you are using it's almost certain that you have access to such a library of I/O functions.

Do understand that the I/O facilities with different operating systems would be different. Thus, the way DOS displays output on screen would be different than the way UNIX does it. Fortunately, the **printf( )** function that we use on a DOS based C compiler works even with a UNIX based C compiler. This is because, the standard library function **printf( )** for DOS based C compiler has been written keeping in mind the way DOS outputs characters to screen. Similarly, the **printf( )** function for a UNIX based compiler has been written keeping in mind the way UNIX outputs characters to screen. We as users do not have to bother about which **printf( )** has been written in what manner. We should just use **printf( )** and it would take care of the rest of the details. Same is true about all other standard library functions available for I/O.

There are numerous library functions available for I/O. These can be classified into three broad categories:

(a) Console I/O functions - functions to receive input from keyboard and write output to VDU.

(b) Disk I/O functions functions to perform I/O operations on a floppy disk or hard disk.

(c) Port I/O functions - functions to perform I/O operations on various ports.

In this chapter we would take a close look at the Console I/O functions.

Console I/O Functions

Figure 6.1 shows how the Console I/O functions can be further classified.

Console Input/Output functions

Formatted functions		
Type	**Input**	**Output**
char	scanf( )	printf( )
int	scanf( )	printf( )
float	scanf( )	printf( )
string	scanf( )	printf( )

Unformatted functions		
Type	**Input**	**Output**
char	getch( ) getche( ) getchar( )	putch( ) putchar()
int	-	-
float	-	-
string	gets( )	puts( )

Figure 6.1

The basic difference between formatted and unformatted I/O functions is that the formatted functions allow the input read from the keyboard or the output displayed on the VDU to be formatted as per our requirements. For example, if values of average marks and percentage marks are to be displayed on the screen, then the details like where this output would appear on the screen, how many spaces would be present between the two values, the number of places after the decimal points etc. can be controlled using formatted functions.

Now let us discuss these console I/O functions in detail.

Unformatted Console I/O Functions

There are several standard library functions available under this category - those which can deal with a single character and those which can deal with a string of characters. For openers let us look at those which handle one character at a time.

getchar( ) And putchar( )

So far for input we have consistently used the **scanf( )** function. However, for some situations the **scanf( )** function has one glaring weakness... you need to hit the Enter key before the function can digest what you have typed. However, we often want a function that will read a single character the instant it is typed without waiting for the Enter key to be hit. **getch( )** and **getche( )** are two functions which serve this purpose. These functions return the character that has been most recently typed. The 'e' in **getche( )** function means it echoes (displays) the character that you typed to the screen. As against this **getch( )** just returns the character that you typed without echoing it on the screen. **getchar( )** works similarly and echos the character that you typed on the screen, but unfortunately requires Enter key to be typed following the character that you typed. Here is a sample program which illustrates the use of these functions.

```
main( )
{
    char ch ;

    printf ( "Press any key to continue" ) ;
    getch( ) ; /* will not echo the character */

    printf ( "\nType any character" ) ;
    ch = getche( ) ; /* will echo the character typed */

    printf ( "\nType any character" ) ;
```

```
    getchar( ) ; /* will echo character, must be followed  by enter key */
}
```

And here is a sample run of this program...

```
Press any key to continue
Type any character A
Type any character B
```

putch( ) and **putchar( )** form the other side of the coin. They print a character on the screen. As far as the working of **putch( )** and **putchar( )** is concerned it's exactly same. The following program illustrates this.

```
main( )
{
    char ch = 'A' ;

    putch ( ch ) ;
    putchar ( ch ) ;
    putch ( 'Z' ) ;
    putchar ( 'Z' ) ;
}
```

And here is the output...

```
AAZZ
```

The limitation of **putch( )** and **putchar( )** is that they can output only one character at a time.

gets( ) And puts( )

gets( ) receives a string from the keyboard. Why is it needed? Because **scanf( )** function has some limitations while receiving string of characters, as the following example illustrates...

```
main( )
{
    /* array which can store 50 characters in it */
    char name[50] ;

    printf ( "Enter name" ) ;
    scanf ( "%s", name ) ;
    printf ( "%s", name ) ;
}
```

And here is the output...

```
Enter name Jonty Rhodes
Jonty
```

Surprised? Where did "Rhodes" go? It never got stored in the array **name[ ]**, because the moment the blank was typed after "Jonty" **scanf( )** assumed that the name being entered has ended. The result is that there is no way (at least not without a lot of trouble on the programmers part) to enter a multi-word string into a single variable (**name** in this case) using **scanf( )**. The solution to this problem is to use **gets( )** function. As said earlier, it gets a string from the keyboard. It is terminated when an Enter key is hit. Thus, spaces and tabs are perfectly acceptable as part of the input string. More exactly, **gets( )** gets a newline ('\n') terminated string of characters from the keyboard and replaces the '\n' with '\0'. Why a '\0' is placed at the end of the string is something which we will understand only in the next chapter. The **puts( )** function works exactly opposite to **gets( )** function. It outputs a string to the screen.

Here is a program which illustrates the usage of these functions:

```
main( )
{
    char footballer[40] ;

    puts ( "Enter name" ) ;
```

```
        gets ( footballer ) ; /* sends base address of array*/
        puts ( "Happy footballing!" ) ;
        puts ( footballer ) ;
    }
```

Following is the sample output:

```
Enter name
Jonty Rhodes
Happy footballing!
Jonty Rhodes
```

Why did we use two **puts( )** functions to print "Happy footballing!" and "Jonty Rhodes"? Because, unlike **printf( )**, **puts( )** can output only one string at a time. If we attempt to print two strings using **puts( )**, only the first one gets printed. Similarly, unlike **scanf( )**, **gets( )** can be used to read only one string at a time.

Formatted Console I/O Functions

As can be seen from Figure 6.1 the functions **printf( )**, **scanf( )**, and a variation of **printf( )** called **sprintf( )** fall under the category of formatted functions. These functions allow us to supply the input in a fixed format and let us obtain the output in the specified form. Let us discuss these functions one by one.

We have talked a lot about **printf( )**, used it regularly, but without having introduced it formally. Well, better late than never. It's general form looks like this..

```
printf ( "format string", list of variables ) ;
```

The format string can contain:

- characters that are simply printed as they are

- conversion specifications that begin with a % sign
- escape sequences that begin with a \ sign

For example, look at the following program:

```
main( )
{
    int avg = 346 ;
    float per = 69.2 ;

    printf ( "Average = %d\nPercentage = %f", avg, per ) ;
}
```

The output of the program would be...

```
Average = 346
Percentage = 69.200000
```

How does **printf( )** function interprets the contents of the format string. For this it examines the format string from left to right. So long as it doesn't come across either a '%' or a '\' it continues to dump the characters that it encounters, on to the screen. In this example **Average =** is dumped on the screen. The moment it comes across a conversion specification in the format string it picks up the first variable in the list of variables and prints its value in the specified format. In this example, the moment **%d** is met the variable **avg** is picked up and its value is printed. Similarly, the moment an escape sequence is met it takes the appropriate action. In this example, the moment **\n** is met it places the cursor at the beginning of the next line. This process continues till the end of format string is reached.

Conversion Specifications

The 'd' and 'f' used in the **printf( )** are called conversion characters. They tell **printf( )** to print the value of **avg** as a decimal integer and the value of **per** as a float. Following is the list of conversion characters that can be used with the **printf( )** funcion.

Data type		**Conversion character**
Integer	short signed	%d or %i
	short unsigned	%u
	long signed	%ld
	long unsigned	%lu
	unsigned hexadecimal	%x
	unsigned octal	%o
Real	float	%f
	double	%lf
character	signed character	%c
	unsigned character	%c
string		%s

Figure 6.2

We can provide following optional specifiers in the conversion specifications.

Specifier	**Description**
dd	digits specifying field width
	decimal point separating field width from precision (precision stands for the number of places after the decimal point)
dd	digits specifying precision
	minus sign for left justifying the output in the specified field width

Figure 6.3

Now a short explaination about these conversion specifications. The field width specifier tells **printf( )** how many columns on screen should be used while printing a value. For example, **%10d** says, "print the variable as a decimal integer in a field of 10 columns." If the value to be printed happens not to fill up the entire field, the value is right justified and is padded with blanks on the left. If we include the minus sign in conversion specification (as in **%-10d**), this means left justification is desired and the value will be padded with blanks on the right. Here is an example which should make this point clear.

```
main( )
{
    int weight = 63 ;

    printf ( "weight is %d kg\n", weight ) ;
    printf ( "weight is %2d kg\n", weight ) ;
    printf ( "weight is %4d kg\n", weight ) ;
    printf ( "weight is %6d kg\n", weight ) ;
    printf ( "weight is %-6d kg\n", weight ) ;
}
```

The output oι the program would look like this ...

```
                   1         2         3
Columns   0123456789012345678901234567890
          weight is 63 kg
          weight is 63 kg
          weight is   63 kg
          weight is     63 kg
          weight is 63     kg
```

Specifying the field width can be useful in creating tables of numeric values, as the following program demonstrates.

```
main( )
{
    printf ( "%f %f %f\n", 5.0, 13.5, 133.9 ) ;
```

```
        printf ( "%f %f %f", 305.0, 1200.9, 3005.3 ) ;
    }
```

And here is the output...

```
5.000000 13.500000 133.900000
305.000000 1200.900000 3005.300000
```

Even though the numbers have been printed, the numbers have not been lined up properly and hence are hard to read. A better way would be something like this...

```
main( )
{
    printf ( "%10.1f %10.1f %10.1f\n", 5.0, 13.5, 133.9 ) ;
    printf ( "%10.1f %10.1f %10.1f", 305.0, 1200.9, 3005.3 );
}
```

This results into a much better output...

```
01234567890123456789012345678901
       5.0       13.5      133.9
     305.0     1200.9     3005.3
```

The conversion specifications could be used even while displaying string of characters. The following program would clarify this point:

```
/* Formatting strings with printf( ) */
main( )
{
    static char firstname1[ ] = "Sandy" ;
    static char surname1[ ] = "Malya" ;
    static char firstname2[ ] = "AjayKumar" ;
    static char surname2[ ] = "Gurubaxani" ;

    printf ( "%20s%20s\n", firstname1, surname1 ) ;
    printf ( "%20s%20s\n", firstname2, surname2 ) ;
```

```
}
```

And here's the output...

```
01234567890123456789012345678901234567890123456789
               Sandy                   Malya
           AjayKumar              Gurubaxani
```

The conversion specification **%20s** reserves 20 columns for printing a string and then prints the string in these 20 columns with right justification. This helps lining up names of different lengths properly. Obviously, the format **%-20s** would have left justified the string.

Escape Sequences

We saw earlier how the newline character, '\n', when inserted in a **printf( )**'s format string, takes the cursor to the beginning of the next line. The newline character is an 'escape sequence', so called because the backslash symbol (\) is considered an 'escape' character: it causes an escape from the normal interpretation of a string, so that the next character is recognised as one having a special meaning.

The following example shows usage of '\n' and a new escape sequence '\t', called 'tab'. A '\t' moves the cursor to the next tab stop. A 80 column screen usually has 10 tab stops. In other words, the screen is divided into 10 zones of 8 columns each. Printing a tab takes the cursor to the beginning of next printing zone. For example, if cursor is positioned in column 5, then printing a tab takes it to col 8.

```
main( )
{
    printf ( "You\tmust\tbe\tcrazy\nto\thate\tthis\tbook" ) ;
}
```

And here's the output...

```
            1         2         3         4
01234567890123456789012345678901234567890
You      must      be      crazy
to       hate      this    book
```

The cursor jumps over eight columns when it encounters the '\t' character. This is another useful technique for lining up columns of output. The '\n' character causes a new line to begin following "crazy". The tab and newline are probably the most often used escape sequences, but there are others as well. The following figure shows a complete list of these escape sequences.

Esc. Seq.	Purpose	Esc. Seq.	Purpose
\n	New line	\t	Tab
\b	Backspace	\r	Carriage return
\f	Form feed	\a	Alert
\'	Single quote	\"	Double Quote
\\	Backslash		

Figure 6.4

The first few of these escape sequences are more or less self-explanatory. '\b' moves the cursor one position to the left of its current position. '\r' takes the cursor to the beginning of the line in which it is currently placed. '\a' alerts the user by sounding the speaker inside the computer. Form feed advances the computer stationery attached to the printer to the top of the next page. Characters that are ordinarily used as delimiters... the single quote, double quote, and the backslash can be printed by preceding them with the backslash. Thus, the statement,

```
printf ( "He said, \"Let's do it!\"" ) ;
```

will print...

```
He said, "Let's do it!"
```

So far we have been describing **printf( )**'s specification as if we are forced to use only **%d** for an integer, only **%c** for a char, only **%s** for a string and so on. This is not true at all. In fact, **printf( )** uses the specification that we mention and attempts to perform the specified conversion, and does its best to produce a proper result. Sometimes the result is nonsensical, as in case when we ask to print a string using **%d**. Sometimes the result is useful, as in case we ask **printf( )** to print ascii value of a character using **%d**. Sometimes the result is disastrous and the entire program blows up.

The following program shows a few of these conversions, some sensible, some weird.

```
main( )
{
    char ch = 'z' ;
    int i = 125 ;
    float a = 12.55 ;
    static char s[ ] = "hello there !" ;

    printf ( "%c %d %f\n", ch, ch, ch ) ;
    printf ( "%s %d %f\n", s, s, s ) ;
    printf ( "%c %d %f\n",i ,i, i ) ;
    printf ( "%f %d\n", a, a ) ;
}
```

And here's the output ...

```
z 122 -93628317825017830000000000000000000000000000.000000
hello there ! 3280 -93628317825017830000000000000000000000000000.000000
} 125 -93628317825017830000000000000000000000000000.000000
12.550000 0
```

I will leave it to you to analyse the results by yourselves. Some of the conversions you would find are quite sensible.

The sprintf( ) Function

This function works similar to the **printf( )** function except for one small difference. Instead of sending the output to the screen as **printf( )** does, this function writes the output to an array of characters.

For example, look at the following problem:

```
main( )
{
    int i = 10 ;
    char ch = 'A' ;
    float a = 3.14 ;
    char str[20] ; /* Array of characters */

    printf ( "%d %c %f\n", i, ch, a ) ;
    sprintf ( str, "%d %c %f", i, ch, a ) ;
    printf ( "%s", str ) ;
}
```

In this Program the **printf( )** prints out the values of **i, ch** and **a** on the screen, whereas **sprintf( )** stores these values in the character array **str**. Since the string **str** is present in memory what is written into **str** using **sprintf( )** doesn't get displayed on the screen. Once **str** has been built, its contents can be displayed on the screen. In our program this achieved by the second **printf( )** statement. More details about strings and their usage is covered in the next chapter.

The scanf( ) Function

Let us now turn our attention to **scanf( )**. **scanf( )** allows us to enter data from keyboard that will be formatted in a certain way.

The general form of **scanf( )** statement is as follows:

```
scanf ( "format string", list of addresses of variables ) ;
```

For example:

```
scanf ( "%d %f %c", &c, &a, &ch ) ;
```

Note that we are sending addresses of variables (addresses are obtained by using '**&**' the 'address of' operator) to **scanf( )** function. This is necessary because the values received from keyboard must be dropped into variables corresponding to these addresses.The values that are supplied through the keyboard must be separated by either blank(s), tab(s), or newline(s). Do not include these escape sequences in the format string.

All the format specifications that we learnt in **printf( )** function apply for **scanf( )** function as well.

Exercise

[A] What will be the output of the following programs:

(1)
```
main( )
{
    float a = 3.14 ;
    printf ( "\na = %f", a ) ;
    printf ( "\na = %6.2f", a ) ;
    printf ( "\na = %-6.2f", a ) ;
    printf ( "\na = %6.1f", a ) ;
    printf ( "\na = %6.0f", a ) ;
}
```

(2)
```
main( )
{
    printf ( "%20s\n", "short leg" ) ;
    printf ( "%20s\n", "long leg" ) ;
    printf ( "%20s\n", "deep fine leg" ) ;
    printf ( "%20s\n", "backward short leg" ) ;
    printf ( "%20s\n", "legs all the same!" ) ;
}
```

(3)
```
main( )
{
    printf ( "Hello\nHi\n" ) ;
    printf ( "Hello\rHi" ) ;
}
```

(4)
```
main( )
{
    printf ( "Hello\b\b\b\b\b" ) ;
    printf ( "Hi!\b\b\bBye" ) ;
}
```

(5)
```
main( )
{
    printf ( "I\tam\ta\tboy" ) ;
}
```

(6)
```
#include "stdio.h"
main( )
{
    char str1[30], str2[30] ;

    printf ( "Enter a sentence\n" ) ;
    scanf ( "%s", str1 ) ;
    printf ( "%s", str1 ) ;
    fflush ( stdin ) ;
    printf ( "\nEnter a sentence\n" ) ;
    gets ( str2 ) ;
    printf ( "%s", str2 ) ;
}
```

(7)
```
main( )
{
    puts ( "Hello...", "Good bye!" ) ;
    printf ( "%s %s", "Hello...", "Good bye!" ) ;
}
```

(8)
```
main( )
{
    printf ( "Carriage\b\b\b\b ybag" ) ;
    printf ( "\\/\\/\\/\\/\\/" ) ;
}
```

[B] State whether the following statements are true or false:

(1) Escape sequences can be used in **scanf( )** statement.

(2) **scanf( )** can be used to receive multiword strings.

(3) **puts( )** prints a string and positions the cursor at the beginning of the next line.

(4) The **sprintf( )** function can write any data type in a string.

(5) The output of **sprintf( )** function is displayed either on screen or on printer.

(6) It's necessary to hit the enter key after supplying a character to the **getchar( )** function.

CHAPTER

7 Arrays

Single Dimensional Arrays
A Simple Program Using Array
More On Arrays
Two Dimensional Arrays
Multi Dimensional Arrays

The C language provides a capability called 'array' that enables the user to design a set of similar data types. This chapter describes how arrays of various types can be created and manipulated in C.

Single Dimensional Arrays

For understanding the arrays properly, let us consider the following program:

```
main( )
{
    int y ;

    y = 5 ;
    y = 10 ;
    printf ( "y = %d", y ) ;
}
```

No doubt, this program will print the value of **y** as 10. Why so? Because when a value 10 is assigned to **y**, the earlier value of **y** i.e. 5

is lost. Thus, ordinary variables (the ones which we have used so far) are capable of holding only one value at a time (as in the above example). However, there are situations in which we would be wanting to store more than one value at a time in a single variable.

For example, suppose we wish to arrange the percentage marks obtained by 100 students in ascending order. In such a case we have two options to store these marks in memory:

(a) Construct 100 variables to store percentage marks obtained by 100 different students. i.e. each variable containing one student's marks.

(b) Construct one variable (called array or subscripted variable) capable of storing or holding all the hundred values.

Obviously, the second alternative is better. A simple reason for this is, it would be much easier to handle one variable than handling 100 different variables. Moreover, there are certain logics which cannot be dealt with, without the use of an array. Now a formal definition of an array: An array is a collective name given to a group of 'similar quantities'. These similar quantities could be percentage marks of 100 students, or salaries of 300 employees, or ages of 50 employees. What is important is that the quantities must be 'similar'. Each member in the group is referred to by its position in the group. For example, assume the following group of numbers which represent percentage marks obtained by five students.

per = { 48, 88, 34, 23, 96 }

If we want to refer to the second number of the group, the usual notation used is per_2. Similarly, the fourth number of the group is referred as per_4. However, in C, the fourth number is referred as **per[3]**. This is because in C the counting of elements begins with 0 and not with 1. Thus, in this example **per[3]** refers to 23 and **per[4]** refers to 96. In general, the notation would be **per[i]**, where, **i** can take a value 0, 1, 2, 3, or 4, depending on the position of the element being referred. Here **per** is the subscripted varaible (array), whereas **i** is its subscript.

Thus, an array is a collection of similar elements. These similar elements could be all **ints**, or all **floats**, or all **chars** etc. Usually, the array of characters is called a 'string', whereas an array of **ints** or **floats** is called simply an array. Remember that all elements of any given array must be of the same type. i.e. we cannot have an array of 10 numbers, of which 5 are **ints** and 5 are **floats**.

A Simple Program Using Array

Let us try to write a program to find average marks obtained by a class of 30 students in a test.

```
main( )
{
    float avg,, sum = 0 ;
    int i ;
    int marks[30] ; /* array declaration */

    for ( i = 0 ; i <= 29 ; i++ )
    {
        printf ( "\nEnter marks " ) ;
        scanf ( "%d", &marks[i] ) ; /* store data in array */
    }

    for ( i = 0 ; i <= 29 ; i++ )
        sum = sum + marks[i] ; /* read data from an array*/

    avg = sum / 30 ;
    printf ( "Average marks = %f", avg ) ;
}
```

There is a lot of new material in this program, so let us take it apart slowly.

Array Declaration

To begin with, like other variables an array needs to be declared, so that the compiler will know what kind of an array and how large an array we want. In our program we have done this with the statement:

```
int marks[30] ;
```

Here, **int** specifies the type of the variable, just as it does with ordinary variables and the word **marks** specifies the name of the variable. The **[30]** however is new. The number 30 tells how many elements of the type **int** will be in our array. This number is often called the 'dimension' of the array. The bracket ([ ]) tells the compiler that we are dealing with an array.

Accessing Elements Of An Array

Once an array is declared, let us see how individual elements in the array can be referred. This is done with subscript, the number in the brackets following the array name. This number specifies the element's position in the array. All the array elements are numbered, starting with 0. Thus, **marks[2]** is not the second element of the array but the third. In our program we are using the variable **i** as a subscript to refer to various elements of the array. This variable can take different values and hence can refer to the different elements in the array in turn. This ability to use variables as subscripts is what makes arrays so useful.

Entering Data Into An Array

Here is the section of code that places data into the array:

```
for ( i = 0 ; i <= 29 ; i++ )
{
    printf ( "\nEnter marks" ) ;
    scanf ( "%d", &marks[i] ) ;
}
```

The **for** loop causes the process of asking for and receiving a students marks from the user to be repeated 30 times. The first time through the loop, **i** has a value 0, so the **scanf( )** statement will cause the value typed to be stored in the array element **marks[0]**, the first element of the array. This process will be repeated until **i** becomes 29. This is last time through the loop, which is a good thing, because there is no array element like **marks[30]**.

In the **scanf( )** statement, we have used the "address of" operator (&) on the element **marks[i]** of the array, just as we have used it earlier on other variables (**&rate**, for example). In so doing, we are passing the address of this particular array element to the **scanf( )** function, rather than its value; which is what **scanf( )** requires.

Reading Data From An Array

The balance of the program reads the data back out of the array and uses it to calculate the average. The **for** loop is much the same, but now the body of the loop causes each student's marks to be added to a running total stored in a variable called **sum**. When all the marks have been added up, the result is divided by 30, the number of students, to get the average.

```
for ( i = 0 ; i <= 29 ; i++ )
    sum = sum + marks[i] ;

avg = sum / 30 ;
printf ( "Average marks = %f" , avg ) ;
```

To fix our ideas, let us revise whatever we have learnt about arrays:

(a) An array is a collection of similar elements.
(b) The first element in the array is numbered 0, so the last element is 1 less than the size of the array.
(c) An array is also known as a subscripted variable.
(d) Before using an array its type and dimension must be declared.
(e) However big an array its elements are always stored in contiguous memory locations. This is a very important point which we would discuss in more detail later on.

More On Arrays

Array is a very popular data type with C programmers. This is because of convenience with which arrays lend themselves to programming. The features which make arrays so convenient to program would be discussed below, along with the possible pitfalls in using them.

Array Initialisation

So far we have used arrays that did not have any value in them to begin with. We managed to store values in them during program execution. Let us now see how to initialise an array while declaring it. Following are a few examples which demonstrate this.

```
static int num[6] = { 2, 4, 12, 5, 45, 5 } ;
static int n[ ] = { 2, 4, 12, 5, 45, 5 } ;
static float press[ ] = { 12.3, 34.2 -23.4, -11.3 } ;
```

Note the following points carefully:

(a) Till the array elements are not given any specific values, they are supposed to contain garbage values.

(b) If the array is initialised where it is declared, mentioning the dimension of the array is optional as in the 2nd example above.

(c) If the array is initialised where it is declared, its storage class must be either **static** or **extern**.

Array Elements In Memory

Consider the following array declaration:

```
int arr[8] ;
```

What happens in memory when we make this declaration? 16 bytes get immediately reserved in memory. 16, because each of the 8 integers would be 2 bytes long. And since the array is not being initialised all eight values present in it would be garbage values. This so happens because the storage class of this array is assumed to be **auto**. If the storage class is declared to be **static** then all the array elements would have a default initial value as zero. Whatever be the initial values all the array elements would always be present in contiguous memory locations. This arrangement of array elements in memory is shown in Figure 7.1.

12	34	66	-45	23	346	77	90
4002	4004	4006	4008	4010	4012	4014	4016

Figure 7.1

Bounds Checking

In C there is no check to see if the subscript used for an array exceeds the size of the array. Data entered with a subscript exceeding the array size will simply be placed in memory outside the array; probably on top of other data, or on the program itself. This will lead to unpredictable results, to say the least, and there will be no error message to warn you that you are going beyond the array size. In some cases the computer may just hang. Thus, the following program may turn out to be suicidal.

```
main( )
{
    int num[40], i ;

    for ( i = 0 ; i <= 100 ; i++ )
        num[i] = i ;
}
```

So do remember that, to see to it that we do not reach beyond the array size is entirely the programmer's botheration and not the compiler's.

Strings

The way a group of integers can be stored in an integer array, similarly a group of characters can be stored in a character array. Character arrays are often called 'strings'. Most languages (like Basic, Fortran etc.) internally treat strings as character arrays, but somehow conceal this fact from the programmer. Character arrays or strings are the data types used by programming languages to manipulate text such as words and sentences.

A string constant is a one dimensional array of characters terminated by a null ('\0').

For example,

```
static char name[ ] = { 'C', 'L', 'I', 'N', 'T', 'O', 'N', '\0' } ;
```

Since we are initialising an array at the place we are declaring it, the storage class of the array **name** should either be **static** or **extern**. Each character in the array occupies one byte of memory and the last character is always '\0'. What character is this? It looks like two characters, but it is actually an escape sequence like '\n'. It is called 'null character'. Note that '\0' and '0' are not same. Ascii value of '\0' is 0, whereas Ascii value of '0' is 48. Note that the array elements of a character array are also stored in contiguous memory locations as shown in the following figure.

C	L	I	N	T	O	N	\0
4001	4002	4003	4004	4005	4006	4007	4008

Figure 7.2

The terminating null ('\0') is important, because it is the only way the functions that work with string can know where a string ends. In tact, a string not terminated by a '\0' is not really a string, but merely a collection of characters.

C concedes the fact that you would use strings very often and hence provides a shortcut for initialising strings. For example, the string initialised above can also be initialised as,

```
static char[ ] = "CLINTON" ;
```

Note that, in this declaration '\0' is not necessary. C inserts the null automatically.

In what way are character arrays different than numeric arrays? Can elements in a character array be accessed in the same way as the elements of a numeric array? Do I need to take any special care of '\0'? Why numeric arrays don't end with '\0'? Declaring strings is okay, but how do I manipulate them? Questions galore! Well, let us settle some of these issues right away with the help of sample programs.

```
/* Program to demonstrate printing of string */
```

```
main( )
{
    static char name[ ] = "Krishnan" ;
    int i ;

    i = 0 ;
    while ( i <= 7 )
    {
        printf ( "%c", name[i] ) ;
        i = i + 1 ;
    }
}
```

And here is the output...

```
Krishnan
```

No big deal. We have initialised a character array, and then printed out the elements of this array within a **while** loop. Can we write the **while** loop without using the final value 7? We can; because we know that each character array always ends with a '\0'. Following program illustrates this.

```
main( )
{
    static char name[ ] = "Krishnan" ;
    int i ;

    i = 0 ;
    while ( name[i] != '\0' )
    {
        printf ( "%c", name[i] ) ;
        i = i + 1 ;
    }
}
```

And here is the output...

```
Krishnan
```

This program doesn't rely on the length of the string (no. of characters in string) to print out its contents and hence is definitely more general than the earlier one.

Even though there are so many ways (as shown above) to refer to the elements of a character array, rarely is any one of them used to print out an array. This is because **printf ( )** function has got a sweet and simple way of doing it, as shown below. Note that **printf ( )** doesn't print the '\0'.

```
main( )
{
    static char name[ ] = "Klinsman" ;
    printf ( "%s", name ) ;
}
```

The %s is a format specification for printing out a string. The same specification can be used to receive a string from the keyboard, as shown below.

```
main( )
{
    char name[25] ;

    printf ( "Enter your name " ) ;
    scanf ( "%s", name ) ;
    printf ( "\nHello %s !", name ) ;
}
```

And here is the output...

```
Enter your name Debashish
Hello Debashish !
```

Note that the declaration **char name[25]** sets aside 25 characters under the array **name[ ]**, whereas the **scanf( )** function fills in the characters typed at keyboard into this array until the enter key is hit. Naturally, we should pass the base address of the array to the function.

While entering the string using **scanf( )** we must be cautious about two things:

(a) The length of the string should not exceed the dimension of the character array. This is because the C compiler doesn't perform bounds checking on character arrays. Hence, if you carelessly exceed the bounds there is always a danger of overwriting something important, and in that event you would have nobody to blame but yourselves.

(b) **scanf( )** is not capable of receiving multi-word strings. Therefore names such as Debashish Roy would not be acceptable. To get past this limitation the function **gets( )** can be used.

Two Dimensional Arrays

So far we have looked at arrays with only one dimension. It is also possible for arrays to have two or more dimensions. The two dimensional array is also called a matrix.

Here is a sample program that stores roll number and marks obtained by a student side by side in a matrix.

```
main( )
{
    int stud[4][2] ;
    int i, j ;

    for ( i = 0 ; i <= 3 ; i++ )
```

```
        {
            printf ( "\n Enter rollno and marks" ) ;
            scanf ( "%d %d", &stud[i][0], &stud[i][1] ) ;
        }

        for ( i = 0 ; i <= 3 ; i++ )
            printf ( "%d %d\n", stud[i][0], stud[i][1] ) ;
    }
```

There are two parts to the program - in the first part through a **for** loop we read in the values of rollno and marks, whereas, in second part through another **for** loop we print out these values.

Look at the **scanf( )** statement used in the first **for** loop:

```
scanf ( "%d %d", &stud[i][0], &stud[i][1] ) ;
```

In **stud[i][0]** and **stud[i][1]** the first subscript of the variable **stud,** is row number which changes for every student. The second subscript tells which of the two columns are we talking about... the zeroeth column which contains the rollno or the first column which contains the marks. Remember, the counting of rows and columns begin with zero.

The complete array arrangement is shown below.

	col. no. 0	col. no. 1
row no. 0	1234	56
row no. 1	1212	33
row no. 2	1434	80
row no. 3	1312	78

Figure 7.3

Thus, 1234 is stored in **stud[0][0]**, 56 is stored in **stud[0][1]** and so on. The above arrangement highlights the fact that a two dimensional array is nothing but a collection of a number of one dimensional arrays placed one below the other.

In our sample program the array elements have been stored rowwise and accessed rowwise. However, you can store and access the array elements columnwise as well. Traditionally, the array elements are being stored and accessed rowwise, therefore we would also stick to the same strategy.

Initialising A 2 Dimensional Array

How do we initialise a two dimensional array? As simple as this...

```
static int stud[4][2] = {
                        { 1234, 56 },
                        { 1212, 33 },
                        { 1434, 80 },
                        { 1312, 78 }
                    } ;
```

or even this would work...

```
static int stud[4][2] = { 1234,56,1212,33,1434,80,1312,78 } ;
```

of course with a corresponding loss in readability.

It is important to remember that while initialising an array it is necessary to mention the second (column) dimension, whereas the first dimension (row) is optional.

Thus the declarations,

```
static int arr[2][3] = { 12, 34, 23, 45, 56, 45 } ;
static int arr[ ][3] = { 12, 34, 23, 45, 56, 45 } ;
```

are perfectly acceptable,

whereas,

```
static int arr[2][ ] = { 12, 34, 23, 45, 56, 45 } ;
static int arr[ ][ ] = { 12, 34, 23, 45, 56, 45 } ;
```

would never work.

Memory Map Of A 2 Dimensional Array

Let us reiterate the arrangement of array elements in a two dimensional array of students, which contains roll nos. in one column and the marks in the other.

The array arrangement shown in Figure 7.3 is only conceptually true. This is because memory doesn't contain rows and columns. In memory whether it is a one-dimensional or a two-dimensional array the array elements are stored in one continuous chain. The arrangement of array elements of a two-dimensional array in memory is shown below:

s[0][0]	s[0][1]	s[1][0]	s[1][1]	s[2][0]	s[2][1]	s[3][0]	s[3][1]
1234	56	1212	33	1434	80	1312	78
5002	5004	5006	5008	5010	5012	5014	5016

Figure 7.4

Multi Dimensional Arrays

We aren't going to show a programming example that uses a three dimensional array. This is because, in practice, one rarely uses this array. However, an example of initialising a three dimensional array will consolidate your understanding of subscripts:

```
static int arr[3][4][2] = {
                        {
                            { 2, 4 },
                            { 7, 8 },
                            { 3, 4 },
                            { 5, 6 }
                        },
                        {
                            { 7, 6 },
                            { 3, 4 },
                            { 5, 3 },
                            { 2, 3 }
                        },
                        {
                            { 8, 9 },
                            { 7, 2 },
                            { 3, 4 },
                            { 5, 1 },
                        }
                    } ;
```

A three dimensional array can be thought of as an array of arrays of arrays. The outer array has three elements, each of which is a two dimensional array of four rows, each of which is a one dimensional array of five elements. In other words, a one dimensional array of two elements is constructed first. Then four such one dimensional arrays are placed one below the other to give a two dimensional array containing four rows. Then, three such two dimensional arrays are placed one behind the other to yield a three dimensional array containing three 2-dimensional arrays. In the array declaration note how the commas have been given. Figure 7.5 would possibly help you in visualising the situation better.

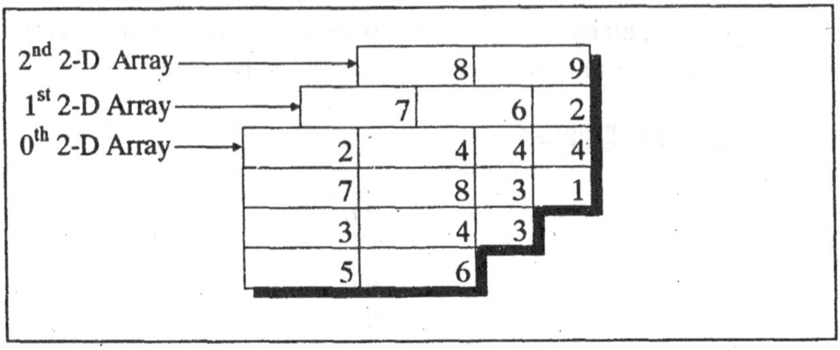

Figure 7.5

Again remember that the arrangement shown above is only conceptually true. In memory the same array elements are stored linearly as shown in Figure 7.6.

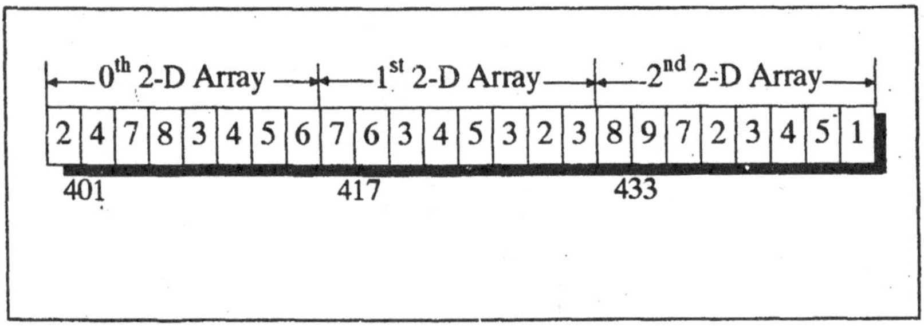

Figure 7.6

How would you refer to the array element 1 in the above array? The first subscript should be [2], since the element is in third two dimensional array; the second subscript should be [3] since the element is in fourth row of the two dimensional array; and the third subscript should be [1] since the element is in second position in the one dimensional array. We can therefore say that the element 1 can be referred as **arr[2][3][1]**. It may be noted here that the counting of array elements even for a 3-D array begins with zero.

Exercise

[A] What will be the output of the following programs:

(1)
```
main( )
{
    static int sub[5] = { 10, 20, 30, 40, 50 } ;
    int i ;
    for ( i = 0 ; i <= 4 ; i++ ) ;
    {
        if ( i <= 4 )
        {
            sub[i] = i * i ;
            printf ( "%d\n", sub[i] ) ;
        }
    }
}
```

(2)
```
main( )
{
    int size = 10 ;
    int arr[size] ;
    for ( i = 1 ; i <= size ; i++ )
    {
        scanf ( "%d", &arr[i] ) ;
        printf ( "\n%d", arr[i] ) ;
    }
}
```

(3)
```
main( )
{
    static int b[ ] = { 10, 20, 30, 40, 50 } ;
    int i ;
    for ( i = 0 ; i <= 4 ; i++ )
        printf ( "%d ", i[b] ) ;
```

```
}
```

(4)
```
main( )
{
    int arr(25), i ;
    for ( i = 0 ; i <= 100 ; i++ )
    {
        arr(i) = 100 ;
        printf ( "%d ", arr(i) ) ;
    }
}
```

(5)
```
main( )
{
    static int n[3][3] = {
                            2, 4, 3,
                            6, 8, 5,
                            3, 5, 1
                         } ;
    /* Assume that array begins at address 404 */
    printf ( "%d %d %d", n, n[2], n[2][2] ) ;
}
```

(6)
```
main( )
{
    int n[3][3], i, j ;
    static int m[3][3] ;
    for ( i = 0 ; i < 3 ; i++ )
    {
        for ( j = 0 ; j < 3 ; j++ )
            printf ( "\n %d %d", n[i][j], m[i][j] ) ;
    }
}
```

(7)
```
main( )
{
```

```
    static char city[20] = "Nagpur" ;
    int i = 0 ;
    while ( city[i] )
        printf ( "%c", city[i++] ) ;
}
```

(8)

```
main( )
{
    static char city[20] = "Nagpur" ;
    int i = 0 ;
    while ( i[city] )
        printf ( "%c", city[i++] ) ;
}
```

(9)

```
main( )
{
    static int n[3][2][4] = {
                                {
                                    2, 1, 4, 7,
                                    2, 5, 8, 9
                                },
                                {
                                    8, 6, 4, 4
                                    2, 5, 3, 5
                                },
                                {
                                    2, 4, 5, 6,
                                    1, 9, 8, 7
                                },
                            } ;
    printf ( "%d %d %d", n[0][1][2], n[2][1][0], n[1][0][2] ) ;
}
```

[B] Attempt the following:

(1) The first difference D1 of a sequence A of N elements is obtained by subtracting each element. except the last, from the

next element in the array. The second difference D2 is defined as the first difference of D1, and so on. For example, if

A: 1, 2, 4, 7, 11, 16, 22, then
D1: 1, 2, 3, 4, 5, 6
D2: 1, 1, 1, 1, 1
D3: 0, 0, 0, 0

Write a program that reads a sequence of 25 elements in an array and finds its first, second, and third differences.

(2) A common problem in statistics is that of generating frequency distribution of the given data. Assuming that the data consists of 50 positive integers in the range 1 to 25, write a program that prints the number of times each integer occurs in the data.

(3) A square matrix, that is, one having the same number of rows and columns, is called a diagonal matrix if its only non-zero elements are on the diagonal from upper left to lower right. It is called upper triangular, if all elements below the diagonal are zeroes, and lower triangular, if all elements above the diagonal are zeroes. Write a program that reads a matrix and determines if it is one of these three special matrices.

(4) The Miniaturization Unlimited sells 5 types of memory chips through its retail outlets in 10 cities. The weekly sales of the company are stored in a 5 x 10 x 7 array SALES such that SALES(L, K, M) denotes the sales of the Lth memory chip in the Kth city on the Mth day of the week. Write a program that computes:

(a) The total weekly sale of each type of memory chip
(b) The total weekly sale in each city
(c) The average daily sale of the company

CHAPTER

8 Functions

General FormOf A Function
Functions With Arguments
Function Declaration And Prototypes
Call By Value And Call By Reference
Scope Rules Of Functions
Calling Functions With Arrays
argc And argv - Arguments To main( )
Recursion

Knowingly or unknowingly we rely on so many persons for so many things. Man is an intelligent species, but still cannot perform all of life's tasks all alone. He has to rely on others. You may call a mechanic to fix up your bike, hire a gardener to mow your lawn, or rely on a store to supply you groceries every month. A computer program (except for the simplest one) finds itself in a similar situation. It cannot handle all the tasks by itself. Instead, it requests other programlike entities - called 'functions' in C - to get its tasks done. In this chapter we will study these functions. We will look at a variety of features of these functions, starting with the simplest one and then working towards those which demonstrate the virility of C functions.

General Form Of A Function

Function is a self-contained block of program that performs a coherent task of some kind. Every C program can be thought of as a collection of these functions. As we noted earlier, using a function is something like hiring a person to do a specific job for you. Sometimes the interaction with this person is very simple; sometimes it's complex.

Suppose you have a task which is always performed exactly in the same way... say a bimonthly servicing of your motorbike. When you want it to be done, you go to the service station and say, "It's time, do it now". You don't need to give instructions, because the mechanic knows his job. You don't need to be told when the job is done. You assume the bike would be serviced in the usual way, the mechanic does it and that's that.

Let us now look at a simple C function which operates in much the same way as the mechanic. Actually, we will be looking at two things: a program that calls or activates the function and the function itself.

```
main( )
{
    message( ) ,
    printf ( "Cry, and you stop the monotony." ) ;
}
message( )
{
    printf ( "Smile, and the world smiles with you." ) ;
}
```

And here's the output...

```
Smile, and the world smiles with you. Cry, and you stop the monotony.
```

Here, through **main( )** we are calling the function **message( )**. What do we mean when we say that **main( )** 'calls' the function **message( )**? We mean that the control passes to the function **message( )**. The activity of **main( )** is temporarily suspended; it falls asleep while the **message( )** function wakes up and goes to work. When the **message( )** function runs out of statements to execute, the control returns to **main( )**, which comes to life again and begins executing its code at the exact point where it left off. Thus, **main( )** becomes the 'calling' function, whereas **message( )** becomes the 'called' function.

Looking at the function **message( )** now we can specify the general form of a function. Here it is...

```
function ( arg1, arg2, arg3 )
type arg1, arg2, arg3 ;
{
    statement 1 ;
    statement 2 ;
    statement 3 ;
    statement 4 ;
}
```

Though the function **message( )** didn't have any arguments within the pair of parentheses, some functions may have them. If the arguments are present, before beginning with the statements in the functions it is necessary to declare the type of the arguments through type declaration statements.

We would discuss these arguments later in the chapter. Before that let us spend some more time on simpler functions which do not have arguments. If you have grasped the concept of 'calling' a function you are prepared for a call to more than one functions. Consider the following example:

```
main( )
{
    printf ( "I am in main\n" ) ;
    italy( ) ;
    brazil( ) ;
    argentina( ) ;
}
italy( )
{
    printf ( "I am in italy\n" ) ;
}
brazil( )
{
```

```
        printf ( "I am in brazil\n" ) ;
}
argentina( )
{
        printf ( "I am in argentina\n" ) ;
}
```

The output of the above program when executed would be as under:

```
I am in main
I am in italy
I am in brazil
I am in argentina
```

From this program a number of conclusions can be drawn:

- Any C program contains at least one function.
- If a program contains only one function, it must be **main( )**.
- In a C program if there are more than one functions present, then one (and only one) of these functions must be **main( )**, because program execution always begins with **main( )**.
- There is no limit on the number of functions that might be present in a C program.
- Each of the function is called in the sequence specified by the function calls in the **main( )**.
- After each function has done its thing, control returns to **main( )**.When **main( )** runs out of function calls, the program ends.

As we have noted earlier the program execution always begins with **main( )**. Except for this fact all C functions enjoy a state of perfect equality. No precedences, no priorities, nobody is nobody's boss. One function can call another function it has already called but has in the meantime left temporarily in order to call a third function which will sometime later call the function that has called it, if you understand what I mean. No? Well, let's illustrate with an example.

```
main( )
{
    printf ( "I am in main\n" ) ;
    italy( ) ;
    printf ( "I am finally back in main\n" ) ;
}
italy( )
{
    printf ( "I am in italy\n" ) ;
    brazil( ) ;
    printf ( "I am back in italy\n" ) ;
}
brazil( )
{
    printf ( "I am in brazil\n" ) ;
    argentina( ) ;
}
argentina( )
{
    printf ( "I am in argentina\n" ) ;
}
```

And the output would look like...

```
I am in main
I am in italy
I am in brazil
I am in argentina
I am back in italy
I am finally back in main
```

Here, **main( )** calls other functions, which in turn call still other functions. Trace carefully the way control passes from one function to another. Since the compiler always begins the program execution with **main( )**, every function in a program must be called directly or indirectly by **main( )**. In other words, the **main( )** function drives other functions.

Let us now summarise what we have learnt so far.

(a) C program is a collection of one or more functions.

(b) A funcion gets called when the function name is followed by a semicolon. For example,

```
main( )
{
    argentina( ) ;
}
```

(c) A function is defined when function name is followed by a pair of braces in which one or more statements my be present. For example,

```
argentina( )
{
    statement 1 ;
    statement 2 ;
    statement 3 ;
}
```

(d) Any function can be called from any other function. Even **main( )** can be called from other functions. For example,

```
main( )
{
    message( ) ;
}
message( )
```

```
{
    printf ( "Can't imagine life without C\n" ) ;
    main( ) ;
}
```

(e) A function can be called any number of times. For example,

```
main( )
{
    message( ) ;
    message( ) ;
}
message( )
{
    printf ( "Jewel Thief!!\n" ) ;
}
```

(f) The order in which the functions are defined in a program and the order in which they get called need not necessarily be same. For example,

```
main( )
{
    message1( ) ;
    message2( ) ;
}
message2( )
{
    printf ( "But the butter was bitter" ) ;
}
message1( )
{
    printf ( "Mary bought some butter\n" ) ;
}
```

Here, even though **message1( )** is getting called before **message2( )**, still, **message1( )** has been defined after **message2( )**.

However, it is advisable to define the functions in the same order in which they are called. This makes the program easier to understand.

(g) A function can call itself. Such a process is called 'recursion'. We would discuss this aspect of C functions later in this chapter.

(h) A function can be called from other function, but a function cannot be defined in another function. Thus, the following program code would be wrong, since **argentina( )** is being defined inside another function **main( )**.

```
main( )
{
    printf ( "I am in main" ) ;
    argentina( )
    {
        printf ( "I am in argentina" ) ;
    }
}
```

(i) There are basically two types of functions:

Library functions Ex. **printf( )**, **scanf( )** etc.
User defined functions Ex. **argentina( )**, **brazil( )** etc.

As the name suggests, library functions are nothing but commonly required functions grouped together and stored in what is called a Library. This library of functions is present on the disk and is written for us by people who write compilers for us. Almost always a compiler comes with a library of standard functions. The procedure of calling both types of functions is exactly same.

Why Use Functions

Why write separate functions at all? Why not squeeze the entire logic into one function, **main( )**? Two reasons.

(a) Writing functions avoids rewriting the same code over and over. Suppose you have a section of code in your program that calculates area of a triangle. If, later in the program, you want to calculate the area of a different triangle, you won't like it if you are required to write the same instructions all over again. Instead, you would prefer to jump to a 'section of code' that calculates area and then jump back to the place from where you left off. This section of code is nothing but a function.

(b) Using functions it is easier to write programs and keep track of what they are doing. If the operation of a program can be divided into separate activities, and each activity placed in a different function, then each could be written and checked more or less independently. Separating the code into modular functions also makes the program easier to design and understand.

What is the moral of the story? Don't try to cram the entire logic in one function. It is a very bad style of programming. Instead, break a program into small units and write functions for each of these isolated subdivisions. Don't hesitate to write functions that are called only once. What is important is that these functions perform some logically isolated task.

Functions With Arguments

The functions that we have used so far haven't been very flexible. We call them and they do what they are designed to do. Like our mechanic who always services the motor-bike in exactly the same way, we haven't been able to influence the functions in the way they carry out their tasks. It would be nice to have a little more control over what functions do, in the same way it would be nice to be able to tell the mechanic, "Also change the engine oil, I am going for an outing". In short, now we want to communicate between the 'calling' and the 'called' functions.

The mechanism used to convey information to the function is the 'argument'. You have unknowingly used the arguments in the **printf( )** and **scanf( )** functions; the format string and the list of variables used inside the parentheses in these functions are arguments. The arguments are sometimes also called 'parameters'.

Consider the following program. In this program, in **main( )** we receive the values of **a, b** and **c** through the keyboard and then output the sum of **a, b** and **c**. However, the calculation of sum is done in a different function called **calsum( )**. If sum is to be calculated in **calsum( )** and values of **a, b** and **c** are received in **main( )**, then we must pass on these values to **calsum( )**, and once **calsum( )** calculates the sum we must return it from **calsum( )** back to **main( )**.

```
/* Sending and receiving values between functions */
main( )
{
    int a, b, c, sum ;

    printf ( "Enter any three numbers " ) ;
    scanf ( "%d %d %d", &a, &b, &c ) ;

    sum = calsum ( a, b, c ) ;

    printf ( "\nSum = %d", sum ) ;
}

calsum ( x, y, z )
int x, y, z ;
{
```

```
        int d ;

        d = x + y + z ;
        return ( d ) ;
    }
```

And here is the output...

```
Enter any three numbers 10 20 30
Sum = 60
```

There are a number of things to note about this program:

(a) In this program, from the function **main( )** the values of **a, b** and **c** are passed on to the function **calsum( )**, by making a call to the function **calsum( )** and mentioning **a, b** and **c** in the parentheses:

```
sum = calsum ( a, b, c ) ;
```

In the **calsum( )** function these values get collected in three variables **x, y** and **z**:

```
calsum ( x, y, z )
int x, y, z ;
```

(b) The variables **a, b** and **c** are called 'actual arguments', whereas the variables **x, y** and **z** are called 'formal arguments'. Any number of arguments can be passed to a function being called. However, the type, order and number of the actual and formal arguments must always be same.

Instead of using different variable names **x, y** and **z**, we could have used the same variable names **a, b** and **c**. But the compiler would still treat them as different variables since they are in different functions.

(c) In the earlier programs the moment closing brace (}) of the called function was encountered the control returned to the calling function. No separate **return** statement was necessary to send back the control.

This approach is fine if the called function is not going to return any meaningful value to the calling function. In the above program, however, we want to return the sum of **x, y** and **z.** Therefore, it is necessary to use the **return** statement.

The **return** statement serves two purposes:

(1) On executing the **return** statement it immediately transfers the control back to the calling program.
(2) It returns the value present in the parentheses after **return**, to the calling program. In the above program the value of sum of three numbers is being returned.

(d) There is no restriction on the number of **return** statements that may be present in a function. Also, the **return** statement need not always be present at the end of the called function. The following program illustrates these facts.

```
fun( )
{
    char ch ;

    printf ( "Enter any alphabet " ) ;
    scanf ( "%c", &ch ) ;

    if ( ch >= 65 && ch <= 90 )
        return ( ch ) ;
    else
        return ( ch + 32 ) ;
}
```

In this function different **return** statements will be executed depending on whether **ch** is capital or not.

(e) Whenever the control returns from a function some value is definitely returned. If a meaningful value is returned then it should be accepted in the calling program by equating the called function to some variable. For example,

```
sum = calsum ( a, b, c ) ;
```

(f) All the following are valid **return** statements.

```
return ( a ) ;
return ( 23 ) ;
return ( 12.34 ) ;
return ;
```

In the last statement a garbage value is returned to the calling function since we are not passing any specific value. Note that in this case the parentheses after **return** are dropped.

(g) If we want that a called function should not return any value, in that case, we must mention so by using the keyword **void** as shown below.

```
void display( )
{
	printf ( "Heads I win..." ) ;
	printf ( "Tails you lose" ) ;
}
```

(h) A function can return only one value at a time. Thus, the following statements are invalid.

```
return ( a, b ) ;
return ( x, 12 ) ;
```

There is a way to get around this limitation, which would be discussed at a later stage when we learn pointers.

(i) If the value of a formal argument is changed in the called function, the corresponding change does not take place in the calling function. For example.

```
main( )
{
    int a ;
    a = 30 ;

    fun ( a ) ;
    printf ( "%d", a ) ;
}

fun ( b )
int b ;
{
    b = 60 ;
    printf ( "%d\n", b ) ;
}
```

The ouput of the above program would be:

```
60
30
```

Thus, even though the value of **b** is changed in **fun( )**, the value of **a** in **main( )** remains unchanged. This means that when values are passed to a called function the values present in actual arguments are not physically moved to the formal arguments; just a photocopy of values in actual argument is made into formal arguments.

Function Declaration And Prototypes

With a sound basis of the preliminaries of C functions, let us now get into their intricacies. Any C function by default returns an **int** value. More specifically, whenever a call is made to a function, the compiler assumes that this function would return a value of the type **int**. If we desire that a function should return a value other than an **int**, then it is necessary to explicitly mention so in the calling function as well as in the called function. Suppose we want to find out square of a number using a function. This is how this simple program would look like:

```
main( )
{
    float a, b ;

    printf ( "\nEnter any number " ) ;
    scanf ( "%f", &a ) ;

    b = square ( a ) ;
    printf ( "\nSquare of %f is %f", a, b ) ;
}

square ( x )
float x ;
{
    float y ;

    y = x * x ;
    return ( y ) ;
}
```

And here are three sample runs of this program...

```
Enter any number 3
```

```
Square of 3 is 9.000000
Enter any number 1.5
Square of 1.5 is 2.000000
Enter any number 2.5
Square of 2.5 is 6.000000
```

The first of these answers is correct. But square of 1.5 is definitely not 2. Neither is 4 a square of 2.5. This happened because, any C function, by default, always returns an integer value. Therefore, even though the function **square( )** calculates the square of 1.5 as 2.25, the problem crops up when this 2.25 is to be returned to **main( )**. **square( )** is not capable of returning a **float** value. How do we overcome this? The following program segment illustrates how to make **square( )** capable of returning a **float** value.

```
main( )
{
    float square( ) ;
    float a, b ;

    printf ( "\nEnter any number " ) ;
    scanf ( "%f", &a ) ;

    b = square ( a ) ;
    printf ( "\nSquare of %f is %f", a, b ) ;
}

float square ( x )
float x ;
{
    float y ;

    y = x * x ;
    return ( y ) ;
}
```

And here is the output...

```
Enter any number 1.5
Square of 1.5 is 2.250000
Enter any number 2.5
Square of 2.5 is 6.250000
```

Now the expected answers i.e. 2.25 and 6.25 are obtained. Note that the function **square( )** must be declared as **float** in the **main( )** as well. The statement **float square( )** means that it is a function which will return a **float** value.

In practice you may seldom be required to return a value other than an **int**, but just in case you are required to, employ the above method. In some programming situations we want that a called function should not return any value. This is made possible by making use of the keyword **void**. This is illustrated in the following program.

```
main( )
{
    void gospel( ) ;

    gospel( ) ;
}

void gospel( )
{
    printf ( "Viruses are electronic bandits...\n" ) ;
    printf ( "who eat nuggets of information...\n" ) ;
    printf ( "and  chunks of bytes...\n" ) ;
    printf ( "when you least expect...\n" ) ;
}
```

Here, the **gospel( )** function has been defined to return **void**; means it would return nothing. Therefore, it would just flash the four messages about viruses and return the control back to the **main( )** function.

Call By Value And Call By Reference

By now we are well familiar with how to call functions. But, if you observe carefully, whenever we called a function and passed something to it we have always passed the values of variables to the called function. Such function calls are called 'calls by value'. By this what we mean is, on calling a function we are passing values of variables to it. The examples of call by value are shown below:

```
sum = calsum ( a, b, c ) ;
f = factr ( a ) ;
```

We have also learnt that variables are stored somewhere in memory. So instead of passing the value of a variable, can we not pass the location number (also called address) of the variable to a function? If we are able to do so it would become a 'call by reference'. What purpose a 'call by reference' serves we would find out a little later. But first we must equip ourselves with knowledge of how to make a 'call by reference'. This feature of C functions needs at least an elementary knowledge of 'pointers'. So let us first acquire the basics of pointers after which we would take up this topic once again.

An Introduction To Pointers

Which feature of C do beginners find most difficult to understand? The answer is easy: pointers. Other languages have pointers but few use them so frequently as C does. Hence we have an entire chapter (Chapter 9) devoted to it. Here, we would just have an introduction to the concept of pointers. Most of the material covered would be discussed in greater depth in the next chapter. To begin with let's try to understand pointers in terms of programming concepts that we have already learnt.

Consider the declaration,

```
int i = 3 ;
```

This declaration tells the C compiler to:

(a) Reserve space in memory to hold the integer value.
(b) Associate the name **i** with this memory location.
(c) Store the value 3 at this location.

We may represent **i**'s location in the memory by the following memory map.

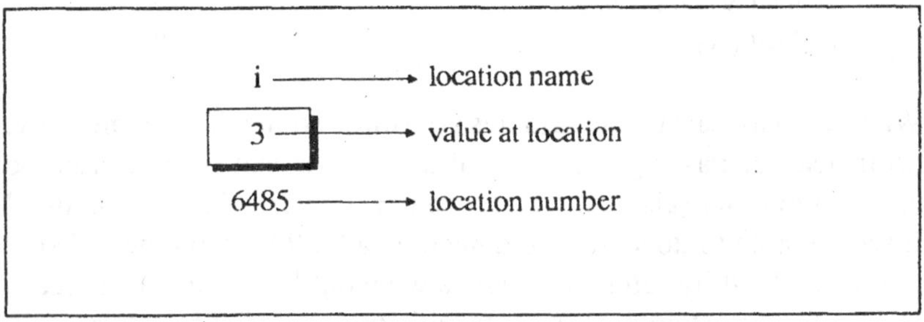

Figure 8.1

We see that the computer has selected memory location 6485 as the place to store the value 3. The location number 6485 is not a number to be relied upon, because some other time the computer may choose a different location for storing the value 3. The important point is, **i**'s address in memory is a number.

We can print this address number through the following program:

```
main( )
{
    int i = 3 ;
    printf ( "Address of i = %d\n", &i ) ;
    printf ( "Value of i = %d\n", i ) ;
}
```

The output of the above program would be:

```
Address of i = 6485
Value of i = 3
```

Look at the first **printf( )** statement carefully. '&' used in this statement is C's 'address of' operator. The expression **&i** returns the address of the variable **i**, which in this case happens to be 6485. We have been using this '&' all the time in the **scanf( )** statement.

The other pointer operator available in C is **'*'** , called 'Value at address' operator. It gives the value stored at a particular address. The 'value at address' operator is also called 'indirection' operator.

Observe carefully the output of the following program:

```
main( )
{
    int i = 3 ;

    printf ( "Address of i = %d\n", &i ) ;
    printf ( "Value of i = %d\n", i ) ;
    printf ( "Value of i = %d\n", *( &i ) ) ;
}
```

The output of the above program would be:

```
Address of i = 6485
Value of i = 3
Value of i = 3
```

Note that printing the value of ***(&i)** is same as printing the value of **i**.

The expression **&i** gives the address of the variable **i**. This address can be collected in a variable, by saying,

```
j = &i ;
```

But remember that **j** is not an ordinary variable like any other integer variable. It is a variable which contains the address of other variable (**i** in this case).

Since **j** is a variable the compiler must provide it space in the memory. Once again, the following memory map would illustrate the contents of **i** and **j**.

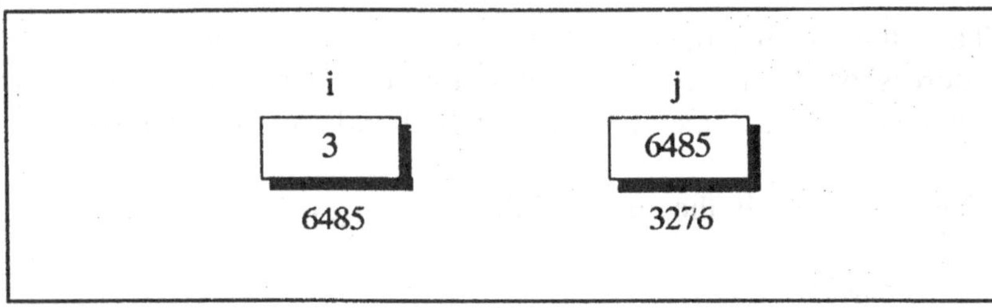

Figure 8.2

As you can see, **i**'s value is 3 and j's value is **i**'s address.

But wait, we can't use **j** in a program without declaring it. And since **j** is a variable which contains the address of **i**, it is declared as,

```
int *j ;
```

This declaration tells the compiler that **j** will be used to store the address of an integer value. In other words **j** points to an integer. How do we justify the usage of * in the declaration,

```
int *j ;
```

Let us go by the meaning of *. It stands for 'value at address' . Thus, **int *j** would mean, the value at the address contained in **j** is an **int**.

Here is a program that demonstrates the relationships we have been discussing.

```
main( )
```

```
{
    int i = 3 ;
    int *j ;

    j = &i ;

    printf ( "Address of i = %d\n", &i ) ;
    printf ( "Address of i = %d\n", j ) ;
    printf ( "Address of j = %d\n", &j ) ;
    printf ( "Value of j  = %d\n", j ) ;
    printf ( "Value of i  = %d\n", i ) ;
    printf ( "Value of i  = %d\n", *( &i ) ) ;
    printf ( "Value of i  = %d\n", *j ) ;
}
```

The output of the above program would be:

```
Address of i = 6485
Address of i = 6485
Address of j = 3276
Value of j = 6485
Value of i = 3
Value of i = 3
Value of i = 3
```

Work through the above program carefully, taking help of the memory locations of **i** and **j** shown earlier. This program summarises everything we have discussed so far. If you don't understand the program's output, or the meanings of **&i**, **&j**, ***j** and ***(&i**), re-read the last few pages. Everything we say about C pointers from here onwards will depend on your understanding these expressions thoroughly.

Look at the following declarations,

```
int *alpha ;
char *ch :
```

```
float *s ;
```

Here, **alpha, ch** and s are declared as pointer variables, i.e. variables capable of holding addresses. Remember that, addresses (location nos.) are always going to be whole numbers, therefore pointers always contain whole numbers. Now we can put these two facts together and say: pointers are variables which contain addresses, and since addresses are always whole numbers, pointers would always contain whole numbers.

The declaration **float *s** does not mean that **s** is going to contain a floating point value. What it means is, s is going to contain the address of a floating point value. Similarly, **char *ch** means that **ch** is going to contain the address of a char value. Or in other words, the value at address stored in **ch** is going to be a **char**.

Back To Function Calls

Having had the first meeting with pointers let us now get back to what we had originally set out to learn - the two types of function calls: call by value and call by reference. Arguments can generally be passed to functions in one of the two ways:

(a) sending the values of the arguments
(b) sending the addresses of the arguments

In the first method the 'value' of each of the actual arguments in the calling function is copied into corresponding formal arguments of the called function. With this method the changes made to the formal arguments in the called function have no effect on the values of actual arguments in the calling function.

The following program illustrates the 'Call by Value'.

```
main( )
{
```

```
        int a = 10 ;
        int b = 20 ;

        swapv ( a, b ) ;

        printf ( "a = %d\n", a ) ;
        printf ( "b = %d\n", b ) ;
}

swapv ( x, y )
int x, y ;
{
        int t ;

        t = x ;
        x = y ;
        y = t ;

        printf ( "x = %d\n", x ) ;
        printf ( "y = %d\n", y ) ;
}
```

The output of the above program will be:

```
x = 20
y = 10
a = 10
b = 20
```

Note that values of **a** and **b** remain unchanged even after exchanging the values of **x** and **y**.

In the second method (call by reference) the addresses of actual arguments in the calling function are copied into formal arguments of the called function. This means that using these addresses we would have an access to the actual arguments and hence we would be able to manipulate them.

The following program illustrates this fact.

```
main( )
{
    int a = 10 ;
    int b = 20 ;

    swapr ( &a, &b ) ;

    printf ( "a = %d\n", a ) ;
    printf ( "b = %d\n", b ) ;
}

swapr( x, y )
int *x, *y ;
{
    int t ;

    t = *x ;
    *x = *y ;
    *y = t ;
}
```

The output of the above program will be:

```
a = 20
b = 10
```

Note that this program manages to exchange the values of **a** and **b** using their addresses stored in **x** and **y**.

Usually in C programming we make a call by value. This means in general you cannot alter the actual arguments. But if desired, it can always be achieved through a call by reference.

Using a 'call by reference' intelligently we can make a function return more than one value at a time, which is not possible ordinarily. This is shown in the example given below.

```
main( )
{
    int radius ;
    float area, perimeter ;

    printf ( "Enter radius of a circle " ) ;

    areaperi ( radius, &area, &perimeter ) ;

    printf ( "\nArea = %f\n", area ) ;
    printf ( "\nPerimeter = %f\n", perimeter ) ;
}

areaperi ( r, a, p )
int r ;
float *a, *p ;
{
    *a = 3.14 * r * r ;
    *p = 2 * 3.14 * r ;
}
```

And here is the output...

```
Enter radius of a circle 5
Area = 78.500000
Perimeter = 31.400000
```

Here, we are making a mixed call, in the sense, we are passing the value of **radius** but, addresses of **area** and **perimeter**. And since we are passing the addresses, any change that we make in values stored at addresses contained in the variables **a** and **p**, would make the change effective in **main( )**. That is why when the control returns from the function **areaperi( )** we are able to output the values of **area** and **perimeter**.

Thus, we have been able to return two values from a called function, and hence, get past the limitation of the **return** statement, which can return only one value from a function at a time.

Scope Rules Of Functions

Look at the following program:

```
main( )
{
    int i = 20 ;
    display ( i ) ;
}

display ( j )
int j ;
{
    int k = 35 ;
    printf ( "%d", j ) ;
    printf ( "%d", k ) ;
}
```

In this program is it necessary to pass the value of the variable **i** to the function **display( )**? Will it not become automatically available to the function **display( )**? No. Because by default the scope of a variable is local to the function in which it is defined. The presence of **i** is known only to the function **main( )** and not to any other function. Similarly, the variable **k** is local to the function **display( )** and hence it is not available to **main( )**. That is why to make the value of **i** available to **display( )** we have to explicitly pass it to **display( )**. Likewise, if we want **k** to be available to **main( )** we will have to return it to **main( )** using the **return** statement. In general we can say that the scope of a variable is local to the function in which it is defined.

The scope rules change if the place where the variables are declared is changed. For example, if the variables **i** and **k** in the above program are declared on the top of **main( )**, then their values would be available to **main( )** as well as to **display( )**. Such variables are called 'external' variables. Following program shows how to declare these variables.

```
int i = 20, k = 35 ;
main( )
{
    printf ( "%d\n", i ) ;
    printf ( "%d\n", k ) ;
    display( );
}

display( )
{
    printf ( "%d\n", i ) ;
    printf ( "%d\n", k ) ;
}
```

Note that now there is no need to pass **i** to **display( )**. The values of the variables **i** and **k** are now automatically available to **main( )** as well as to **display( )**.

Calling Functions With Arrays

Array elements can be passed to a function by calling the function by value, or by reference. In the call by value we pass values of array elements to the function, whereas in the call by reference we pass addresses of array elements to the function. These two calls are illustrated below:

```
/* Demonstration of Call by value */
main( )
{
    int i ;
    static int marks[ ] = { 55, 65, 75, 56, 78, 78, 90 } ;

    for ( i = 0 ; i <= 6 ; i++ )
        display ( marks[i] ) ;
}

display ( m )
int m ;
{
    printf ( "%d\n", m ) ;
}
```

And here's the output...

```
55
65
75
56
78
78
90
```

Here, we are passing an individual array element at a time to the function **display( )** and getting it printed in the function **display( )**. Note that since at a time only one element is being passed, in the function **display( )** this element is collected in an ordinary integer variable **m**.

And now the call by reference.

```
/* Demonstration of Call by reference */
main( )
{
```

```
    int i ;
    static int marks[ ] = { 55, 65, 75, 56, 78, 78, 90 } ;

    for ( i = 0 ; i <= 6 ; i++ )
        disp ( &marks[i] ) ;
}

disp ( n )
int *n ;
{
    printf ( "%d\n", *n ) ;
}
```

And here's the output...

```
55
65
75
56
78
78
90
```

Here, we are passing addresses of individual array elements to the function **display( )**. Hence, the variable in which this address is collected (**n**) is declared as a pointer variable. And since **n** contains the address of array element, to print out the array element we are using the 'value at address' operator (*).

Read the following program carefully. The purpose of the function is just to display the array elements on the screen. The program is only partly complete. You are required to write the function **show( )** on your own. Try your hand at it.

```
main( )
{
    int i ;
```

```
    static int marks[ ] = { 55, 65, 75, 56, 78, 78, 90 } ;

    for ( i = 0 ; i <= 6 ; i++ )
        disp ( &marks[i] ) ;
}

disp ( n )
int *n ;
{
    show ( &n ) ;
}
```

Pointers And Arrays

To be able to see what pointers have got to do with arrays, let us first learn some pointer arithmetic. Consider the following example:

```
main( )
{
    int i = 3, *x ;

    printf ( "Value of i = %d\n", i ) ;
    x = &i ;
    printf ( "Original value in x = %d\n", x ) ;
    x++ ;
    printf ( "New value in x = %d\n", x ) ;
}
```

Suppose **i** is stored in memory at address 1002, the output would be...

```
Value of i = 3
Original value in x = 1002
New value in x = 1004
```

Observe the last line of the output carefully. 1004 is original value in **x** plus 2. This so happens because every time a pointer is incremented it points to the immediately next location of its type. That is why, when the integer pointer **x** is incremented, it points to an address two locations after the current location, since an **int** is always 2 bytes long. This is a very important result and can be effectively used while passing the entire array to a function.

The way a pointer can be incremented, it can be decremented as well, to point to earlier locations.

Now we will try to correlate the following two facts, which we have already learnt:

(a) Array elements are always stored in contiguous memory locations.
(b) A pointer when incremented always points to an immediately next location of its type.

Suppose we have an array **num[ ]** = { 24, 34, 12, 44, 56, 17 }. The following figure shows how this array is located in memory.

24	34	12	44	56	17
4001	4003	4005	4007	4009	4011

Figure 8.3

Here is a program that prints out the memory locations in which the elements of this array are stored.

```
main( )
{
    static int num[ ] = { 24, 34, 12, 44, 56, 17 } ;
    int i = 0 ;

    while ( i <= 5 )
```

```
        {
            printf ( "element no. %d ", i ) ;
            printf ( "address = %d\n", &num[i] ) ;
            i++ ;
        }
}
```

The output of this program would look like this:

```
element no. 0 address = 4001
element no. 1 address = 4003
element no. 2 address = 4005
element no. 3 address = 4007
element no. 4 address = 4009
element no. 5 address = 4011
```

Note that the array elements are stored in contiguous memory locations, each element occupying two bytes, since it is an integer array. When you run this program, you make get different addresses, but what is promised is that each subsequent address would be 2 bytes greater than its immediate predecessor.

Our next two programs show two ways in which we can access the array elements of this array.

```
main( )
{
    static int num[ ] = { 24, 34, 12, 44, 56, 17 } ;
    int i = 0 ;

    while ( i <= 5 )
    {
        printf ( "address = %d ", &num[i] ) ;
        printf ( "element = %d\n", num[i] ) ;
        i++ ;
    }
}
```

The output of this program would look like this:

```
address = 4001 element = 24
address = 4003 element = 34
address = 4005 element = 12
address = 4007 element = 44
address = 4009 element = 56
address = 4011 element = 17
```

This method of accessing array elements by using subscripted variables is already known to us. This method has in fact been given here for easy comparison with the next method, which accesses the array elements using pointers.

```
main( )
{
    static int num[ ] = { 24, 34, 12, 44, 56, 17 } ;
    int i = 0, *j ;

    j = &num[0] ; /* assign address of zeroeth element */

    while ( i <= 5 )
    {
        printf ( "address = %d ", j ) ;
        printf ( "element = %d\n", *j ) ;
        i++ ;
        j++ ; /* increment pointer to point to the next location */
    }
}
```

The output of this program would look like this:

```
address = 4001 element = 24
address = 4003 element = 34
address = 4005 element = 12
address = 4007 element = 44
address = 4009 element = 56
```

```
address = 4011 element = 17
```

In this program, to begin with we have collected the base address of the array (address of the 0th element) in the variable **j** using the statement,

```
j = &num[0] ; /* assigns address 4001 to j */
```

When we are inside the loop for the first time **j** contains the address 4001, and the value at this address is 24. These are printed using the statements,

```
printf ( "address = %d ", j ) ;
printf ( "element = %d\n", *j ) ;
```

On incrementing **j** it points to the next memory location of its type (that is location no. 4003). But location no. 4003 contains the second element of the array, therefore when the **printf( )** statements are executed for the second time they print out the second element of the array and its address (i.e. 34 and 4003)... and so on till the last element of the array has been printed.

Obviously, a question arises as to which of the above two methods should be used when? Accessing array elements by pointers is **always** faster than accessing them by subscripts. However, from the point of view of convenience in programming we should observe the following:

Array elements should be accessed using pointers if the elements are to be accessed in a fixed order, say from beginning to end, or from end to beginning, or every alternate element or any such definite logic.

Instead, it would be easier to access the elements using a subscript if there is no fixed logic in accessing the elements. However, in this case also, accessing the elements by pointers would work faster than subscripts.

Passing An Entire Array To A Function

Earlier we saw two programs - one in which we passed individual elements of an array to a function, and another in which we passed addresses of individual elements to a function. Let us now see how to pass an entire array to a function rather than its individual elements. Consider the following example:

```
/* Demonstration of passing an entire array to a function */
main( )
{
    static int num[ ] = { 24, 34, 12, 44, 56, 17 } ;
    dislpay ( &num[0], 6 ) ;
}

display ( j, n )
int *j, n ;
{
    int i = 1 ;

    while ( i <= n )
    {
        printf ( "element =\n", *j ) ;
        i++ ;
        j++ ; /* increment pointer to point to next location */
    }
}
```

Here, the **display( )** function is used to print out the array elements. Note that the address of the zeroeth element is being passed to the **display( )** function. The **while** loop is same as the one used in the earlier program to access the array elements using pointers. Thus, just passing the address of the zeroeth element of the array to a function, is as good as passing the entire array to the function. It is also necessary to pass the total number of elements in the array, otherwise the **display( )** function would not know when to terminate the **while** loop. Note that the address of the zeroeth element (many a times called the base address) can also be passed by just passing the name of the array. Thus, the following two function calls are same:

```
display ( &num[0], 6 ) ;
display ( num, 6 ) ;
```

The Real Thing

If you have grasped the concept of storage of array elements in memory and the arithmetic of pointers, here is some real food for thought. Once again consider the following array.

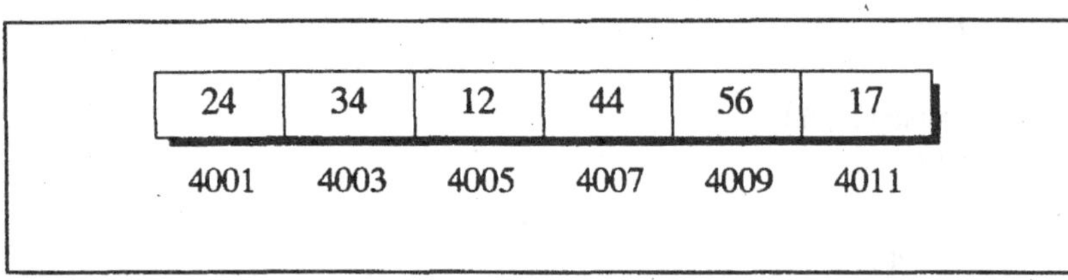

Figure 8.4

This is how we would declare the above array in C,

```
static int num[ ] = { 24, 34, 12, 44, 56, 17 } ;
```

We also know that on mentioning the name of the array we get its base adddress. Thus, by saying ***num** we would be able to refer to the zeroeth element of the array, that is, 24. One can easily see that ***num** and ***(num + 0**) both refer to 24.

Similarly by saying ***(num + 1**), we can refer the first element of the array, that is, 34. In fact, this is what the C compiler does internally. When we say, **num[i]**, the C compiler internally converts it to ***(num + i**). This means that all the following notations are same:

```
num[i]
*( num + i )
*( i + num )
i[num]
```

And here is a program to prove my point.

```
/* Accessing array elements in different ways */
main( )
{
    static int num[ ] = { 24, 34, 12, 44, 56, 17 } ;
    int i = 0 ;

    while ( i <= 5 )
    {
        printf ( "address = %d ", &num[i] ) ;
        printf ( "element = %d ", num[i] ) ;
        printf ( "%d ", *( num + i ) ) ;
        printf ( "%d ", *( i + num ) ) ;
        printf ( "%d\n", i[num] ) ;

        i++ ;
    }
}
```

The output of this program would be:

```
address = 4001 element = 24 24 24 24
address = 4003 element = 34 34 34 34
address = 4005 element = 12 12 12 12
address = 4007 element = 44 44 44 44
address = 4009 element = 56 56 56 56
address = 4011 element =  17 17 17 17
```

argc And argv - Arguments To main( )

Can we not pass arguments to **main( )** the way we pass them to other functions? We can. For this we specify the arguments at command prompt when we execute the program. For example, suppose 'PR1.EXE' is the name of the executable file, and we wish to pass the arguments 'Cat', 'Dog' and 'Parrot' to **main( )** in this file. We can do so through the following comand at the command prompt:

```
C> PR1.EXE Cat Dog Parrot
```

Now if we are passing arguments to **main( )**, it must collect them in variables. Usually only two variables are used to collect these arguments. These are called **argc** and **argv.** Out of these **argc** contains the count (number) of arguments being passed to **main( )**, whereas **argv** contains addresses of strings passed to **main( )**. In the above example **argc** would contain 4, whereas **argv[0]**, **argv[1]**, **argv[2]**, and **argv[3]** would contain base addresses of PR1.EXE, Cat, Dog and Parrot respectively. If we so desire we can print these arguments from within **main( )** as shown in the following program.

```
main ( argc, argv )
int argc ;
char *argv[ ] ;
{
    int i ;

    for ( i = 0 ; i < argc ; i++ )
        printf ( "%s\n", argv[i] ) ;
}
```

Note the declaration of **argv[ ]**. It has been declared as an array of pointers to strings. The concept of array of pointers is covered in detail in Chapter 9. Also observe the format specification used in

printf( ). We are using **%s** because we wish to print out the various strings that are being passed to **main( )**.

It is not necessary that we should always use the variable names **argc** and **argv**. In place of them any other variable names can as well be used.

Recursion

In C, it is possible for the functions to call themselves. A function is called 'recursive' if a statement within the body of a function calls the same function. Sometimes called 'circular definition', recursion is thus the process of defining something in terms of itself.

A simple example of recursion is the function **rec( )**, shown below which computes the factorial value of an integer. As we know the factorial of a number is the product of all the integers between 1 and that number. For example, 3 factorial is 3 * 2 * 1, or 6. For the sake of understanding let us first look at the non-recursive function for calculating the factorial value of an integer.

```
main( )
{
    int a, fact ;

    printf ( "\nEnter any number " ) ;
    scanf ( "%d", &a ) ;

    fact = factorial ( a ) ;

    printf ( "Factorial value = %d", fact ) ;
}

factorial ( x )
int x ;
```

```
{
    int f = 1, i ;

    ror ( i = x ; i >= 1 ; i-- )
        f = f * i ;

    return ( f ) ;
}
```

And here is the output...

```
Enter any number 3
Factorial value = 6
```

Work through the above program carefully, till you understand the logic of the program properly. Recursive factorial function can be understood only if you are thorough with the above logic.

Following is the recursive version of the function to calculate the factorial value.

```
main( )
{
    int a, fact ;

    printf ( "\nEnter any number " ) ;
    scanf ( "%d", &a ) ;

    fact = rec ( a ) ;
    printf ( "Factorial value = %d", fact ) ;
}

rec ( x )
int x ;
{
    int f ;
```

```
        if ( x == 1 )
            return ( 1 ) ;
        else
            f = x * rec ( x - 1 ) ;

        return ( f ) ;
}
```

And here is the output for four runs of the program...

```
Enter any number 1
Factorial value = 1
Enter any number 2
Factorial value = 2
Enter any number 3
Factorial value = 6
Enter any number 5
Factorial value = 120
```

Let us understand this recursive factorial function thoroughly.

In the first run when the number entered through **scanf( )** is 1, let us see what action does **rec( )** takes. The value of **a** (i.e. 1) is copied into **x**. Since **x** turns out to be 1 the condition **if (x == 1)** is satisfied and hence 1 (which indeed is the value of 1 factorial) is returned through the **return** statement.

When the number entered through **scanf( )** is 2, the **(x == 1)** test fails, so we reach the statement,

```
f = x * rec ( x - 1 ) ;
```

And here is where we meet recursion. How do we handle the expression **x * rec (x - 1)**? We multiply **x** by **rec (x - 1)**. Since the current value of **x** is 2, it is the same thing as saying that we must calculate the value (2 * rec (1)). We know that the value returned by **rec (1)** is 1, so the expression reduces to (2 * 1), or simply 2. Thus the statement,

```
x * rec ( x - 1 ) ;
```

evaluates to 2, which is stored in the variable **f**, and is returned to **main( )**, where it is duly printed as

```
Factorial value = 2
```

Now perhaps you can see what would happen if the value of **a** is 3, 4, 5 and so on.

In case the value of **a** is 5, **main( )** would call **rec( )** with 5 as its actual argument, and **rec( )** will send back the computed value. But before sending the computed value, **rec( )** calls **rec( )** and waits for a value to be returned. It is possible for the **rec( )** that has just been called to call yet another **rec( )**, the argument **x** being decreased in value by 1 for each of these recursive calls. We speak of this series of calls to **rec( )** as being different invocations of **rec( )**. These successive invocations of the same function are possible because the C compiler keeps track of which invocation calls which. These recursive invocations end finally when the last invocation gets an argument value of 1, which the preceeding invocation of **rec( )** now uses to calculate its own **fact** value and so on up the ladder. So we might say what happens is,

```
rec ( 5 ) returns ( 5 times rec ( 4 ),
      which returns ( 4 times rec ( 3 ),
            which returns ( 3 times rec ( 2 ),
                  which returns ( 2 times rec ( 1 ),
                        which returns ( 1 ) ) ) ) )
```

Foxed? Well, that is recursion for you in its simplest garbs. I hope you agree that it's difficult to visualise how the control flows from one function call to another. Possibly the following figure would make the things a bit clearer.

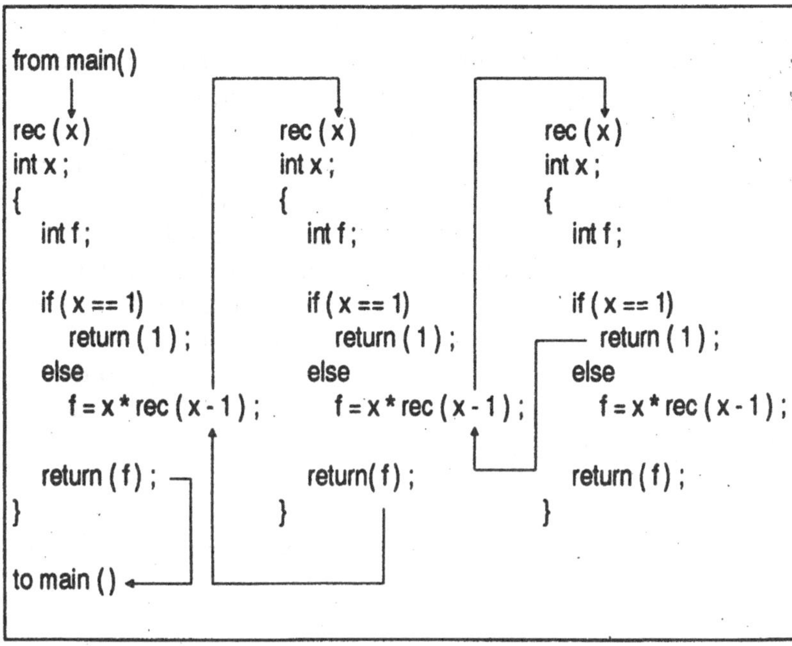

Figure 8.5

Assume that the number entered is 3. Using the figure let's visualise what exactly happens when the recursive function **rec( )** gets called. Go through the figure carefully. The first time when **rec( )** is called from **main( )**, **x** collects 3. From here, since **x** is not equal to 1, the **if** block is skipped and **rec( )** is called again with the argument (**x - 1**), i.e. 2. This is a recursive call. Since **x** is still not equal to 1, **rec( )** is called yet another time, with argument (2 - 1). This time as **x** is 1, control goes back to previous **rec( )** with the value 1, and **f** is evaluated as 2.

Similarly, each **rec( )** evaluates its **f** from the returned value, and finally 6 is returned to main( ). The sequence would be grasped better by following the arrows in the figure. Let it be clear that while executing the program there do not exist so many copies of the function **rec( )**. These have been shown in the figure just to help you keep track of how the control flows during successive recursive calls.

Recursion may seem strange and complicated at first glance, but it is often the most direct way to code an algorithm - and, once you are familiar with recursion, the clearest way of doing so.

When writing recursive functions, you must have an **if** statement somewhere in the recursive function to force the function to return without recursive call being executed. If you don't do this and you call the function, you will fall in an indefinite loop, and will never return from the called function. This is a very common error while writing recursive functions. My advice is to use **printf( )** statement liberally during the development of recursive function, so that you can watch what is going on and can abort execution if you see that you have made a mistake.

A word of advice... some people seem to think recursively more easily than others. If you feel comfortable with recursion, then use it. If you do not, use iterative methods like **for, while** or **do-while**.

Exercise

[A] What will be the output of the following programs:

(1)
```
main( )
{
    int area ;
    float radius = 2.0 ;
    area = areacircle ( radius ) ;
    printf ( "area = %f", area ) ;
}
areacircle ( r )
float r ;
{
    float a ;
    a = 3.14 * r * r ;
    printf ( "a = %f\n", a ) ;
    return ( a ) ;
}
```

(2)
```
main( )
{
    int c ;
    printf ( "c before call = %d\n", c ) ;
    c = message( ) ;
    printf ( "c after call = %d\n", c ) ;
}
message( )
{
    printf ( "Live and let live\n" ) ;
}
```

(3)
```
main( )
{
    C( )
```

```
    {
        c( )
        {
            printf ( "C is a C...\n" ) ;
        }
        printf ( "..is a c...\n" ) ;
    }
    printf ( "..is a sea afterall!" ) ;
}
```

(4)
```
main( )
{
    int i = 3, k, l ;
    k = add ( ++i ) ;
    l = add ( i++ ) ;
    printf ( "i = %d k = %d l = %d", i, k, l ) ;
}
add ( ii )
int ii ;
{
    ++ii ;
    return ( ii ) ;
}
```

(5)
```
main( )
{
    int i = 135, a = 135, k ;
    k = function ( !++i, !a++ ) ;
    printf ( "i = %d a = %d k = %d", i, a, k ) ;
}
function ( j, b )
int j, b ;
{
    int c ;
    c = j + b ;
    return ( c ) ;
}
```

(6)
```
main( )
{
    int k = 35, z ;
    k = func1 ( k = func1 ( k = func1 ( k ) ) ) ;
    printf ( "k = %d", k ) ;
}
func1 ( k )
int k ;
{
    k++ ;
    return ( k ) ;
}
```

(7)
```
main( )
{
    int k = 35, z ;
    z = func ( k ) ;
    printf ( "z = %d", z ) ;
}
func ( m )
int m ;
{
    ++m ;
    return ( m = func1 ( ++m ) ) ;
}
func1 ( m )
int m ;
{
    m++ ;
    return ( m ) ;
}
```

(8)
```
main( )
{
    void message( ) ;
    int c ;
```

```
    printf ( "c before call = %d\n", c ) ;
    c = message( ) ;
    printf ( "c after call = %d", c ) ;
}
void message( )
{
    printf ( "Only he will survive who is C-fit" ) ;
}
```

(9)

```
main( )
{
    int i ;
    printf ( "In the year of lord\n" ) ;
    for ( i = 1 ; i <= 10 ; i++ )
        main( ) ;
}
```

(10)

```
main( )
{
    int i = 5, j = 2 ;
    junk ( i, j ) ;
    printf ( "%d %d", i , j );
}
junk( i, j )
int i, j ;
{
    i = i * i ;
    j = j * j ;
}
```

(11)

```
main( )
{
    int i = 5, j = 2 ;
    junk ( &i, &j ) ;
    printf ( "%d %d", i , j );
}
```

```
junk ( i, j )
int *i, *j ;
{
     *i = *i * *i ;
     *j = *j * *j ;
}
```

(12)
```
main( )
{
     int i = 4 , j = 2 ;
     junk ( &i, j ) ;
     printf ( "%d %d", i, j ) ;
}
junk ( i, j )
int *i, j ;
{
     *i = *i * *i ;
     j = j * j ;
}
```

(13)
```
main( )
{
     float a = 13.5
     float *b, *c ;

     b = &a ; /*suppose the address of a is 1006 */
     c = b ;
     printf ( "%d %d %d \n", &a, b, c ) ;
     printf ( "%d %d %d %d \n", a, *(&a), *b, *c ) ;
}
```

[B] Attempt the following:

(1) Consider a currency system in which there are notes of seven denominations, namely,

Re. 1, Rs. 2, Rs. 5, Rs. 10, Rs. 20, Rs. 50, Rs. 100

If a sum of Rs. N is entered through the keyboard, write a program to compute the smallest number of notes that will combine to give Rs. N.

(2) Write a program to obtain the sum of the first ten terms of the following series using recursion.

$$x - \frac{x^3}{3!} + \frac{x^5}{5!} - \frac{x^7}{7!} + \frac{x^9}{9!} - \ldots$$

(3) Two dates are entered through the keyboard in dd,mm,yy format. Write a program to find out the difference in these two dates in terms of number of days.

(4) Write a function which receives a float and an integer from **main()**, finds the product of these two and returns the product which is printed through **main()**.

(5) A 5 digit positive integer is entered through the keyboard, write a function to calculate sum of digits of the 5 digit number:

(a) Without using recursion
(b) Using recursion

(8) A positive integer is entered through the keyboard, write a program to obtain the prime factors of the number. Modify the function suitably to obtain the prime factors recursively.

(9) Write a recursive function to obtain the first 25 numbers of the Fibonacci sequence. In a Fibonacci sequence the sum of two successive terms gives the third term.

For example, 1 1 2 3 5 8 13 21 34 55 89 ...

CHAPTER

9 Pointers

The & And * Operators
Pointer Expressions
Dynamic Memory Allocation
Pointers Versus Arrays
Pointers And 2 Dimensional Arrays
Arrays Of Pointers
Pointers To Pointers
Pointers To Functions
Functions Returning Pointers
Functions With Variable Number Of Arguments

Which feature of C do beginners find most difficult to understand? The answer is easy: pointers. Other languages have pointers but few use them so freely, with such abandon, as C does. And why not? It is C's clever use of pointers that makes it the excellent language that it is.

The difficulty beginners have with pointers has much to do with C's pointer terminology than the actual concept. For instance, when a C programmer says that a certain variable is a 'pointer', what does that mean? It is hard to see how a variable can point to something, or in a certain direction. It is hard to get a grip on pointers just by listening to programmer's jargon. In our discussion of C pointers, therefore, we will try to avoid this jargon and try to explain them in terms of programming concepts we already understand. The first thing we want to do is explain the rationale of C's pointer notation. Some of the concepts discussed below have already been dealt with to a certain extent in the previous chapter. But inspite of some repitition we thought it worthwhile to start off with pointers right from scratch. Those of you who feel comfortable with pointers may skip the next 2-3 pages. But we would rather have that you don't.

The & And * Operators

Consider the declaration,

```
int i = 3 ;
```

This declaration tells the C compiler to:

(a) Reserve space in memory to hold the integer value.
(b) Associate the name **i** with this memory location.
(c) Store the value 3 at this location.

We may represent **i**'s location in the memory by the following memory map:

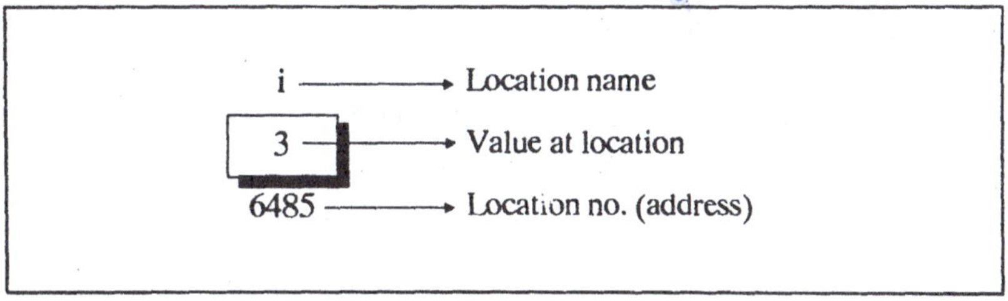

Figure 9.1

We see that the computer has selected memory location 6485 as the place to store the value 3. The location number 6485 is not a number to be relied upon, because some other time the computer may choose a different location for storing the value 3. The important point is, **i**'s address in memory is a number.

We can print this address number through the following program:

```
main( )
{
    int i = 3 ;
```

```
        printf ( "Address of i = %d\n", &i ) ;
        printf ( "Value of i = %d \n", i ) ;
}
```

The output of the above program would be:

```
Address of i = 6485
Value of i = 3
```

Look at the first **printf( )** statement carefully. '**&**' used in this statement is C's 'address of' operator. The expression **&i** returns the address of the variable **i**, which in this case happens to be 6485. We have been using this **&** all the time in the **scanf( )** statement.

The other pointer operator available in C is '*', called 'Value at address' operator. It gives the value stored at a particular address. The 'value at address' operator is also called 'indirection' operator.

Observe carefully the output of the following program:

```
main( )
{
    int i = 3 ;
    printf ( "Address of i = %d \n", &i ) ;
    printf ( "Value of i = %d \n", i ) ;
    printf ( "Value of i = %d \n", *( &i ) ) ;
}
```

The output of the above program would be:

```
Address of i = 6485
Value of i = 3
Value of i = 3
```

Note that printing the value of ***(&i)** is same as printing the value of **i**.

Pointer Expressions

Let us now see how pointers can be used in expressions and what arithmetic and comparison operations can be performed on pointers. Let us begin with the usage of pointers in an assignment statement.

Pointer Assignments

We have seen in the previous section that the expression **&i** returns the address of **i**. If we so desire this address can be collected in a variable by saying,

```
j = &i ;
```

But remember that **j** is not an ordinary variable like any other integer variable. It is a variable which contains the address of other variable (**i** in this case).

Since **j** is a variable the compiler must provide it space in memory. Once again, the following memory map would illustrate the contents of **i** and **j**.

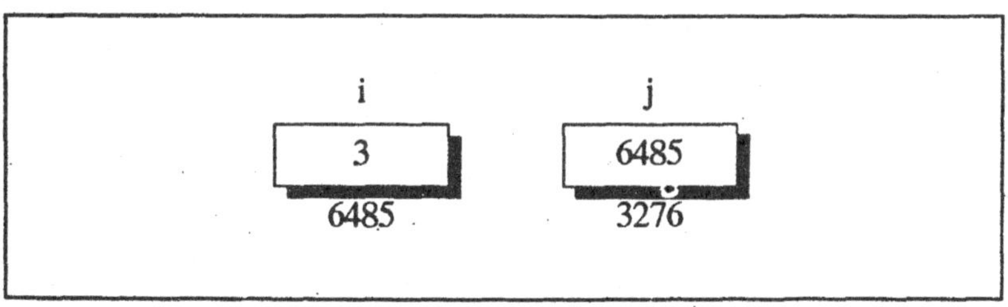

Figure 9.2

As you can see, **i**'s value is 3 and **j**'s value is **i**'s address.

But wait, we can't use **j** in a program without declaring it. And since **j** is a variable which contains the address of **i**, it is declared as,

```
int *j ;
```

This declaration tells the compiler that **j** will be used to store the address of an integer value - in other words j points to an integer. How do we justify the usage of * in the declaration,

```
int *j ;
```

Let us go by the meaning of *. It stands for 'value at address' . Thus, **int *j** would mean, the value at the address contained in **j** is an **int**.

Here is a program that demonstrates the relationships we have been discussing.

```
main()
{
    int i = 3 ;
    int *j ;

    j = &i ;

    printf ( "Address of i = %d \n", &i ) ;
    printf ( "Address of i = %d \n", j ) ;
    printf ( "Address of j = %d \n", &j ) ;
    printf ( "Value of j = %d \n", j ) ;
    printf ( "Value of i = %d \n", i ) ;
    printf ( "Value of i = %d \n", *( &i ) ) ;
    printf ( "Value of i = %d \n", *j ) ;
}
```

The output of the above program would be:

```
Address of i = 6485
Address of i = 6485
Address of j = 3276
Value of j = 6485
Value of i = 3
```

```
Value of i = 3
Value of i = 3
```

Work through the above program carefully, taking help of the memory locations of **i** and **j** shown earlier. This program summarises everything we have discussed so far. If you don't understand the program's output, or the meanings of **&i, &j, *j** and ***(&i)**, re-read the last few pages. Everything we say about C pointers from here onwards will depend on your understanding these expressions thoroughly.

Look at the following declarations,

```
int *alpha ;
char *ch ;
float *s ;
```

Here, **alpha, ch** and s are declared as pointer variables, i.e. variables capable of holding addresses. Remember that, addresses (location numbers) are always going to be whole numbers, therefore pointers always contain whole numbers. Now we can put these two facts together and say: pointers are variables which contain addresses, and since addresses are always whole numbers, pointers would always contain whole numbers.

The declaration **float *s** does not mean that **s** is going to contain a floating point value. What it means is, **s** is going to contain the address of a floating point value. Similarly, **char *ch** means that **ch** is going to contain the address of a **char** value. Or in other words, the value at address stored in **ch** is going to be a **char**.

Pointer Arithmetic

Having imbibed the basics of pointers it's time to venture into something more complicated. Let us start off with some pointer arithmetic. Consider the following example:

```
main( )
{
    int i = 3, *x ;
    float j = 1.5, *y ;
    char k = 'c', *z ;

    printf ( "Value of i = %d\n", i ) ;
    printf ( "Value of j = %f\n", j ) ;
    printf ( "Value of k = %c\n\n", k ) ;

    x = &i ;
    y = &j ;
    z = &k ;

    printf ( "Original value in x = %d\n", x ) ;
    printf ( "Original value in y = %d\n", y ) ;
    printf ( "Original value in z = %d\n\n", z ) ;

    x++ ;
    y++ ;
    z++ ;

    printf ( "New value in x = %d\n", x ) ;
    printf ( "New value in y = %d\n", y ) ;
    printf ( "New value in z = %d\n", z ) ;
}
```

Suppose **i, j** and **k** are stored in memory at addresses 1002, 2004 and 5006, the output would be...

```
Value of i = 3
Value of j = 1.5
Value of k = c

Original value in x = 1002
Original value in y = 2004
Original value in z = 5006
```

```
New value in x = 1004
New value in y = 2008
New value in z = 5007
```

Observe the last three lines of the output. 1004 is original value in **x** plus 2, 2008 is original value in **y** plus 4, and 5007 is original value in **z** plus 1. This so happens because every time a pointer is incremented it points to the immediately next location of its type. That is why, when the integer pointer **x** is incremented, it points to an address two locations after the current location, since an **int** is always 2 bytes long. Similarly **y** points to an address 4 locations after the current location and **z** points 1 location after the current location. This is a very important result and can be effectively used while passing the entire array to a function.

The way a pointer can be incremented, it can be decremented as well, to point to earlier locations. Thus, the following operations can be performed on a pointer:

(a) Addition of a number to a pointer. For example,

```
int i = 4, *j, *k ;
j = &i ;
j = j + 1 ;
j = j + 9 ;
k = j + 3 ;
```

(b) Subtraction of a number from a pointer. For example,

```
int i = 4, *j, *k ;
j = &i ;
j = j - 2 ;
j = j - 5 ;
k = j - 6 ;
```

(c) Subtraction of one pointer from another.

One pointer variable can be subtracted from another provided both variables point to elements of the same array. The resulting value indicates the number of bytes separating the corrseponding array elements. This is illustrated in the following example.

```
main( )
{
    static int arr[ ] = { 10, 20, 30, 45, 67, 56, 74 } ;
    int *i, *j ;

    i = &arr[1] ;
    j = &arr[5] ;
    printf ( "%d %d", j - i, *j - *i ) ;
}
```

Here **i** and **j** have been declared as integer pointers holding addresses of first and fifth element of the array respectively.

Suppose the array begins at location 4002, then the elements **arr[1]** and **arr[5]** would be present at locations 4004 and 4012 respectively since each integer in the array occupies two bytes in memory. The expression **j - i** would print a value 5 and not 10. This is because **j** and **i** are pointing to locations which are 5 integers apart. What would be the result of the expression ***j - *i**? 36, since ***j** and ***i** return the values present at addresses contained in the pointers **j** and **i**.

A word of caution! Do not attempt the following operations on pointers... they would never work out.

(a) Addition of two pointers
(b) Multiplication of a pointer with a constant
(d) Division of a pointer with a constant

Pointer Comparison

Pointer variables can be compared provided both variables point to objects of the same data type. Such comparisons can be useful when both pointer variables point to elements of the same array. The comparison can test for either equality or inequality. Moreover a pointer variable can be compared with zero (usually expressed as NULL). The following program illustrates how the comparison is carried out.

```
main( )
{
    static int arr [ ] = { 10, 20, 36, 72, 45, 36 } ;
    int *j, *k ;

    j = &arr [ 4 ] ;
    k = ( arr + 4 );i ;

    if ( j == k )
        printf ( "The two pointers point to the same location" ) ;
    else
        printf ( "The two pointers do not point to the same location" ) ;
}
```

Dynamic Memory Allocation

Consider the array declaration,

```
int marks[100] ;
```

Such a declaration would typically be used if 100 student's marks are to be stored in memory. The moment we make this declaration 200 bytes are reserved in memory for storing 100 integers in it. However, it may so happen that when we actually run the program we might be interested in storing only 60 students marks. Even in this case 200 bytes would get reserved in memory, which would result in wastage of memory.

Other way round there always exists a possibility that when you run a program you need to store more than 100 student's marks. In this case the array would fall short. Moreover, there is no way to increase or decrease the array size during execution of the program. In other words when we use arrays static memory allocation takes place. What if we want to allocate memory only at the time of execution? This is done using standard library functions **malloc( )** and **calloc( )**. Since these functions allocate memory - on the fly - during execution they are often known as 'Dynamic memory allocation functions'. Let us now see a program which uses the concept of dynamic memory allocation.

```
main( )
{
    int n, avg, i, *p, sum = 0 ;

    printf ( "Enter the number of students " ) ;
    scanf ( "%d", &n ) ;

    p = ( int * ) malloc ( n * 2 ) ;
    if ( p == NULL )
    {
        printf ( "\nMemory allocation unsuccesful" ) ;
        exit( ) ;
    }

    for ( i = 0 ; i < n ; i++ )
        scanf ( "%d", ( p + i ) ) ;

    for ( i = 0 ; i < n ; i++ )
        sum = sum + *p ;

    avg = sum / n ;
```

```
        printf ( "Average marks = %d", avg ) ;
}
```

Here, we first ask for the number of students whose marks are to be entered and then allocate only as much memory as is really required to store these marks. Not a byte more, not a byte less. The allocation job is done by **malloc( )**. It returns a NULL if memory allocation is unsuccessful. If successful it returns the address of the memory chunk that was allocated.

This address we collected in an integer pointer **p**. The expression (**int ***) is used to type cast the address being returned as the address of an integer rather than a character. This type casting is necessary since **malloc( )** by default returns a pointer to a **void**. In the first **for** loop using simple pointer arithmetic we store the marks entered from keyboard into the memory that has been allocated. In the second **for** loop we access the same values and sum them up to find the average marks.

The **calloc( )** functions works exactly similar to **malloc( )** except for the fact that it needs two arguments as against the one argument required by **malloc( )**. For example,

```
int *p ;
p = ( int * ) calloc ( 10, 2 ) ;
```

Here 2 indicates that we wish to allocate memory for storing integers, since an integer is a 2 byte entity. And 10 indicates that we want to reserve space for storing 10 integers.

Another minor difference between **malloc( )** and **calloc( )** is that by default the memory allocated by **malloc( )** contains garbage values whereas that allocated by **calloc( )** contains all zeros.

Pointers Versus Arrays

Look at the following program.

```
main( )
{
    static char arr[10] = "Nagpur" ;
    char *s = "Nagpur" ;

    printf ( "%s\n", arr ) ;
    printf ( "%s", s ) ;
}
```

Here, though the declarations of **arr** and **s** are different the output of both the **printf( )**s is same. What exactly is the difference in the declarations? In the first declaration "Nagpur" gets stored in the array **arr[ ]**, whereas in the second "Nagpur" gets stored at some place in memory and the base address of it is stored in **s**. In other words s points to the zeroth character in the string.

On mentioning the name of the array **arr** we get its base address. Hence the following **printf( )** would print the base address of **arr** and the address stored in s.

```
printf ( "%d %d", arr, s ) ;
```

In that sense **arr** acts as a pointer to a **char**. But the similarity between **arr** and s ends there. The following program outlines this difference.

```
main( )
{
    static char arr[10] = "Nagpur" ;
    char *s = "Nagpur" ;

    s++ ;
```

```
        arr++ ;
        printf ( "%s %s", s, arr ) ;
}
```

Here **s++** increments s such that it starts pointing to 'a' of "Nagpur" and hence **printf( )** would output "agpur". As against this **arr++** would give an error message. This is because all that is known to the C compiler about an array is its base address, and if we do **arr++** we are attempting to change this base address. This the C compiler would never allow.

Another difference between arrays and pointers is the way the **sizeof** operator treats them. Can you imagine the output of the following statement.

```
printf ( "%d %d", sizeof ( s ), sizeof ( arr ) ) ;
```

In this statement the first expression would print 2 since size of any pointer is 2 bytes. However, the second expression would print 7 because the array contains 7 characters including the '\0'.

Pointers And 2 Dimensional Arrays

The C language embodies an unusual but powerful capability: it can treat parts of arrays as arrays. More specifically, each row of a two dimensional array can be thought as a one dimensional array. This is a very important fact if we wish to access array elements of a two dimensional array using pointers.

Thus, the declaration,

```
static int stud[5][2] ;
```

can be thought of as setting up a one dimensional array of 5 elements, each of which is a one dimensional array 2 elements long. We refer to an element of a one dimensional array using a single subscript. Similarly, if we can imagine **stud** to be a one dimensional array then we can refer to its zeroeth element as **stud[0]**, the next element as **stud[1]** and so on. More specifically, **stud[0]** gives the address of the zeroeth one dimensional array, **stud[1]** gives the address of the first one dimensional array and so forth. This fact can be illustrated by the following program.

```
/* Demo: 2 - D array is an array of arrays */
main( )
{
    static int stud[5][2] = {
                            { 1234, 56 },
                            { 1212, 33 },
                            { 1434, 80 },
                            { 1312, 78 }
                            { 1203, 75 }
                        } ;
    int i, j ;

    for ( i = 0 ; i <= 4 ; i++ )
        printf ( "Address of %d th 1-D array = %d\n", stud[i] ) ;
}
```

And here is the output...

```
Address of 0 th 1-D array = 5002
Address of 1 th 1-D array = 5006
Address of 2 th 1-D array = 5010
Address of 3 th 1-D array = 5014
Address of 4 th 1-D array = 5018
```

Let's figure out how the program works. The compiler knows that **stud** is an integer array. So each element of this array occupies 2 bytes. There are two elements in each row, so each row takes 4 bytes. Thus, each row starts 4 bytes further along than the last one. And, since each row is a one dimensional array, each of these one dimensional arrays starts 4 bytes further along than the last one, as can be seen in the memory map of the array shown below.

s[0][0]	s[0][1]	s[1][0]	s[1][1]	s[2][0]	s[2][1]	s[3][0]	s[3][1]
1234	56	1221	33	1434	80	1312	78
5002	5004	5006	5008	5010	5012	5014	5016

Figure 9.3

The compiler knows how many columns are there in the array **stud**, since we specified this in the array declaration. So it interprets the expression **stud[0]** as (**stud + 0**), and **stud[1]** as (**stud + 1**). Therefore, (**stud + 0**) is interpreted as address 5002, and (**stud + 1**) is interpreted as address 5006 and so on.

Now, we have been able to reach each individual row. What remains is to be able to refer to individual elements of a row. Suppose we want to refer to the element **stud[2][1]** using pointers. We know (from the above program) that **stud[2]** would give the address 5010, the address of the second one dimensional array. Obviously (5010 + 1) would give the address 5012. Or (**stud[2] + 1**) would give the address 5012. And the value at this address can be obtained by using the value at address operator, saying ***(stud[2] + 1**). But, we have already studied while learning one dimensional arrays that **num[i]** is same as ***(num + i**). Similarly, ***(stud[2] +1**) is same as, ***(*(stud + 2) + 1**). Thus, all the following expressions refer to the same element,

```
stud[2][1]
* ( stud[2] + 1 )
* ( * ( stud + 2 ) + 1 )
```

Using these concepts the following program prints out each element of a two dimensional array using pointer notation.

```
/* Pointer notation to access 2-D array elements */
main( )
{
    static int stud[5][2] = {
                                 { 1234, 56 },
                                 { 1212, 33 },
                                 { 1434, 80 },
                                 { 1312, 78 },
                                 { 1203, 75 }
                            } ;
    int i, j ;

    for ( i = 0 ; i <= 4 ; i++ )
    {
        for ( j = 0 ; j <= 1 ; j++ )
            printf ( "%d ", *( *( stud + i )+ j ) ) ;
        printf ( "\n" ) ;
    }
}
```

And here is the output...

```
1234 56
1212 33
1434 80
1312 78
1203 75
```

Arrays Of Pointers

The way there can be an array of **ints** or an array of **floats**, similarly there can be an array of pointers. Since a pointer variable always contains an address, an array of pointers would be nothing but a collection of addresses. The addresses present in the array of pointers can be addresses of isolated variables or addresses of array elements or any other addresses. All rules that apply to an ordinary array apply in toto to the array of pointers as well. I think a program would clarify the concept.

```
main( )
{
    int *arr[4] ; /* array of integer pointers */
    int i = 31, j = 5, k = 19, l = 71, m ;

    arr[0] = &i ;
    arr[1] = &j ;
    arr[2] = &k ;
    arr[3] = &l ;
    for ( m = 0 ; m  <= 3 ; m++ )
        printf ( "%d", * ( arr[m] ) ) ;
}
```

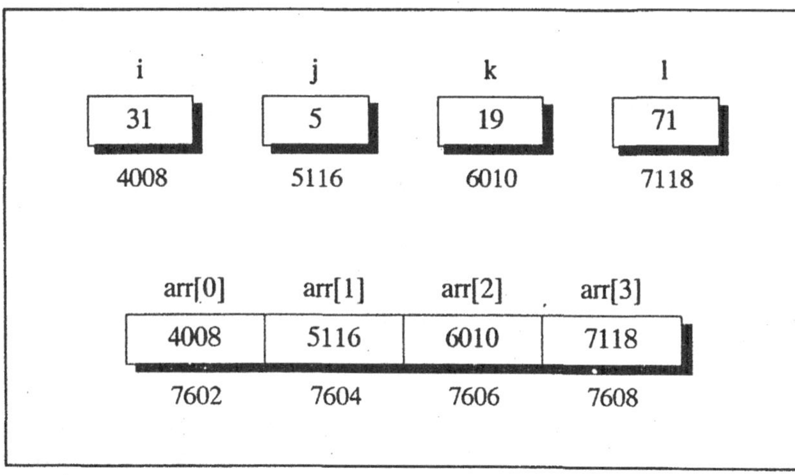

Figure 9.4

Figure 9.4 shows the contents and the arrangement of the array of pointers in memory. As you can observe, **arr** contains addresses of isolated **int** variables **i**, **j**, **k** and **l**.

The **for** loop in the program picks up the addresses present in **arr** and prints the values present at these addresses.

An array of pointers can even contain the addresses of other arrays. The following program would justify this.

```
main( )
{
    static int a[ ] = { 0, 1, 2, 3, 4 } ;
    static int *p[ ] = { a, a + 1, a + 2, a + 3, a + 4 } ;

    printf ( "%d %d %d", p, *p, * ( *p ) ) ;
}
```

I would leave it for you to figure out the output of this program.

An array of pointers is very popularly used for storing several strings in memory. For example, names of students in a class can be stored in an array of pointers as shown below.

```
static char *names[ ] = {
                            "akshay",
                            "parag",
                            "raman",
                            "srinivas",
                            "gopal",
                            "rajesh"
                        } ;
```

In this declaration **names[ ]** is an array of pointers. It contains base addresses of respective names. That is, base address of "akshay" is stored in **name[0]**, base address of "parag" is stored in **name[1]** and so on. This is depicted in the following figure.

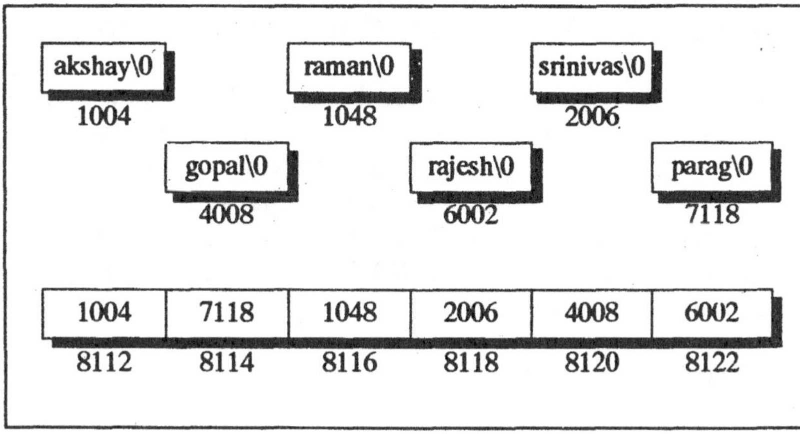

Figure 9.5

Had a two dimensional array of characters **char name[6][20]** been used for storing these names there would have been a lot of wasted memory space. This is because in the 2-D array we have to assume that each row in the array would be 20 characters long (assuming that no name exceeds 20 characters).

As against this, while using an array of pointers only as much space is used by each name as is really required. And then addresses of each string are stored in the array of pointers. This arrangement has been shown in Figure 9.5.

Thus, one reason to store strings using an array of pointers is to make more efficient use of available memory.

Another reason to use array of pointers to store strings is to obtain greater ease in the manipulation of the strings. That is why, even though in principle strings can be stored and handled through a two dimensional array of characters, in actual practise it is the array of pointers to strings which is more commonly used.

Limitation Of Array Of Pointers To Strings

When we are using a two dimensional array of characters we are at liberty to either initialise the strings where we are declaring the array, or receive the strings using **scanf( )** function. However, when we are using an array of pointers to strings we can initialise the strings at the place where we are declaring the array, but we cannot receive the strings from keyboard using **scanf( )**. Thus, the following program would never work out.

```
main( )
{
    char *names[6] ;
    int i ;

    for ( i = 0 ; i <= 5 ; i++ )
    {
        printf ( "Enter name " ) ;
        scanf ( "%s", names[i] ) ;
    }
}
```

The program doesn't work because, when we are declaring the array it is containing garbage values. And it would be definitely wrong to send these garbage values to **scanf( )** as the addresses where it should store the strings received from the keyboard.

Pointers To Pointers

The concept of pointer can be further extended. Pointer we know is a variable which contains address of a variable. This variable itself could be another pointer. Thus, we now have a pointer which contains another pointer's address. The following example should make this point clear.

```
main( )
{
	int i = 3 ;
	int *j ;
	int **k ;

	j = &i ;
	k = &j ;

	printf ( "Address of i = %d \n", &i ) ;
	printf ( "Address of i = %d \n", j ) ;
	printf ( "Address of i = %d \n", *k ) ;
	printf ( "Address of j = %d \n", &j ) ;
	printf ( "Address of j = %d \n", *k ) ;
	printf ( "Address of k = %d \n\n", &k ) ;

	printf ( "Value of j = %d \n", j ) ;
	printf ( "Value of k = %d \n", k ) ;
	printf ( "Value of i = %d \n", i ) ;
	printf ( "Value of i = %d \n", *( &i ) ) ;
	printf ( "Value of i = %d \n", *j ) ;
	printf ( "Value of i = %d \n", **k ) ;
}
```

The output of the above program would be:

```
Address of i = 6485
Address of i = 6485
Address of i = 6485
Address of j = 3276
Address of j = 3276
Address of k = 7234

Value of j = 6485
Value of k = 3276
Value of i = 3
Value of i = 3
```

```
Value of i = 3
Value of i = 3
```

Figure 9.6 would help you in tracing out how the program prints the above output.

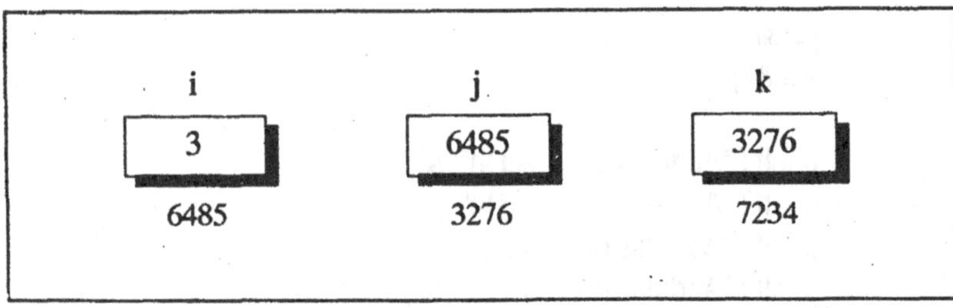

Figure 9.6

Observe how the variables **i**, **j** and **k** have been defined.

```
int i ;
int *j ;
int **k ;
```

Here, **i** is an ordinary **int**, **j** is a pointer to an **int**, whereas **k** is a pointer to a **int pointer**. In principle, there could be a pointer to a pointer's pointer, a pointer to a pointer's pointer's pointer. There is no limit on how far can we go on extending this definition. Possibly, till the point we can comprehend it. And that point of comprehension is usually a pointer to a pointer. Beyond this one rarely requires to extend the definition of a pointer. But just in case...

Pointers To Functions

Every type of variable that we have discussed so far, with the exception of register, has an address. We have seen how we can reference variables of type **char, int, float** etc... through their addresses - that is by using pointers. Pointers can also point to C functions. And why not? C functions have addresses. If we know the function's address we can point to it, which provides another way to invoke it. Let us see how this can be done.

```
/* Demo to get address of a function */
main( )
{
    int display( ) ;
    printf ( "Address of function display is %d", display )
    display( ) ;  /* usual way of invoking a function */
}

display( )
{
    puts ( "Long live viruses!!" ) ;
}
```

The output of the program would be:

```
Address of function display is 1125
Long live viruses!!
```

Note that to obtain the address of a function all that we have to do is to mention the name of the function, as has been done in the **printf( )** statement above. This is similar to mentioning the name of the array to get its base address.

Now let us see how using the address of a function we can manage to invoke it. This is shown in the program given below:

```
/* Invoking function using pointer to a function */
main( )
{
    int display( ) ;
    int ( *func_ptr )( ) ;

    func_ptr = display ; /* assign address of function */
```

```
    printf ( "Address of function display is %d", func_ptr );
    ( *func_ptr )( ) ;  /* invokes the function display( ) */
}

display( )
{
    puts ( "Long live viruses!!" ) ;
}
```

The output of the program would be:

```
Address of function display is 1125
Long live viruses!!
```

In **main( )** we declare the function **display( )** as a function returning an **int**. But what are we to make of the declaration,

```
int ( *func_ptr )( ) ;
```

that comes in the next line? We are obviously declaring something that, like **display( )**, will return an **int**, but what is it? And why is ***func_ptr** enclosed in parentheses?

If we glance down a few lines in our program, we see the statement,

```
func_ptr = display ;
```

so we know that **func_ptr** is being assigned the address of **display( )**. Therefore, **func_ptr** must be a pointer to the function **display( )**.

Thus, all that the declaration

```
int ( *func_ptr )( ) ;
```

means is, that **func_ptr** is a pointer to a function, which returns an **int**. And to invoke the function we are just required to write the statement,

```
( *func_ptr )( ) ;
```

Pointers to functions are certainly awkward and offputting. And why use them at all when we can invoke a function in a much simpler manner? What is the possible gain of using this esoteric feature of C? There are two possible uses:

(a) in writing memory resident programs
(b) in writing viruses, or vaccines to remove the viruses

Both these topics form interesting and powerful C applications and would call for separate chapters on each if full justice is to be given to them. Much as we would have liked to, for want of space we would have to exclude these topics.

Functions Returning Pointers

The way functions return an **int**, a **float**, a **double** or any other data type, it can even return a pointer. However, to make a function return a pointer it has to be explicitly mentioned in the calling function as well as in the function declaration. The following program illustrates this.

```
main( )
{
    int *p ;
    int *fun( ) ;

    p = fun ( ) ;
}

int *fun( )
{
    int i = 20 ;
    return ( &i ) ;
```

```
}
```

This program just indicates how an integer pointer can be returned from a function. Beyond that it doesn't serve any useful purpose. This concept can be put to use while handling strings. For example look at the following program which copies one string into another and returns the pointer to the target string.

```
main( )
{
    char *str ;
    char *copy( ) ;
    static char source[ ] = "Jaded" ;

    str = copy ( target, source ) ;
    printf ( "%s", str ) ;
}

char *copy ( t, s )
char *t, *s ;
{
    char *r ;

    r = t ;
    while ( *s != '\0' )
    {
        *t = *s ;
        t++ ;
        s++ ;
    }
    *t = '\0' ;
    return ( r ) ;
}
```

Here, we send the base addresses of **source** and **target** strings to **copy( )**. In the **copy( )** function the **while** loop copies the characters in the source string into the target string. Since during copying **t** is continuously incremented, before entering into the loop the initial value of **t** is safely stored in the character pointer **r**. Once copying is over this character pointer is returned to **main( )**.

Functions With Variable Number Of Arguments

We have used **printf( )** so often without realising how it works properly irrespective of how many arguments we pass to it. How do we go about writing such routines which can take variable number of arguments? And what have pointers got to do with it? There are three macros available in the file "stdarg.h" called **va_start**, **va_arg** and **va_list** which allow us to handle this situation. (Macros are discussed in detail in Chapter 12). These macros provide a method for accessing the arguments of the function when a function takes a fixed number of arguments followed by a variable number of arguments. The fixed number of arguments are accessed in the normal way, whereas the optional arguments are accessed using the macros **va_start** and **va_arg**. Out of these macros **va_start** is used to initialise a pointer to the beginning of the list of optional arguments. On the other hand the macro **va_arg** is used to advance the pointer to the next argument. Let us put these concepts into action using a program. Suppose we wish to write a function **findmax( )** which would find out the maximum value from a set of values, irrespective of the number of values passed to it.

```
# include "stdarg.h"
main( )
{
    int max ;

    max = findmax ( 5, 23, 15, 1, 92, 50 ) ;
    printf ( "\nMax = %d", max ) ;
```

```
        max = findmax ( 3, 100, 300, 29 ) ;
        printf ( "\nMax = %d", max ) ;
}

findmax ( tot_num )
int tot_num ;
{
        int max, count, num ;

        va_list ptr ;

        va_start ( ptr, tot_num ) ;
        max = va_arg ( ptr, int ) ;

        for ( count = 1 ; count < tot_num ; count++ )
        {
                num = va_arg ( ptr, int ) ;
                if ( max < num )
                        max = num ;
        }
        return ( max ) ;
}
```

Here we are making two calls to **findmax( )** first time to find maximum out of 5 values and second time to find maximum out of 3 values. Note that for each call the first argument is the count of arguments following the first argument. The value of the first argument passed to **findmax( )** is collected in the variable **tot_num**. **findmax()** begins with a declaration of pointer **ptr** of the type **va_list**. Observe the next statement carefully:

```
va_start ( ptr, tot_num ) ;
```

This statement sets up **ptr** such that it points to the first variable argument in the list. If we are considering the first call to **finndmax( )** **ptr** would now point to 23. The next statement **max = va_arg (ptr, int)** would assign the integer being pointed to by **ptr** to **max**. Thus

23 would be assigned to **max**, and **ptr** would now start pointing to the next argument i.e., 15. The rest of the program is fairly straight forward. We just keep picking up successive numbers in the list and keep comparing them with the latest value in **max**, till all the arguments in the list have been scanned. The final value in **max** is then returned to **main( )**.

How about another program to fix your ideas? This one calls a function **display( )** which is capable of printing any number of arguments of any type.

```
#include "stdarg.h"
main( )
{
    printf ( "\n" ) ;
    display ( 1, 2, 5, 6 ) ;
    printf ( "\n" ) ;
    display ( 2, 4, 'A', 'a', 'b', 'c' ) ;
    printf ( "\n" ) ;
    display ( 3, 3, 2.5, 299.3, -1.0 ) ;
}

display ( type, num )
int type, num ;
{
    int i, j ;
    char c ;
    float f ;
    va_list ptr ;

    va_start ( ptr, num ) ;

    switch ( type )
    {
        case 1 :
            for ( j = 1 ; j <= num ; j++ )
            {
```

```
                i = va_arg ( ptr, int ) ;
                printf ( "%d ", i ) ;
            }
            break ;

        case 2 :
            for ( j = 1 ; j <= num ; j++ )
            {
                c = va_arg ( ptr, char ) ;
                printf ( "%c ", c ) ;
            }
            break ;

        case 3 :
            for ( j = 1 ; j <= num ; j++ )
            {
                f = ( float ) va_arg ( ptr, double ) ;
                printf ( "%f ", f ) ;
            }
    }
}
```

Here we pass two fixed arguments to the function **display( )**. The first one indicates the data type of the arguments to be printed and the second indicates the number of such arguments to be printed. Once again through the statement **va_start (ptr, num)** we set up **ptr** such that it points to the first argument in the variable list of arguments. Then depending upon whether the value of **type** is 1, 2 or 3 we print out the arguments as **ints, chars** or **floats**.

Exercise

[A] What will be the output of the following programs:

(1)
```
main( )
{
    static char a[ ] = "BOMBAY" ;
    char *b = "BOMBAY" ;

    printf ( "\n %d %d", sizeof ( a ), sizeof ( b ) ) ;
}
```

(2)
```
main( )
{
    static int a[ ] = { 0, 1, 2, 3, 4 } ;
    static int *p[ ] = { a, a + 1, a + 2, a + 3, a + 4 } ;
    int **ptr = p ;
    printf ( "%d %d\n", a, *a ) ;
    printf ( "%d %d %d\n", p, *p, **p ) ;
    printf ( "%d %d %d\n", ptr, *ptr, **ptr ) ;
}
```

(3)
```
main( )
{
    static int a[ ] = { 0, 1, 2, 3, 4 } ;
    static int *p[ ] = { a, a+ 1, a + 2, a + 3, a + 4 } ;
    int **ptr = p ;
    ptr++ ;
    printf ( "%d %d %d\n", ptr - p, *ptr - a, **ptr ) ;

    *ptr++ ;
    printf ( "%d %d %d\n", ptr - p, *ptr - a, **ptr ) ;

    *++ptr ;
    printf ( "%d %d %d\n", ptr - p, *ptr - a, **ptr ) ;
```

```
        ++*ptr ;
        printf ( "%d %d %d\n", ptr - p , *ptr - a, **ptr ) ;
    }
```

(4)
```
    main( )
    {
        static int a[ ] = { 0, 1, 2, 3, 4 } ;
        static int *p[ ] = {  a, a + 1, a + 2, a + 3, a + 4 } ;
        int **ptr ;
        ptr = p

        **ptr++ ;
        printf ( "%d %d %d\n", ptr - p, *ptr - a, **ptr ) ;
        *++*ptr ;
        printf ( "%d %d %d\n",  ptr - p, *ptr - a, **ptr ) ;
        ++**ptr ;
        printf ( "%d %d %d\n", ptr - p, *ptr - a, **ptr ) ;
    }
```

(5)
```
    main( )
    {
        static int a[3][3] = {
                                1, 2, 3,
                                4, 5, 6,
                                7, 8, 9
                            } ;
        int *ptr[3] = { a[0], a[1], a[2] } ;
        int **ptr1 = ptr ;
        int i ;
        for ( i = 0 ; i <= 2 ; i++ )
            printf ( "%d",*ptr[i] ) ;

        printf ( "\n" ) ;
        for ( i = 0 ; i <= 2 ; i++ ) ;
            printf ( "%d", *a[i] ) ;
        printf ("\n" ) ;
        for ( i = 0 ; i <= 2 ; i++ ) ;
```

```
    {
        printf ( "%d", **ptr1 ) ;
        ptr++ ;
    }
}
```

(6)
```
main( )
{
    static char *s[ ] = {
                            "ice",
                            "green",
                            "cone",
                            "please"
                        } ;
    static char **ptr[ ] = { s + 3, s + 2, s + 1, s } ;
    char ***p = ptr ;
    printf ( "%s\n", **++p ) ;
    printf ( "%s\n", *--*++p + 3 ) ;
    printf ( "%s\n", *p[-2] + 3 ) ;
    printf ( "%s\n", p[-1][-1] + 1 ) ;
}
```

(7)
```
main( )
{
    static char str[ ] = "For your eyes only" ;
    int i ;
    char *p ;
    for ( p = str, i = 0 ; p + i <= str + strlen ( str ) ; p++, i++ )
        printf ( "%c", *(p + i ) ) ;
}
```

(8)
```
main( )
{
    static char mess[6][30] = {
                                "Don't walk  in front of me...",
                                "I may not follow;",
```

```
                                    "Don't walk behind me....",
                                    "I may not lead;",
                                    "Just walk beside me....",
                                    "And be my friend."
                                };
        printf ( "%c %c", *( mess[2] + 9 ), *(*( mess + 2 ) + 9 ) );
    }
```

(9)
```
    main( )
    {
        int n[25] ;
        n[0] = 100 ;
        n[24] = 200 ;
        printf ( "%d %d", *n, *( n + 24 ) + *( n + 0 ) ) ;
    }
```

(10)
```
    main( )
    {
        static int b[ ] = { 10, 20, 30, 40, 50 } ;
        int i, *k ;
        k = &b[4] - 4 ;
        for ( i = 0 ; i <= 4 ; i++ )
        {
            printf ( "%d ", *k ) ;
            k++ ;
        }
    }
```

(11)
```
    main( )
    {
        static int a[ ] = { 2, 4, 6, 8, 10 } ;
        int i ;
        for ( i = 0 ; i <= 4 ; i++ )
        {
            *( a + i ) = a[i] + i[a] ;
            printf ( "%d ", *( i + a ) ) ;
```

```
        }
    }
```

(12)
```
main( )
{
    static int a[5] = { 2, 4, 6, 8, 10 } ;
    int i, b = 5 ;
    for ( i = 0 ; i < 5 ; i++ )
    {
        f ( a[i], &b ) ;
        printf ( "%d %d\n", a[i], b ) ;
    }
}

f ( x, y )
int x, *y ;
{
    x = *( y ) += 2 ;
}
```

(13)
```
main( )
{
    static int a[5] = { 2, 3, 4, 5, 6 } ;
    int i ;
    change ( a ) ;
    for ( i = 4 ; i = 0 ; i-- )
        printf( "%d ", a[i] ) ;
}

change ( b )
int *b ;
{
    int i ;
    for ( i = 0 ; i <= 4 ; i++ )
    {
        *b = *b + 1 ;
        b++ ;
```

```
        }
    }
```

(14)
```
main( )
{
    int arr[ ] = { 0, 1, 2, 3, 4 } ;
    int i, *ptr ;
    for ( ptr = &arr[0] ; ptr <= &arr[4] ; ptr++ )
        printf ( "%d ", *ptr ) ;
}
```

(15)
```
main( )
{
    int arr[ ] = { 0, 1, 2, 3, 4 } ;
    int i, *ptr ;
    for ( ptr = &arr[0], i = 0 ; i <= 4 ; i++ )
        printf ( "%d ", ptr[i] ) ;
}
```

(16)
```
main( )
{
    int arr[ ] = { 0, 1, 2, 3, 4 } ;
    int i, *p ;
    for ( p = arr, i = 0 ; p + i <= arr + 4 ; p++, i++ )
        printf ( "%d ", *( p + i ) ) ;
}
```

(17)
```
main( )
{
    int arr[ ] = { 0, 1, 2, 3, 4 } ;
    int i, *ptr ;
    for ( ptr = arr + 4 ; ptr = arr ; ptr-- )
        printf ( "%d ", *ptr ) ;
}
```

(18)
```
main( )
```

```
{
    int arr[ ] = { 0, 1, 2, 3, 4 } ;
    int i, *ptr ;
    for ( ptr = arr + 4, i = 0 ; i <= 4 ; i++ )
        printf ( "%d ", ptr[-i] ) ;
}
```

(19)
```
main( )
{
    char str[20] ;
    int i ;
    for ( i = 0 ; i <= 18 ; i++ )
        i[str] = 'C' ;
    i[str] = '\0' ;
    printf ( "%s", str ) ;
}
```

(20)
```
main( )
{
    static char str[10] = { 0, 0, 0, 0, 0, 0, 0, 0, 0, 0 } ;
    char *s ;
    int i ;
    s = str ;
    for ( i = 0 ; i <= 9 ; i++ )
    {
        if ( *s )
            printf ( "%c", *s ) ;
        s++ ;
    }
}
```

(21)
```
main( )
{
    static char s[ ] = "C smart !!" ;
    int i ;
    for ( i = 0 ; s[i] ; i++ )
```

```
        printf ( "%c %c %c %c\n", s[i], *( s + i ) , i[s], *( i + s ) ;
}
```

(22)
```
main( )
{
    static char s[ ] = "Oinks Grunts and Guffaws" ;
    printf ( "%c\n", *( &s[2] ) ) ;
    printf ( "%s\n", s + 5 ) ;
    printf ( "%s\n", s ) ;
    printf ( "%c\n", *( s + 2 ) ) ;
    printf ( "%d\n", s ) ;
}
```

(23)
```
main( )
{
    static char s[25] = "The cocaine man" ;
    int i = 0 ;
    char ch ;
    ch = s[++i] ;
    printf ( "%c %d\n", ch, i ) ;
    ch = s[i++] ;
    printf ( "%c %d\n", ch, i ) ;
    ch = i++[s] ;
    printf ( "%c %d\n", ch, i ) ;
    ch = ++i[s] ;
    printf ( "%c %d\n", ch, i ) ;
}
```

[B] Attempt the following:

(1) Write a program to find determinant of a square matrix of any size. (Hint: Use the **calloc()** function).

CHAPTER

10 Structures, Unions And Enumerated Data Types

Structures
Unions
Enumerated Data Types
typedef Statement

Structures

Which mechanic is good enough who knows how to repair only one type of vehicle? None. Same thing is true about C language. It wouldn't have been so popular had it been able to handle only all **ints**, or all **floats** or all **chars** at a time. In fact when we handle real world data, we don't usually deal with little atoms of information by themselves - things like integers, characters and such. Instead we deal with entities that are collections of things, each thing having its own attributes, just as the entity we call a 'book' is a collection of things such as a title, an author, a call no., a publisher, number of pages, date of publication etc. As you can see all this data is dissimilar, for example author is a string, whereas number of pages is an integer. For dealing with such collections, C provides a data type called 'structure'. A structure gathers together, different atoms of information that comprise a given entity. And structures and their distant cousins, unions are the topics of this chapter.

In this chapter we are also going to take a brief look at two more features of C - the enumerated data type and the **typedef** statement. Let us begin with the structures first.

Basics Of Structures

We have seen earlier how ordinary variables can hold one piece of information and how arrays can hold a number of pieces of information of the same data type. These two data types can handle a great variety of situations. But quite often we deal with entities that are collection of dissimilar data types.

For example, suppose you want to store data about a book. You might want to store its name (a string), its price (a float) and number of pages in it (an int) and so on. If data about say 3 such books is to be stored, then we can follow two approaches:

(a) Construct individual arrays, one for storing names, another for storing prices and still another for storing number of pages.
(b) Use a structure variable.

Let us examine these two approaches one by one. For the sake of programming convenience assume that the names of books would be single character long.

```
main( )
{
    char name[3] ;
    float price[3] ;
    int pages[3], i ;

    printf ( "Enter names, prices and no. of pages of 3 books\n") ;

    for ( i = 0 ; i <= 2 ; i++ )
        scanf ( "%c %f %d", &name[i], &price[i], &pages[i] );

    printf ( "\n\nAnd this is what you entered\n" ) ;
    for ( i = 0 ; i <= 2 ; i++ )
        printf ( "%c %f %d\n", name[i], price[i], pages[i] );
```

And here is the sample run...

```
Enter names, prices and no. of pages of 3 books
A 100.00 354
C 256.50 682
F 233.70 512

And this is what you entered
A 100.000000 354
C 256.500000 682
F 233.700000 512
```

This approach no doubt allows you to store names, prices and number of pages. But as you must have realised, it is an unwieldy approach that obscures the fact that you are dealing with a group of characteristics related to a single entity: the book.

The program becomes more difficult to handle as the number of items relating to the employee goes on increasing. For example, we would be required to use a number of arrays, if we also decide to store the sex of the employee, his address, his telephone number, his blood group and so on. To solve this problem, C provides a special data type... the structure.

A structure contains a number of data types grouped together. These data types may or may not be of the same type. The following example illustrates the use of this data type.

```
main( )
{
    struct book
    {
        char name ;
        float price ;
        int pages ;
    } ;
    struct book b1, b2, b3 ;
```

```
        printf ( "Enter names, prices & no. of pages of 3 books\n" ) ;
        scanf ( "%c %f %d", &b1.name, &b1.price, &b1.pages ) ;
        scanf ( "%c %f %d", &b2.name, &b2.price, &b2.pages ) ;
        scanf ( "%c %f %d", &b3.name, &b3.price, &b3.pages ) ;

        printf ( "\n\nAnd this is what you entered" ) ;
        printf("\n%c %f %d", b1.name, b1.price, b1.pages ) ;
        printf("\n%c %d %f", b2.name, b2.price, b2.pages ) ;
        printf("\n%c %d %f", b3.name, b3.price, b3.pages ) ;
}
```

And here is the output...

```
Enter names, prices and no. of pages of 3 books
A 100.00 354
C 256.50 682
F 233.70 512

And this is what you entered
A 100.000000 354
C 256.500000 682
F 233.700000 512
```

This program demonstrates the two fundamental aspects of structures:

(a) declaration of a structure
(b) accessing of structure elements

Let us now look at these concepts one by one.

Declaring A Structure

In our example program, the following statement declares the structure type:

```
struct book
{
    char name ;
    float price ;
    int pages ;
} ;
```

This statement defines a new data type called **struct book**. Each variable of this data type will consist of a character variable called **name**, a float variable called **price** and an integer variable called **pages**. The general form of a structure declaration statement is given below:

```
struct <structure name>
{
    structure element 1 ;
    structure element 2 ;
    structure element 3 ;
    ......
    ......
} ;
```

Once the new strutcture data type has been defined one or more variables can be declared to be of that type. For example the variables **b1, b2, b3** can be declared to be of the data type **struct book**, as,

```
struct book b1, b2, b3 ;
```

This statement sets aside space in memory. It makes available space to hold all the elements in the structure: in this case, 7 bytes ... one for **name**, four for **price** and two for **pages**. These bytes are always in adjacent memory locations.

If we so desire, we can combine the declaration of the structure type and the structure variables in one statement.

For example,

```
struct book
{
    char name ;
    float price ;
    int pages ;
} ;

struct book b1, b2, b3 ;
```

is same as...

```
struct book
{
    char name ;
    float price ;
    int pages ;
} b1, b2, b3 ;
```

or even...

```
struct
{
    char name ;
    float price ;
    int pages ;
} b1, b2, b3 ;
```

Like primary variables and arrays, structure variables can also be initialised where they are declared. The format used is quite similar to that used to initiate arrays.

```
struct book
{
    char name[10] ;
    float price ;
```

```
        int pages ;
    } ;
    struct book b1 = { "Basic", 130.00, 550 } ;
    struct book b2 = { "Physics", 150.80, 800 } ;
```

Note that if the structure variables are declared and initialised inside a function, their storage class must be **static**.

Note the following points while declaring a structure type:

(a) The closing brace in the structure type declaration must be followed by a semicolon.

(b) It is important to understand that a structure type declaration does not tell the compiler to reserve any space in memory. All a structure declaration does is, it defines the 'form' of the structure.

(c) Usually structure type declaration appears at the top of the source code file, before any variables or functions are defined. In very large programs they are usually put in a separate header file, and the file is included (using the preprocessor directive **#include**) in whichever program we want to use this structure type.

Accessing Structure Elements

Having declared the structure type and the structure variables, let us see how the elements of the structure can be accessed.

In arrays we can access individual elements of an array using a subscript. Structures use a different scheme. They use a dot (.) operator. So to refer to **pages** of the structure defined in our sample program we have to use,

```
b1.pages
```

Similarly, to refer to **price** we would use,

```
b1.price
```

Note that before the dot there must always be a structure variable and after the dot there must always be a structure element.

How Structure Elements Are Stored

Whatever be the elements of a structure, they are always stored in contiguous memory locations. This can be illustrated by the following program:

```
/* memory map of structure elements */
main( )
{
    struct book
    {
        char name ;
        float price ;
        int pages ;
    } ;
    static struct book b1 = { 'B', 130.00, 550 } ;

    printf ( "Address of name = %d\n", &b1.name ) ;
    printf ( "Address of price = %d\n", &b1.price ) ;
    printf ( "Address of pages = %d", &b1.pages ) ;
}
```

And here is the output:

```
Address of name = 1001
Address of price = 1002
Address of pages = 1006
```

Actually the structure elements are stored in memory as shown in the following figure:

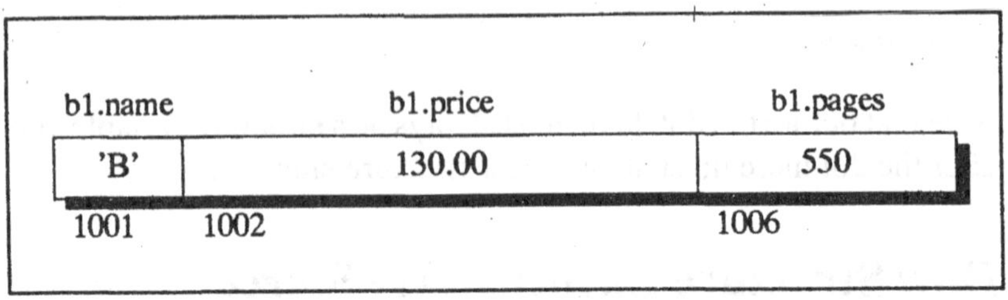

Figure 10.1

The values of a structure variable can be assigned to another structure variable of the same type using the assignment operator. It is not necessary to copy the structure elements piece-meal. Obviously programmers prefer assignment to piece-meal copying. This is shown in the following example:

```
main( )
{
    struct employee
    {
        char name[10] ;
        int age ;
        float salary ;
    } ;
    static struct employee e1 = { "Sanjay", 30, 5500 } ;
    struct employee e2, e3 ;

    /* piece meal copying */
    strcpy ( e2.name, e1.name ) ;
    e2.age = e1.age ;
    e2.salary = e1.salary ;

    /* copying all elements at one go */
    e3 = e2 ;

    printf ( "%s %d %f\n", e1.name, e1.age, e1.salary) ;
    printf ( "%s %d %f\n", e2.name, e2.age, e2.salary) ;
    printf ( "%s %d %f\n", e3.name, e3.age, e3.salary) ;
```

```
}
```

And here is the output...

```
Sanjay 30 5500
Sanjay 30 5500
Sanjay 30 5500
```

Ability to copy the contents of all structure elements of one variable into the corresponding structure elements of another variable is rather surprising, since C does not allow assigning the contents of one array to another just by equating the two. As we saw carlier, for copying arrays we have to copy the contents of the array element by element.

This copying of all structure elements at one go has been possible only because the structure elements are stored in contiguous memory locations. Had this not been so, we would have been required to copy structure variables element by element. And who knows, had this been so, structures would not have become popular at all.

Array Of Structures

Our sample program showing usage of structure is rather simple minded. All it does is, it receives values into various structure elements and output these values. But that's all we intended to do anyway... show how structure types are created, how structure variables are declared and how individual elements of a structure variable are referenced.

In our sample program, to store data of 100 books we would be required to use 100 different structure variables from **b1** to **b100**, which is definitely not very convenient. A better approach would be to use an array of structures. Following program shows how to use an array of structures.

```
/* usage of an array of structures */
```

```
main( )
{
	struct book
	{
		char name ;
		float price ;
		int pages ;
	} ;

	struct book b[100] ;
	int i ;

	for ( i = 0 ; i <= 99 ; i++ )
	{
		printf ( "\nEnter name, price and pages " ) ;
		scanf ( "%c %f %d", &b[i].name, &b[i].price, &b[i].pages ) ;
	}

	for ( i = 0 ; i <= 99 ; i++ )
		printf ( "\n%c %f %d", b[i].name, b[i].price, b[i].pages ) ;
}
```

Now a few comments about the program:

(a) Notice how the array of structures is declared...

```
struct book b[100] ;
```

This provides space in memory for 100 structures of the type **struct book**.

(b) The syntax we use to reference each element of the array **b** is similar to the syntax used for arrays of **ints** and **chars**. For example, we refer to zeroeth book's price as **b[0].price**. Similarly, we refer first book's pages as **b[1].pages**.

(c) It should be appreciated what careful thought Dennis Ritchie has put into C language. He first defines array as a collection of similar elements; then realises that dissimilar data types which are often found in real life cannot be handled using arrays, therefore creates a new data type called structure. But even using structures programming convenience is not achieved, because a lot of variables (**b1** to **b100** for storing data about hundred books) need to be handled. And therefore he allows us to create an array of structures; an array of similar data types which themselves are a collection of dissimilar data types. Hats off to the genius!

(d) In an array of structures all elements of the array are stored in adjacent memory locations. Since each element of this array is a structure, and since all structure elements are always stored in adjacent locations you can very well visualise the arrangement of array of structures in memory. Thus in our example, in memory **b[0]**'s **name, price** and **pages** would be immediately followed by **b[1]**'s **name, price** and **pages**, and so on.

Passing Structure Elements To Functions

Can we pass structure elements to a function? Certainly. Here is how it can be done...

```
/* Passing individual structure elements */
main( )
{
    struct book
    {
        char name[25] ;
        char author[25] ;
        int callno ;
    } ;
    static struct book b1 = { "Let us C", "YPK", 101 } ;
```

```
        display ( b1.name, b1.author, b1.callno ) ;
    }

    display ( s, t, n )
    char *s, *t ;
    int n ;
    {
        printf ( "%s\n%s\n%d", s, t, n ) ;
    }
```

And here is the output...

```
Let us C
YPK
101
```

Observe that in the declaration of structure type, **name** and **author** have been declared as arrays. Therefore, when we call the function **display( )** using,

```
display ( b1.name, b1.author, b1.callno ) ;
```

we are passing the base addresses of the arrays **name** and **author** but the value stored in **callno**. Thus, this is a mixed call: a call by reference as well as a call by value.

It can be immediately realised that to pass individual elments would become more tedious as the number of structure elements go on increasing. A better way would be to pass the entire structure variable at a time. This is discussed in the following section.

Passing Entire Structure To Functions

In case of structures having numerous structure elements passing these individual elements would be tedious. In such cases we may pass an entire structure to a function as shown in the following program.

```
struct book
{
    char name[25] ;
    char author[25] ;
    int callno ;
} ;

main( )
{
    static struct book b1 = { "Let us C", "YPK", 101 } ;
    display ( b1 ) ;
}
display ( b )
struct book b ;
{
    printf ( "%s \n%s \n%d", b.name, b.author, b.callno ) ;
}
```

And here is the output...

```
Let us C
YPK
101
```

Note that here the calling of function **display**( ) becomes quite compact,

```
display ( b1 ) ;
```

Having collected what is being passed to the **display**( ) function, the question comes, how do we define the formal arguments in the function. We cannot say,

```
struct book b1 ;
```

because the data type **struct book** is not known to the function **display( )**. Therefore, it becomes necessary to define the structure type **struct book** outside **main( )**, so that it becomes known to all functions in the program.

Structure Pointers

The way we can have a pointer pointing to an **int**, or a pointer pointing to a **char**, similarly we can have a pointer pointing to a **struct**. Such pointers are known as 'structure pointers'.

Let us look at a program which demonstrates the usage of structure pointer.

```
main( )
{
	struct book
	{
		char name[25] ;
		char author[25] ;
		int callno ;
	} ;
	static struct book b1 = { "Let us C", "YPK", 101 } ;
	struct book *ptr ;

	ptr = &b1 ;
	printf ( "%s %s %d\n", b1.name, b1.author, b1.callno ) ;
	printf ( "%s %s %d\n", ptr -> name, ptr -> author, ptr -> callno ) ;
}
```

The first **printf( )** is as usual. The second **printf( )** however is peculiar. We can't use **ptr.name** or **ptr.callno** because **ptr** is not a structure variable but a pointer to a structure, and the dot operator requires a structure variable on its left. In such cases C provides an operator **->**, called an arrow operator to refer to the structure elements. Remember that on the left hand side of the '**.**' structure operator, there must always be a structure variable, whereas on the left hand side of the '->' operator there must always be a pointer to a structure. The arrangement of the structure variable and pointer to structure in memory is shown in the figure given below.

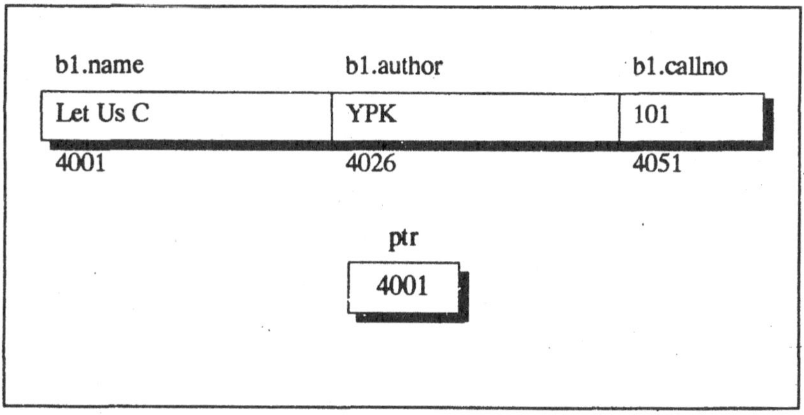

Figure 10.2

Can we not pass the address of a structure variable to a function? We can. The following program demonstrates this.

```
/* Passing address of a structure variable */
struct book
{
    char name[25] ;
    char author[25] ;
    int callno ;
} ;

main( )
{
    static struct book b1 = { "Let us C", "YPK", 101 } ;
    display ( &b1 ) ;
}

display ( b )
```

```
struct book *b ; /* pointer to a structure */
{
    printf ( "%s \n%s \n%d", b-> name, b -> author, b -> callno ) ;
}
```

And here is the output...

```
Let us C
YPK
101
```

Again note that to access the structure elements using pointer to a structure we have to use the '->' operator.

Also the structure **struct book** should be declared outside **main( )** such that this data type is available to **display( )** while declaring pointer to the structure.

Structures Within Structures

One structure can be nested within another structure. Using this facility complex data types can be created. Following program shows nested structures at work:

```
main( )
{
    struct address
    {
        char phone[15] ;
        char city[25] ;
        int pin ;
    } ;

    struct emp
    {
        char name[25] ;
```

```
        struct address a ;
    } ;
    static struct emp e = { "jeru", "531046", "nagpur", 10 };

    printf ( "name = %s phone = %s\n", e.name, e.a.phone ) ;
    printf ( "city = %s pin = %d", e.a.city, e.a.pin ) ;
}
```

And here is the output...

```
name = jeru phone = 531046
city = nagpur pin = 10
```

Notice the method used to access the elements of a structure that is a part of another structure. Here, the dot operator is used twice, as in the expression,

```
e.a.pin or e.a.city
```

Of course, the nesting process need not stop at this level. We can nest a structure within a structure, within another structure, which is in still another structure and so on... till the time we can comprehend the structure ourselves. Such construction however gives rise to variable names that can be surprisingly self descriptive, for example:

```
maruti.engine.bolt.large.qty
```

This clearly signifies that we are referring to the quantity of large sized bolts which fit on an engine of a maruti car.

Uses Of Structures

Where are structures useful? The immediate application that comes to the mind is Database Management. That is, to maintain data about employees in an organisation, books in a library, items in a store, financial accounting transactions in a company etc. But mind you, use of structures stretches much beyond database management. They can be used for a variety of applications like:

(a) changing the size of the cursor
(b) clearing the contents of the screen
(c) placing the cursor at appropriate position on screen
(d) drawing any graphics shape on the screen
(e) receiving a key from the keyboard
(f) checking the memory size of the computer
(g) finding out the list of equipment attached to the computer
(h) formatting a floppy
(i) hiding a file from the directory
(j) displaying the directory of a disk
(k) sending the output to printer
(l) interacting with the mouse

And that is certainly a very impressive list! At least impressive enough to make you realise how important a data type a structure is and to be thorough with it if you intend to program any of the above applications. To be able to progrmam these applications one needs thorough knowledge of internal details of operating system. You are referred to the book 'Let Us C' written by Y. P. Kanetkar for the same, where most of these applications are discussed in detail.

Unions

Unions are derived data types, the way structures are. But Unions have the same relationship to structures that you might have with a distant cousin who resembled you but turned out to be smuggling contraband in mexico. That is, unions and structures look alike, but are engaged in totally different enterprises.

Both structures and unions are used to group a number of different variables together. But while a structure enables us to to treat a number of different variables stored at different places in memory, a union enables us to treat the same space in memory as a number of different variables. That is, a union offers a way for a section of memory to be treated as a variable of one type on one occasion, and as a different variable, of a different type, on another occasion.

Let us take a look at a simple example which uses a union.

```
main( )
{
	union a
	{
		int i ;
		char ch[2] ;
	} ;
	union a key ;

	key.i = 512 ;
	printf ( "key.i= %d\n", key.i ) ;
	printf ( "key.ch[0] = %d\n", key.ch[0] ) ;
	printf ( "key.ch[1] = %d\n", key.ch[1] ) ;
}
```

And here is the output...

```
key.i= 512
key.ch[0] = 0
key.ch[1] = 2
```

As you can see, first we declared a data type **union a**, and then a variable 'key' to be of the type **union a.** This is similar to the way we declare first the structure type and then the structure variables. Also, the union elements are accessed exactly the same way in which the structure elements are accessed, using a '.' operator. However, the similarity ends here. To illustrate this let us compare the following data types:

```
struct a
```

```
{
    int i ;
    char ch[2] ;
} ;
struct a key ;
```

This data type would occupy 4 bytes in memory, 2 for **key.i** and one each for **key.ch[0]** and **key.ch[1]**, as shown below.

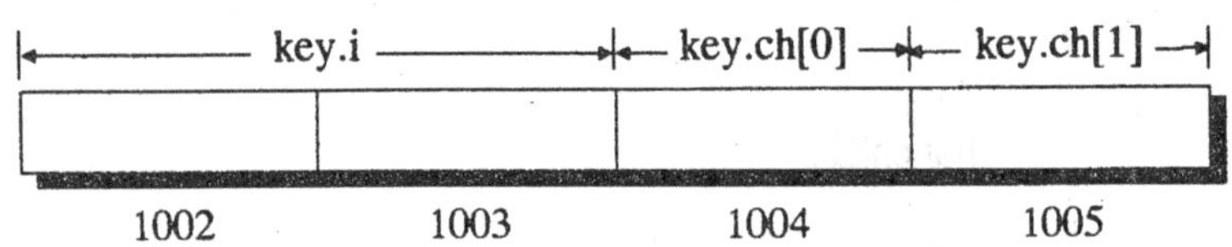

Figure 10.3

Now we declare a similar data type, but instead of using a structure we use a union.

```
union a
{
    int i ;
    char ch[2] ;
} ;
union a key ;
```

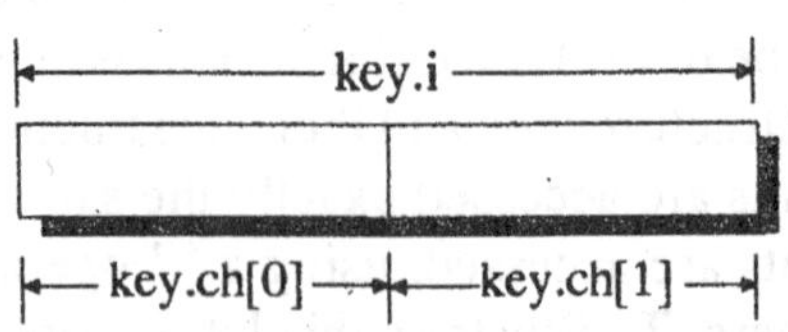

Figure 10.4

This data type would occupy only 2 bytes in memory. Note that the same memory locations which are used for **key.i** are also being used by **key.ch[0]** and **key.ch[1]**. It means that the memory locations used by **key.i** can also be accessed using **key.ch[0]** and **key.ch[1]**. What purpose does this serve? Well, now we can access the two bytes simultaneously (by using **key.i**) or the same two bytes individually (using **key.ch[0]** and **key.ch[1]**).

Now this is a frequent requirement while interacting with the hardware. i.e. sometimes we are required to access two bytes simultaneously and sometimes each byte individually. Faced with such a situation, using union is the answer, usually.

Perhaps, you would be able to understand the union data type more thoroughly if we take a fresh look at the output of the above program. Here it is...

```
key.i= 512 ;
key.ch[0] = 0 ;
key.ch[1] = 2 ;
```

Let us understand this output in detail. 512 is an integer, a 2 byte number. It's binary equivalent will be 0000 0010 0000 0000. We would expect that this binary number when stored in memory would look as shown in Figure 10.5.

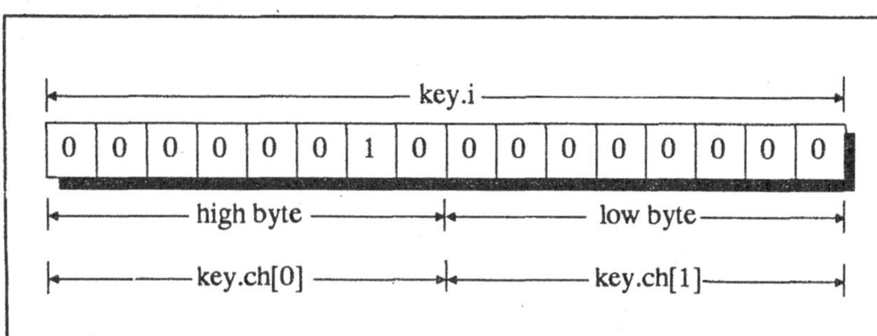

Figure 10.5

If the number is stored in this manner then the output of **key.ch[0]** and **key.ch[1]** should have been 2 and 0. But, if you look at the output of the program written above, it is exactly the opposite. Why is it so? Because, when a two byte number is stored in memory, the low byte is stored before the high byte. It means, actually 512 would be stored in memory as shown below:

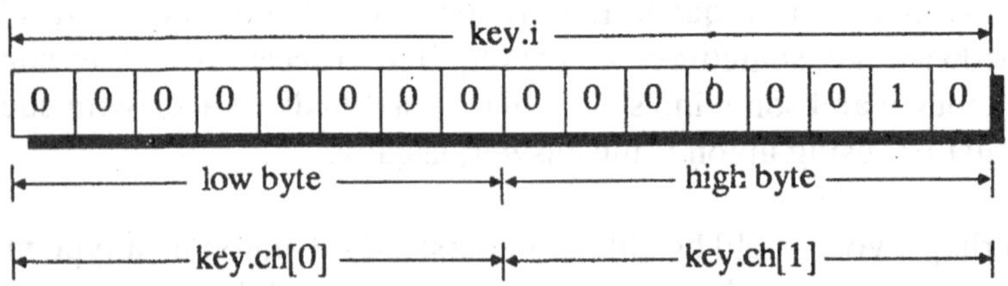

Figure 10.6

Now we can see why value of **key.ch[0]** is printed as 0 and value of **key.ch[1]** is printed as 2.

One last thing. We can't assign different values to the different union elements at the same time. i.e. if assign a value to **key.i**, it gets automatically assigned to **key.ch[0]** and **key.ch[1]**. Vice versa, if we assign a value to **key.ch[0]** or **key.ch[1]**, it is bound to get assigned to **key.i**. Here is a program which illustrates this fact.

```
main( )
{
    union a
    {
        int i ;
        char ch[2] ;
    } ;
    union a key ;

    key.i = 512 ;
```

```
        printf ( "key.i= %d\n", key.i ) ;
        printf ( "key.ch[0] = %d\n", key.ch[0] ) ;
        printf ( "key.ch[1] = %d\n\n", key.ch[1] ) ;

        key.ch[0] = 50 ; /* assign a new value to key.ch[0] */

        printf ( "key.i= %d\n", key.i ) ;
        printf ( "key.ch[0] = %d\n", key.ch[0] ) ;
        printf ( "key.ch[1] = %d\n", key.ch[1] ) ;
}
```

And here is the output...

```
key.i= 512
key.ch[0] = 0
key.ch[1] = 2

key.i= 562
key.ch[0] = 50
key.ch[1] = 2
```

Before we move on to the next section, do remember now, that a union provides a way to look at the same data in several different ways. For example, there can be a union as shown below.

```
union data
{
    long f ;
    int i[2] ;
    char ch[4] ;
} ;

union data b ;
```

In what different ways can the data be accessed from it? Sometimes as a complete set of four bytes (**b.f**), sometimes as two sets of 2 bytes each (**b.i[0]** and **b.i[1]**) and sometimes as four sets of 1 byte each (**b.ch[0], b.ch[1], b.ch[2]** and **b.ch[3]**).

Union Of Structures

Just as one structure can be nested within another, a union too can be nested in another union. Not only that, there can be a union in a structure, or a structure in a union. Here is an example of stuctures nested in a union.

```
main( )
{
	struct a
	{
		int i ;
		char c[2] ;
	} ;

	struct b
	{
		int j ;
		char d[2] ;
	} ;

	union z
	{
		struct a key ;
		struct b data ;
	} ;

	union z strange ;

	strange.key.i = 512 ;
	strange.data.d[0] = 0 ;
	strange.data.d[1] = 32 ;
```

```
    printf ( "%d\n", strange.key.i ) ;
    printf ( "%d\n", strange.data.j ) ;

    printf ( "%d\n", strange.key.c[0] ) ;
    printf ( "%d\n", strange.data.d[0] ) ;

    printf ( "%d\n", strange.key.c[1] ) ;
    printf ( "%d\n", strange.data.d[1] ) ;
}
```

And here is the output...

```
512
512
0
0
32
32
```

Just as we do with nested structures, we access the elements of the union in this progam using the '.' operator twice. Thus,

```
strange.key.i
```

refers to the varible **i** in the structure **key** in union **strange**. I leave it to you to analyse the output of the above program.

Uses Of Unions

As we know the elements of a structure use different memory locations whereas that of a union use same memory locations. Thus, unions conserve memory space. They are useful for applications involving multiple elements, where values need not be assigned to all the elements at any one time. Let us take the example of raising a number to a power. Thus, we wish to evaluate $y = x^n$, where x and y are **floats** and **n** is either an **int** or a **float**.

If **n** is an **int**, **y** can be evaluated by multiplying **x** by itself an appropriate number of times. For example, x^3 can be expressed as **x * x * x**. If **n** is a **float**, then we can write **log y = n log x** which is same as **y** = $e^{(n \log x)}$. In this case, **x** must be a positive quantity, since we cannot take log of zero or a negative quantity. Let us now write a program which puts this logic to work.

```
#include "stdio.h"
#include "math.h"
union exp
{
    float fexp ;         /* floating point exponent */
    int nexp ;           /* integer exponent */
} ;
struct val
{
    float x ;            /* value to be raised to a power */
    char flag ;          /* 'f' if exponent is floating point, 'i' if integer */
    union exp e ;        /* union containing exponent */
} ;

main( )
{
    struct val a ;
    int i ;
    float n, y ;
    float power( ) ;

    printf ( "y = x^n\n\nEnter value of x and n" ) ;
    scanf ( "%f %f", &a.x, &n ) ;

    i = (int) n ;
    a.flag = ( i == n ) ? 'i' : 'f' ;

    if ( a.flag == 'i' )
        a.e.nexp = i ;
    else
```

```
        a.e.fexp = n ;

    if ( a.flag == 'f' && a..x <= 0.0 )
        printf ( "Cannot raise a nonpositive number to a \
                floating-point power " ) ;
    else
    {
        y = power ( a ) ;
        printf ( "\ny = %.4f", y ) ;
    }
}

/* function to carry out exponentiation */
float power ( a )
struct val a ;
{
    int i ;
    float y = 1 ;

    if ( a.flag == 'i' )    /* integer exponent */
    {
        if ( a.e.nexp == 0 )        /* zero exponent */
            y = 1.0 ;
        else
        {
            for ( i = 0 ; i <  abs ( a.e.nexp ) ; i++ )
                y = v * a.x ;

            if ( a.e.nexp  <  0 )       /* negative integer exponent */
                y = 1.0 / y ;
        }
    }
    else                            /* floating point exponent */
        y = exp ( a.e.fexp * log ( a.x ) ) ;

    return ( y ) ;
}
```

The program opens with a **scanf( )** to collect the values of **x** and **n**. Next it is tested whether **n** is an **int** or not, and the value of **flag** is appropriately set up. Note that **flag** indicates the type of exponent currently represented by the union. If flag contains 'i' then the union represents the integer exponent and if it contains 'f', then the union represents the floating point exponent. Then the function **power( )** is called to calculate the value of $\mathbf{x^n}$.

In **power( )** the method used to carry out the calculations depends on the value assigned to **a.flag**. If **a.flag** is assigned a value 'i', then exponentiation is carried out by multiplying **a.x** by itself, **n** times. Otherwise, the exponentiation is carried out using the formula $y = e^{(n \log x)}$. Notice that the function takes into account the possibility that the exponent may be zero or a negative quantity.

It should be pointed out that most C compilers include a standard library function called **pow( )**, which is used to raise a number to a power. The current program is of course not meant to replace **pow( )**. It is presented here to illustrate the use of a union in a progamming situation.

Unions are also used wherever the requirement is to access the same memory locations in more than one way. This is often required while calling Basic Input/Output System functions (often simply called BIOS routines) present in the Read Only Memory (ROM) of the computer. While calling these routines values have to be placed in the microprocessor's internal memory which is organised in the form of registers. These registers are usually 16 bits (2 bytes) long. However, some ROM BIOS routines require two different values in 2 bytes of a CPU register, whereas some other require one value in the entire 2 byte register. Therefore, while calling a ROM BIOS routine what is done is a variable which is a look-alike of CPU registers is created using a **union**. And then this variable's individual bytes or both the bytes are accessed as per the requirement of the ROM BIOS routine being called.

Many DOS based application softwares need to access DOS's internal data structures. The breakup of these internal data structures however is not consistent and often changes from one version of DOS to another. Therfore, to make the application programs compatible with different versions of DOS, these programs create **unions** which take into account the variations in the breakup of these DOS data structures. These programs when executed first test the version number of DOS being used on the machine and then access the appropriate part of the **union**.

Writing programs for the two afore-mentioned applications of **unions** is beyond the scope of this book.

Enumerated Data Types

The enumerated data type gives you an opportunity to invent your own data type and define what values the variable of this data type can take. This can help in making the program listings more readable, which can be an advantage when a program gets complicated or when more than one programmer would be working on it. Using enumerated data type can also help you reduce programming errors.

As an example, one could invent a data type called **mar_status** which can have four possible values - single, married, divorced or widowed. Don't confuse these values with variable names; married for instance has the same relationship to the variable **mar_status** as the number 15 has with an integer variable.

The format of the **enum** definition is similar to that of a structure. Here's how the example stated above can be implemented:

```
enum mar_status
{
    single,
    married.
```

```
        divorced,
        widowed
    } ;
    enum mar_status person1, person2 ;
```

Like structures this declaration has two parts:

(a) The first part declares the data type and specifies its possible values. These values are called 'enumerators'.
(b) The second part declares variables of this data type.

Now we can give values to these variables:

```
    person1 = married ;
    person2 = divorced ;
```

Remember we can't use values that aren't in the original declaration. Thus, the expression,

```
    person1 = unknown ;
```

would cause an error.

Internally, the compiler treats the enumerators as integers. Each value on the list of permissible values corresponds to an integer, starting with 0. Thus, in our example, single, is stored as 0, married is stored as 1, divorced as 2 and widowed as 3.

This way of assigning numbers can be overridden by the programmer by initialising the enumerators to different integer values as shown below.

```
    enum mar_status
    {
        single = 100,
        married = 200,
        divorced = 300,
```

```
        widowed = 400
};
enum mar_status person1, person2 ;
```

Uses Of Enumerated Data Type

Enumerated variables are usually used to clarify the operation of a program. For example, if we need to use employee departments in a payroll program, it makes the listing easier to read if we use values like Assembly, Manufacturing, Accounts rather than the integer values 0, 1, 2, etc.

The following program illustrates the point I am trying to make.

```
main( )
{
    enum emp_dept
    {
        assembly,
        manufacturing,
        accounts,
        stores
    } ;
    struct employee
    {
        char name[30] ;
        int age ;
        float bs ;
        enum emp_dept department ;
    } ;
    struct employee e ;

    strcpy ( e.name, "Lothar Mattheus" ) ;
    e.age = 28 ;
    e.bs = 8575.50 ;
    e.department = manufacturing ;
```

```
        printf ( "Name = %s\n", e.name ) ;
        printf ( "Age = %d\n", e.age ) ;
        printf ( "Basic salary = %f\n", e.bs ) ;
        printf ( "Dept = %d\n", e.department ) ;

        if ( e.department == accounts )
            printf ( "Lothar is an accounant " ) ;
        else
            printf ( "Lothar is not an accounant " ) ;
}
```

And here is the output of the program...

```
Name = Lothar Mattheus
Age = 28
Basic salary = 8575.50
Dept = 1
Lothar is not an accountant
```

Let us now dissect the program. We first defined the data type **enum emp_dept** and specified the four possible values, namely, assembly, manufacturing, accounts and stores. Then we defined a variable **department** of the type **enum emp_dept** in a structure. The structure **employee** has three other elements containing employee information.

The program first assigns values to the variables in the structure. The statement,

```
e.department = manufacturing ;
```

assigns the value manufacturing to **e.department** variable. This is much more informative to anyone reading the program than a statement like,

```
e.department = 1 ;
```

The next part of the program shows an important weakness of using **enum** variables... there is no way to use the enumerated values directly in input/output functions like **printf( )** and **scanf( )**.

The **printf( )** function is not smart enough to perform the translation; the department is printed out as 1 and not manufacturing. Of course we can write a function to print the correct enumerated values, using a **switch** statement, but that would reduce the clarity of the program. Even with this limitation, however, there are many situations in which enumerated variables are god sent!

typedef Statement

There is one more technique which in some situations can help to clarify the source code of a C program. This techinque is to make use of the **typedef** declaration. Its purpose is to redefine the name of an existing variable type.

For example, consider the following statement in which the type **unsigned long int** is redefined to be of the type **TWOWORDS**:

```
typedef unsigned long int TWOWORDS ;
```

Now we can declare variables of the type **unsigned long int** by writing,

```
TWOWORDS var1, var2 ;
```

instead of

```
unsigned long int var1, var2 ;
```

Thus, **typedef** provides a short and meaningful way to call a data type. Usually, uppercase letters are used to make it clear that we are dealing with a renamed data type.

While the increase in readability is probably not great in this example, it can be significant when the name of a particular data type is long and unwieldy, as it often is with structure declarations. For example, consider the following structure declaration:

```
struct employee
{
    char name[30] ;
    int age ;
    float bs ;
} ;

struct employee e ;
```

This structure declaration can be made more handy to use when renamed using **typedef** as shown below:

```
struct employee
{
    char name[30] ;
    int age ;
    float bs ;
} ;

typedef struct employee EMP ;
EMP e1, e2 ;

e1.age = 40 ;
printf ( "%d", e1.age ) ;
```

Thus, by reducing the length and apparent complexity of data types, **typedef** can help to clarify source listing and save time and energy spent in understanding a program.

Exercise

[A] What will be the output of the following program segments:

(1)
```
main( )
{
    struct a
    {
        char arr[10] ;
        int i ;
        float b ;
    } v[2] ;

    /* assume that first structure begins at address 1004 */
    printf ( "%d %d %d\n", v[0].arr, &v[0].i, &v[0].b ) ;
    printf ( "%d %d %d\n", v[1].arr, &v[1].i, &v[1].b ) ;
}
```

(2)
```
main( )
{
    struct a
    {
        char ch[7] ;
        char *str ;
    } ;

    static struct a s1 = { "Nagpur", "Bombay" } ;

    printf ( "%c %c\n", s1.ch[0], *s1.str ) ;
    printf ( "%s %s\n", s1.ch, s1.str ) ;
}
```

(3)
```
main( )
{
    struct s1
```

```
    {
        char *z ;
        int i ;
        struct s1 *p ;
    } ;
    static struct s1 a[ ] = {
                                { "Nagpur", 1, a + 1 },
                                { "Raipur", 2, a + 2 },
                                { "Kanpur", 3, a }
                            } ;
    struct s1 *ptr = a ;
    printf ( "%s %s %s\n", a[0].z, ptr->z, a[2].p->z ) ;
}
```

(4)
```
main( )
{
    struct s1
    {
        char *str ;
        int i ;
        struct s1 *ptr ;
    } ;
    static struct s1 a[ ] = {
                                { "Nagpur", 1, a + 1 },
                                { "Raipur", 2, a + 2 },
                                { "Kanpur", 3, a }
                            } ;
    struct s1 *p = a ;
    int j ;

    for ( j = 0 ; j <= 2 ; j++ )
    {
        printf ( "%d " , --a[j].i ) ;
        printf ( "%s\n" , ++a[j].str ) ;
    }
}
```

(5)
```
main( )
{
    struct s1
    {
        char *z ;
        int i ;
        struct s1 *p ;
    } ;
    static struct s1 a[ ] = {
                                { "Nagpur", 1, a + 1 },
                                { "Raipur", 2, a + 2 },
                                { "Kanpur", 3, a }
                            } ;
    struct s1 *ptr = a ;

    printf ( "%s\n", ++( ptr->z ) ) ;
    printf ( "%s\n", a[( ++ptr )->i].z ) ;
    printf ( "%s\n", a [--( ptr->p->i )].z ) ;
}
```

(6)
```
main( )
{
    struct s1
    {
        char *str ;
        struct s1 *ptr ;
    } ;
    static struct s1 arr[ ] = {
                                  { "Nikhil", arr+1 } ,
                                  { "Aditya", arr+2 },
                                  { "Sudheer", arr }
                              } ;

    struct s1 *p[3] ;
    int i ;

    for ( i = 0 ; i <= 2 ; i++ )
```

```
            p[i] = arr[i].ptr ;

        printf ( "%s\n", p[0]->str ) ;
        printf ( "%s\n", (*p)->str ) ;
        printf ( "%s\n", (**p) ) ;
    }
```

(7)
```
    struct s1
    {
        char *str ;
        struct s1 *next ;
    } ;
    main( )
    {
        static struct s1 arr[ ] = {
                                    { "Akhil", arr+1 } ,
                                    { "Nikhil", arr+2 },
                                    { "Anant", arr }
                                 } ;

        struct s1 *p[3] ;
        int i ;

        for ( i = 0 ; i <= 2 ; i++ )
            p[i] = arr[i].next ;

        printf ( "%s %s %s", p[0]->str, (*p)->str, (**p).str ) ;

        swap ( *p, arr ) ;

        printf ( "\n%s", p[0]->str ) ;
        printf ( "\n%s", ( *p )->str ) ;
        printf ( "\n%s", ( *p )->next->str ) ;

        swap ( p[0], p[0]->next ) ;

        printf ( "\n%s", p[0]->str ) ;
```

```
    printf ( "\n%s", ( *++p[0] ).str ) ;
    printf ( "\n%s", ++( *++( *p )->next ).str ) ;
}

swap ( p1, p2 )
struct s1 *p1, *p2 ;
{
    char *temp ;

    temp = p1->str ;
    p1->str = p2->str ;
    p2->str = temp ;
}
```

(8)

```
main( )
{
    struct node
    {
        int data ;
        struct node *link ;
    } ;
    struct node *p, *q ;

    p = malloc ( sizeof ( struct node ) ) ;
    q = malloc ( sizeof ( struct node ) ) ;

    printf ( "%d %d", sizeof ( p ), sizeof ( q ) ) ;
}
```

(9)

```
#define NULL 0
main( )
{
    struct node
    {
        int data ;
        struct node *link ;
    } ;
```

```
        struct node *p, *q ;

        p = malloc ( sizeof ( struct node ) ) ;
        q = malloc ( sizeof ( struct node ) ) ;

        p->data = 30 ;
        p->link = q ;
        q->data = 40 ;
        q->link = NULL ;

        printf ( "%d ", p->data ) ;
        p = p->link ;
        printf (" %d", p->data ) ;
    }
```

(10)
```
#define NULL 0
main( )
{
    struct node
    {
        struct node *previous ;
        int data ;
        struct node *next ;
    } ;

    struct node *p, *q ;

    p = malloc ( sizeof ( struct node ) ) ;
    q = malloc ( sizeof ( struct node ) ) ;

    p->data = 75 ;
    q->data = 90 ;

    p->previous = NULL ;
    p->next = q ;
    q->previous = p ;
    q->next = NULL ;
```

```
	while ( p != NULL )
	{
		printf ( "%d\n", p->data ) ;
		p = p->next ;
	}
}
```

(11)
```
#define NULL 0
main( )
{
	struct node
	{
		int data ;
		struct node *next ;
	} ;
	struct node *p, *q ;

	p = malloc ( sizeof ( struct node ) ) ;
	q = malloc ( sizeof ( struct node ) ) ;

	p->data = 10 ;
	q->data = 20 ;
	p->next = q ;
	q->next = p ;

	while ( p != NULL )
	{
		printf ( "%d\n", p->data ) ;
		p = p->next ;
	}
}
```

(12)
```
main( )
{
	struct a
	{
```

```
        int i ;
        char ch[2] ;
    } ;
    union b
    {
        int i ;
        char c[2] ;
    } ;
    printf ( "%d ", sizeof ( struct a ) ) ;
    printf ( "%d", sizeof ( union b ) ) ;
}
```

(13)
```
main( )
{
    union a
    {
        int i ;
        char ch[2] ;
    } ;
    union a u ;

    u.i = 256 ;
    printf ( "%d %d %d", u.i, u.ch[0], u.ch[1] ) ;
}
```

(14)
```
main( )
{
    union a
    {
        int i ;
        char ch[2] ;
    } ;
    union a u ;

    u.ch[0] = 3 ;
    u.ch[1] = 2 ;
    printf ( "%d %d %d", u.ch[0], u.ch[1], u.i ) ;
```

```
}
```

(15)
```
main( )
{
    struct a
    {
        int i ;
        int j ;
    } ;
    struct b
    {
        char x ;
        char y[3] ;
    } ;
    union c
    {
        struct a aa ;
        struct b bb ;
    } ;
    union c u ;

    u.aa.i = 512 ;
    u.aa.j = 512 ;

    printf ( "%d %d\n", u.bb.x, u.bb.y[0] ) ;
    printf ( "%d %d \n", u.bb.y[1], u.bb.y[2] ) ;
}
```

(16)
```
main( )
{
    union
    {
        unsigned long l ;
        unsigned int d[2] ;
        char ch[4] ;
    } a ;
```

```
	strcpy ( a.ch, "ABC" ) ;

	printf ( "%s\n", a.ch ) ;
	printf ( "%u %u\n", a.d[0], a.d[1] ) ;
	printf ( "%lu", a.l ) ;
}
```

CHAPTER

11 File Handling In C

- A Filecopy Program
- Using argc And argv
- String (line) I/O In Files
- The Awkward Newline
- A Brief Review
- Formatted Disk I/O Functions
- Binary Mode VersusText Mode
- Record I/O In Files
- Making It All Make Sense
- Detecting Errors In Reading/Writing

Having dealt with the various Console Input/Output (I/O) functions like **printf( )**, **scanf( )**, **getch( )** etc., let us now turn our attention to Disk I/O. Disk I/O operations are performed on entities called files. There are a large number of standard library functions available for performing Disk or file I/O.

These functions can be broadly divided into two categories :

(a) High level file I/O functions (also called standard I/O or stream I/O functions)

(b) Low level file I/O functions (also called system I/O functions)

High level disk I/O functions are more commonly used in C programs, since they are easier to use than low level disk I/O functions.

The low level disk I/O functions are more closely related to the computer's operating system than the high level disk I/O functions. Low level disk I/O is harder to program than high level disk I/O. However, low level disk I/O is more efficient both in terms of operation and the amount of memory used by the program. This chapter is concerned only with high level disk I/O functions.

The following figure shows the detailed classification of disk I/O functions.

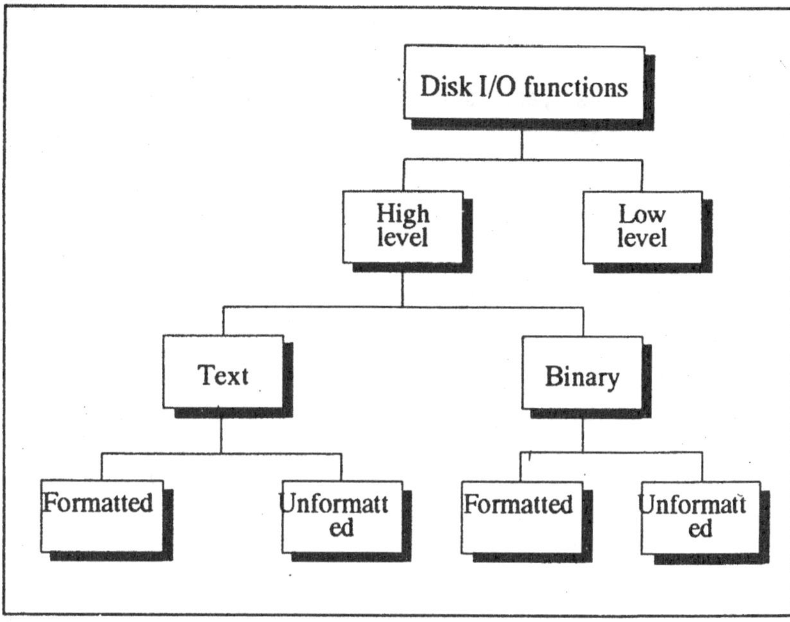

Figure 11.1

As you can see the high level file I/O functions are further categorised into text and binary. This classification arises out of the mode in which a file is opened for input or output. Which of these two modes is used to open the file determines:

(a) How newlines ('\n') are stored.
(b) How end of file is indicated.
(c) How numbers are stored in the file.

We will look at these differences at a later stage in this chapter. Let us now directly jump to writing programs which perform file I/O in high level, unformatted, text mode.

Our first program will read a file and count how many characters, spaces, tabs and newlines are present in the file. We will first list the program and show what it does, and then dissect it line by line. Here is the listing.

```
/* Count chars, spaces, tabs and newlines in a file */
# include "stdio.h"
main( )
{
    FILE *fp ;
    char ch ;
    int nol = 0, not = 0, nos = 0, noc = 0 ;

    fp = fopen ( "PR1.C", "r" ) ;
    while ( 1 )
    {
        ch = getc ( fp ) ;

        if ( ch == EOF )
            break ;

        noc++ ;

        if ( ch == ' ' )
            nob++ ;

        if ( ch == '\n' )
            nol++ ;

        if ( ch == '\t' )
            not++ ;
    }
    fclose ( fp ) ;

    printf ( "Number of characters = %d\n", noc ) ;
    printf ( "Number of blanks = %d\n", nob ) ;
    printf ( "Number of tabs = %d\n", not ) ;
```

```
        printf ( "Number of lines = %d", nol )
    }
```

And here is a sample run...

```
Number of characters = 125
Number of blanks = 25
Number of tabs = 13
Number of lines = 22
```

The above statistics are true for a file "PR1.C", which we had on our diskette. You may give any other filename and obtain different results. More important than the actual statistics, is how the program calculates these. So let us now take a look at how it does it.

Opening A File

Before we can write information to a file on a disk or read it, we must open the file. Opening a file establishes a link between the program and the operating system, about, which file we are going to access and how. We provide the operating system with the name of the file and whether we plan to read or write to it. The link between our program and the operating system is a structure called **FILE** which has been defined in the header file "stdio.h" (standing for standard input/output header file). Therefore, it is necessary to always include this file when we are doing high level disk I/O. When we request the operating system to open a file, what we get back (if the request is indeed granted), is a pointer to the structure **FILE**. That is why, we make the following declaration before opening the file,

```
FILE *fp ;
```

Each file we open will have its own **FILE** structure. The **FILE** structure contains information about the file being used, such as its current size, its location in memory etc.

Now let us understand the following statements,

```
FILE *fp ;
fp = fopen ( "PR1.c", "r" ) ;
```

fp is a pointer variable, which contains address of the structure **FILE** which has been defined in the header file "stdio.h".

fopen( ) will open a file "PR1.C" in 'read' mode, which tells the C compiler that we would be reading the contents of the file. Note that "r" is a string and not a character; hence the double quotes and not single quotes. In fact, **fopen( )** performs three important tasks when you open the file in "r" mode:

(a) Searches the file to be opened on the disk.
(b) If the file is present, it loads the file from the disk into memory. Of course if the file is very big, then it loads the file part by part.
If the file is absent, **fopen( )** returns a NULL. NULL is a macro defined in "stdio.h" which indicates that you failed to open the file.
(c) It sets up a pointer which points to the first character of the chunk of memory where the file has been loaded.

Reading From A File

Once the file has been opened for reading using **fopen( )**, as we have seen the file's contents are brought into memory (partly or wholly) and a pointer points to the very first character. To read the file's contents from memory there exists a standard library function called **getc( )**. This has been used in our sample program through,

```
ch = getc ( fp ) ;
```

getc( ) function reads the character from current pointer position, advances the pointer position so that it now points to the next character, and returns the character that is read, which we collected in the variable **ch**. Note that once the file has been opened, we no longer refer to the file by its name, but through the file pointer **fp**.

Note that we have written the **getc( )** function within an indefinite **while** loop. There has to be a way to break out of this **while**. When shall we break out... the moment we reach the end of file. But what is end of file? End of file is signified by a special character, whose Ascii value is 26. This character is inserted beyond the last character in the file, when it is created. This character can also be generated from the keyboard by typing ctrl Z.

While reading from the file, when **getc( )** encounters this special character, instead of returning the character that it has read, it returns the macro EOF. The EOF macro has been defined in the file "stdio.h".

In our sample program, we go on reading each character from the file till end of file is met. As each character is being read we keep running totals of number of characters, number of blanks, number of tabs and number of lines read. Note that the end of the line is marked by a '\n'. Once out of the loop, we print these running totals.

Trouble Opening The File

There is a possibility that when we try to open a file using the function **fopen( )**, the file may not be opened. While opening the file in "r" mode, this may happen because the file being opened may not be present on the disk at all. And you obviously cannot read a file which doesn't exist.

Similarly, while opening the file for writing, **fopen( )** may fail due to a number of reasons, like, disk space may be insufficient to open a new file, or the disk may be write protected and so on.

Crux of the matter is that it is important for any program that accesses disk files to check whether a file has been opened successfully before trying to read or write to the file. If the file opening fails due to any of the several reasons mentioned above, the **fopen( )** function returns a value NULL (defined in "stdio.h" as #define NULL 0). Here is how this can be handled in a program...

```
#include "stdio.h"
main( )
{
    FILE *fp ;

    fp = fopen ( "pr1.c", "r" ) ;
    if ( fp == NULL )
    {
        puts ( "cannot open file" ) ;
        exit( ) ;
    }
}
```

Closing The File

When we have finished reading from the file, we need to close it. This is done using the function **fclose( )** through the statement,

```
fclose ( fp ) ;
```

This deactivates the file and hence it can no longer be accessed using **getc( )**. Once again we don't use the filename but the file pointer **fp**.

File Opening Modes

In our first program on disk I/O we have opened the file in read ("r") mode. However, "r" is but one of the several modes in which we can open a file. Following is a list of all possible modes in which a file can be opened. The tasks performed by **fopen( )** when a file is opened in each of these modes are also mentioned.

"r" Searches file. If the file exists, loads it into memory and sets up a pointer which points to the first character in it. If file doesn't exist it returns NULL.

Operations possible - reading from the file.

"w" Searches file. If the file exists, its contents are overwritten. If the file doesn't exist, a new file is created. Returns NULL, if unable to open file.

Operations possible - writing to the file.

"a" Searches file. If the file exists, loads it into memory and sets up a pointer which points to the first character in it. If the file doesn't exist, a new file is created. Returns NULL, if unable to open file.

Oprations possible - appending new contents at end of file.

"r+" Searches file. If it exists, loads it into memory and sets up a pointer which points to the first character in it. If file doesn't exist it returns NULL.

Operations possible - reading existing contents, writing new contents, modifying existing contents of the file.

"w+" Searches file. If the file exists, its contents are destroyed. If the file doesn't exist a new file is created. Returns NULL, if unable to open file.

Operations possible - writing new contents, reading them back and modifying existing contents of the file.

"a+" Searches file. If the it exists, loads it into memory and sets up a pointer which points to the first character in it. If the file doesn't exist, a new file is created. Returns NULL, if unable to open file.

Operations possible - reading existing contents, appending new contents to end of file. Cannot modify existing contents.

A Filecopy Program

Now we know a function, **getc( )**, which reads characters rom a file. Its counterpart is a function called **putc( )** which writes characters to a file. As a practical use of these character I/O functions we can copy the contents of one file into another, as demonstrated in the following example. This program takes the contents of a text file and copies them into another text file, character by character.

```
# include "stdio.h"
main( )
{
    FILE *fs, *ft ;
    char ch ;

    fs = fopen ( "pr1.c", "r" ) ;
    if ( fs == NULL)
    {
        puts ( "Cannot open source file" ) ;
        exit( ) ;
    }
    ft = fopen ( "pr2.c", "w" ) ;
    if ( ft == NULL)
    {
        puts ( "Cannot open target file" ) ;
        fclose ( fs ) ;
        exit( ) ;
```

```
        }
        while ( 1 )
        {
            ch = getc ( fs ) ;
            if ( ch == EOF )
                break ;
            else
                putc ( ch, ft ) ;
        }
        fclose ( fs ) ;
        fclose ( ft ) ;
}
```

I hope most of the stuff in the program can be easily understood, since it has already been dealt with in the earlier section. What is new is only the function **putc( )**. Let us see how it works.

Writing To A File

The **putc( )** function is similar to the **putch( )** function, in the sense that both output characters. However, **putch()** function always writes to the VDU, whereas, **putc( )** writes to the file. Which file? The file signifed by **ft**. The writing process continues till all characters from the source file have been written to the target file, following which the loop terminates.

Note that our sample filecopy program is capable of copying only text files. To copy files with extension .EXE or .COM, we need to open the files in binary mode, a topic which would be dealt with in sufficient detail later on.

A Closer Look At fclose( )

Closing the file has several effects. First any characters remaining in the buffer are written to the disk. What buffer? We haven't said anything about the buffer before, because it is invisible to the programmer when using high level disk I/O functions. However, buffer is necessary even if it is invisible.

Consider, for example, how inefficient it would be to actually access the disk every time we want to write a character to it. Every time we write something to a disk, it takes some time for the disk drive to position the read/write head correctly. On a floppy disk system, the drive motor has to actually start rotating the disk from a standstill every time the disk is accessed. If this is to be done for every character we write to the disk, it would take a long time to perform disk I/O. This is where a buffer comes in.

When you send a character off to a file by using **putc( )**, the character is actually stored in a buffer - an area in memory, rather than being immediately written to the disk. When the buffer is full, its contents are written to the disk at once. Or if the program knows that the last character to be written to the disk has been received in the buffer, but it is still not full, it forces the buffer to be written to the disk by 'closing' the file.

A major advantage of using the high level disk I/O functions is that these activities take place automatically, the programmer doesn't need to worry about them.

Another purpose that **fclose( )** serves is, it frees the link used by the particular file, and the associated buffers, so that these are available for other files.

Using argc And argv

To execute the above filecopy program we are required to first type the program, compile it, and then execute it. This program can be improved in two ways:

(a) There should be no need to compile the program everytime to use the filecopy utility. It means the program must be executable at command prompt (A> or C> if you are using MS-DOS, $ if you are using Unix).

(b) Instead of the program prompting us to enter the source and target filenames, we must be able to supply them at command prompt, in the form:

```
C>filecopy PR1.C PR2.C
```

Where, PR1.C is the source filename and PR2.C is the target filename.

The first improvement is simple. In MS-DOS, the executable file (the one which can be executed at DOS prompt and has an extension .EXE) can be created in Quick C by using the option Alt RCX to compile the program (or F9 if you are using Turbo C)

Under uinx this is not required since in Unix every time we compile the program we always get an executable file.

The second improvement is possible by passing the source filename and target filename to the function **main( )**. This is illustrated below:

```
# include "stdio.h"
main ( argc, argv )
int argc ;
char *argv[ ] ;
{
    FILE *fs, *ft ;
    char ch ;

    if ( argc != 3 )
    {
        printf ( "Insufficient atguments" ) ;
        exit( ) ;
    }
```

```
    fs = fopen ( argv[1], "r" ) ;
    if ( fs == NULL)
    {
        puts ( "Cannot open source file" ) ;
        exit( ) ;
    }

    ft = fopen ( argv[2], "w" ) ;
    if ( ft == NULL)
    {
        puts ( "Cannot open target file" ) ;
        fclose ( fs ) ;
        exit( ) ;
    }

    while ( 1 )
    {
        ch = getc ( fs ) ;
        if ( ch == EOF )
            break ;
        else
            putc ( ch, ft ) ;
    }

    fclose ( fs ) ;
    fclose ( ft ) ;
}
```

The arguments that we pass on to **main( )** at the command prompt are called command line arguments. The function **main( )** can have two arguments, traditionally named as **argc** and **argv**. Out of these, **argv** is an array of pointers to strings and **argc** is an **int** whose value is equal to the number of strings to which **argv** points. When the program is executed, the strings on the command line are passed to **main( )**. More precisely, the strings at the command line are stored in memory and address of the first string is stored in **argv[0]**, address of the second string is stored in **argv[1]** and so on. The argument **argc** is set to the number of strings given on the command line. For example, in our sample program, if at the command prompt we give,

```
filcopy PR1.C PR2.C
```

then,

> **argc** would contain 3
> **argv[0]** would contain base address of the string "filecopy"
> **argv[1]** would contain base address of the string "PR1.C"
> **argv[2]** would contain base address of the string "PR2.C"

Whenever we pass on the arguments to **main( )**, it is a good habit to check whether the correct number of arguments have been passed on to **main( )** or not. In our program this has been done through,

```
if ( argc != 3 )
{
    printf ( "Insufficient arguments" ) ;
    exit( ) ;
}
```

Rest of the program is same as the earlier filecopy program. This program is better than the earlier filecopy program on three counts:

(a) There is no need to recompile the program everytime we want to use this utiltiy. It can be executed at command prompt.
(b) Once an executable file is created nobody with malicious intensions can tamper with your C source code program.
(c) We are able to pass source file name and target file name to **main( )**, and utilise them in **main( )**.

One final comment... the **while** loop that we have used in our program can be written in a more compact form, as shown below:

```
while ( ( ch = getc ( fs ) ) != EOF )
```

```
putc ( ch, ft ) ;
```

This avoids the usage of an indefinite loop and a **break** statement to come out of this loop. Here, first **getc (fs)** gets the character from the file, assigns it to the variable **ch**, and then **ch** is compared against **EOF**. Remember that it is necessary to put the expression

```
ch = getc ( fs )
```

within a pair of parentheses, so that first the character read is assigned to variable **ch** and then it is compared with **EOF**.

There is one more way of writing the **while** loop. It is shown below:

```
while ( !feof ( fs ) )
    ch = getc ( fs ) ;
```

Here, **feof( )** is a macro which reutrns a 0 if end of file is not reached. Hence we use the **!** operator to negate this 0 to the truth value. When the end of file is reached **feof( )** returns a non-zero value, **!** makes it 0 and since now the condition evaluates to false the **while** loop gets terminated.

Note that to open a file the following three methods are same, since, essentially a base address of the string (pointer to a string) is being passed to **fopen( )**.

```
fs = fopen ( "PR1.C" , "r" ) ;
fs = fopen ( filename, "r" ) ;
fs = fopen ( argv[1] , "r" ) ;
```

String (line) I/O In Files

For many purposes, character I/O is just what is needed. However, in some situations the usage of functions which read or write entire strings might turn out to be more efficient.

Reading or writing strings of characters from and to files is as easy as reading and writing individual characters. Here is a program that writes strings to a file using the function **fputs( )**.

```
/* Receives strings from keyboard & writes them to file */
# include "stdio.h"
main( )
{
    FILE *fp ;
    char s[80] ;

    fp = fopen ( "POEM.TXT", "w" ) ;
    if ( fp == NULL )
    {
        puts ( "Cannot open file" ) ;
        exit( ) ;
    }

    printf ( "Enter a few lines of text:\n" ) ;
    while ( strlen ( gets(s) ) > 0 )
    {
        fputs ( s, fp ) ;
        fputs ( "\n" ) ;
    }

    fclose ( fp ) ;
}
```

And here is a sample run of the program...

```
Enter a few lines of text:
Shining and bright, they are forever,
so true about diamonds,
more so of memories,
especially yours !
```

Note that each string is terminated by hitting enter. To terminate the execution of the ptogram, hit enter at the beginning of a line. This creates a string of zero length, which the program recognises as the signal to close the file and exit.

We have set up a character array to receive the string; the **fputs( )** function then writes the contents of the array to the disk. Since **fputs( )** does not automatically add a newline character to the end of the string, we must do this explicitly to make it easier to read the string back from the file.

Here is a program that reads strings from a disk file.

```
/* Reads strings from the file and displays them on screen */
# include "stdio.h"
main( )
{
    FILE *fp ;
    char s[80] ;

    fp = fopen ( "POEM.TXT", "r" ) ;
    if ( fp == NULL)
    {
        puts ( "Cannot open file" ) ;
        exit( ) ;
    }

    while ( fgets ( s, 79, fp ) != NULL)
        printf ( "%s" , s ) ;

    fclose ( fp ) ;
```

```
}
```

And here is the output...

```
Shining and bright, they are forever,
so true about diamonds,
more so of memories,
especially yours !
```

The function **fgets( )** takes three arguments. The first is the address where the string is stored, and the second is the maximum length of the string. This argument prevents **fgets( )** from reading in too long a string and overflowing the array. The third argument, as usual, is the pointer to the structure **FILE**. When all the lines from the file have been read, we attempt to read one more line, in which case **fgets( )** returns a NULL.

The Awkward Newline

We had earlier written a program that counts the total number of characters present in a file. If we use that program to count the number of characters present in the above poem (stored in the file "POEM.TXT"), it would give us the character count as 101. The same file if seen in the directory, would be reported by MS-DOS to contain 105 characters.

This discrepancy occurs because of the difference in the way C and DOS represent the end of line. In C the end of line is signalled by single character, the '\n'. In DOS, on the other hand, the end of line is marked by two characters, a carriage return ('\r'), and the linefeed (which is same as the C newline, '\n').

When your program writes a C text file to disk, DOS causes all the newlines to be converted into carriage return - linefeed combinations.

When your program reads in a text file, the carriage return - linefeed combinations are converted back into a single newline character.

Thus, DOS oriented programs like DIR command would count two characters at each end of line, while C oriented programs, like our character count program, will count one. In our poem there are four lines, therefore there is a discrepancy of four characters.

Brief Review

So far we have learnt four functions for disk I/O. These can be categorised as shown below.

Category	Functions
High level, Text, Unformatted, Character I/O	getc( ), putc( ) fgetc( ), fputc( ) Here, **getc( )** and **putc( )** are macros, whereas **fgetc( )** and **fputc( )** are their function versions.
High level, Text, Unformatted, String I/O	fgets( ), fputs( )
High level, Text, Unformatted, int I/O	No standard library function
High level, Text, Unformatted, float I/O	No standard library function

Figure 11.2

Formatted Disk I/O Functions

So far we have dealt with reading and writing only characters and strings. There exist no standard library functions to read or write numbers under the category of high level, unformatted, text I/O functions.

For formatted reading and writing of characters, strings, integers, floats, there exist two functions, **fscanf( )** and **fprintf( )**. Here is a program which illustrates the use of these functions...

```
# include "stdio.h"
main( )
{
    FILE *fp ;
    char another = 'Y' ;
    char name[40] ;
    int age ;
    float bs ;

    fp = fopen ( "EMPLOYEE.DAT", "w" ) ;
    if ( fp == NULL)
    {
        puts ( "Cannot open file" ) ;
        exit( ) ;
    }

    while ( another == 'Y' )
    {
        printf ( "\nEnter name, age and basic salary\n" ) ;
        scanf ( "%s %d %f", name, &age, &bs ) ;
        fprintf ( fp, "%s %d %f\n", name, &age, &bs ) ;

        printf ( "\nAnother employee (Y/N) " ) ;
        fflush ( stdin ) ;
        another = getche( ) ;
    }
    fclose ( fp ) ;
}
```

And here is the output of the program...

```
Enter name, age and basic salary
Anil 34 1550
Another employee (Y/N) Y
Enter name, age and basic salary
Sanjay 24 1200
Another employee (Y/N) Y
Enter name, age and basic salary
Ramesh 26 2000
Another employee (Y/N) N
```

The key to this program is the function **fprintf( )**, which writes the values of three variables to the file. This function is similar to **printf( )**, except that a **FILE** pointer is included as the first argument. As in **printf( )**, we can format the data in a variety of ways, by using **fprintf()**. In fact all the format conventions of **printf( )** function work with **fprintf( )** as well.

Perhaps you are wondering what for have we used the function **fflush( )**. The reason is to get rid of a peculiarity of **scanf( )**. After supplying data for one employee, we would hit the enter key. What **scanf( )** does is it assigns name, age and salary to appropriate variables and keeps the enter key unread in the keyboard buffer. So when it's time to supply Y or N for the question 'Another employee (Y/N)', **getch( )** will read the enter key from the buffer thinking that user has entered the enter key. To avoid this problem we use the function **fflush( )**. It is designed to remove or 'flush out' any data remaining in the buffer. The argument to **fflush( )** must be the buffer which we want to flush out. Here we use 'stdin', which means buffer related with standard input device the keyboard. Now suppose, we want to read back the names, ages and basic salaries of different employees which we stored through the earlier program into the file EMPLOYEE.DAT". Following program does just this:

```
# include "stdio.h"
main( )
{
    FILE *fp ;
```

```
	char name[40] ;
	int age ;
	float bs ;

	fp = fopen ( "EMPLOYEE.DAT", "r" ) ;
	if ( fp == NULL )
	{
		puts ( "Cannot open file" ) ;
		exit( ) ;
	}

	while ( fscanf ( fp, "%s %d %f", name, &age, &bs ) != EOF )
		printf ( "%s %d %f\n", name, &age, &bs ) ;

	fclose ( fp ) ;
}
```

And here is the output...

```
Anil 34 1550.000000
Sanjay 24 1200.000000
Ramesh 26 2000.000000
```

This program uses the **fscanf( )** function to read the data from the disk. This function is similar to **scanf( )**, except that, as with **fprintf( )**, a pointer to **FILE** is included as the first argument.

Binary Mode Versus Text Mode

As we have seen earlier, the high level disk I/O functions can be categorised as text and binary. This classification arises out of the mode in which a file is opened. There are three main areas where text and binary mode files are different:

(a) The handling of newlines

(b) The representation of end of file
(c) The storage of numbers

Let us explore these three differences.

Text Versus Binary Mode: Newlines

We have already seen that, in text mode, a newline character is converted into the carriage return - linefeed combination before being written to the disk. Likewise, the carriage return - linefeed combination on the disk is converted back into a newline when the file is read by a C program. However, if a file is opened in binary mode, as opposed to text mode, these conversions will not take place.

As an example, let us revise our character count program to open a file in binary mode and see what effect it has on the count of characters present in the file. As you may recall, the earlier character count program had counted fewer characters in the file than the DOS DIR ommand. This was because DIR counted each end of line as two characters, while our program counted it as one. The following program would eliminate this discrepancy.

```
# include "stdio.h"
main( )
{
    FILE *fp ;
    char ch ;
    int noc = 0 ;

    fp = fopen ( "POEM.TXT", "rb" ) ;
    if ( fp == NULL)
    {
        puts ( "Cannot open file" ) ;
        exit( ) ;
    }
```

```
while ( 1 )
{
    ch = getc ( fp ) ;
    if ( ch == EOF )
        break ;

    noc++ ;
}
fclose ( fp )
printf ( "Number of characters = %d\n", noc ) ;
}
```

And here is the output...

```
Number of characters = 105
```

There is only one difference between this program and the earlier character count program; we have opened the file in binary mode by using "rb" as an argument to **fopen( )**

While opening the file in text mode we can use either "r" or "rt", but since, text mode is the default mode we usually drop the 't'. Using this program the character count would turn out to be 105, exactly same as that reported by the DIR command. There are four lines in our poem. Therefore, there are four carriage return - linefeed combinations in the file, signifying the end of four lines. Each counts as one in text mode, but two in binary mode, hence the difference of four characters. In binary mode the conversion of carrriage return - linefeed combination into newline or vice versa **does not** take place.

Text Versus Binary Mode: End Of File

The second difference between text and binary modes is in the way the end-of-file is detected. In text mode, a special character, whose ascii value is 26, is inserted after the last character in the file to mark the end of file. If this character is detected at any point in the file, the read function would return the EOF signal to the program.

As against this, there is no such special character present in the binary mode files to mark the end of file. The binary mode files keep track of the end of file from the number of characters present in the directory entry of the file.

There is a moral to be derived from the end of file marker of text mode files. If a file stores numbers in binary mode, it is important that binary mode only be used for reading the numbers back, since one of the numbers we store might well be the number 26 (hexadecimal 1A). If this number is detected while we are reading the file by opening it in text mode, reading would be terminated prematurely at that point.

Thus the two modes are not compatible. See to it that the file that has been written in text mode is read back only in text mode. Similarly, the file that has been written in binary mode must be read back only in binary mode.

Text Versus Binary Mode: Storage Of Numbers

The only function that is available for storing numbers in a disk file is the **fprintf( )** function. It is important to understand how numerical data is stored on the disk by **fprintf( )**. Text and characters are stored one character per byte, as we would expect. Are numbers stored as they are in memory, two bytes for an integer, four bytes for float, and so on? No.

Numbers are stored as srtings of characters. Thus, 1234, even though it occupies two bytes in memory, when transferred to the disk using **fprintf( )**, it would occupy four bytes, one byte per character. Similarly, the floating point number 1234.56 would occupy 7 bytes on disk. Thus, numbers with more digits would require more disk space.

Hence if large amount of numerical data is to be stored in a disk file, using text mode may turn out to be inefficient. The solution is to open the file in binary mode and use those functions which store the numbers in binary format. It means each number would occupy same number of bytes on disk as it occupies in memory.

Record I/O In Files

So far we have seen programs which write characters, strings or numbers to a file. If we desire to write a combination of these, that is a combination of dissimilar data types, what should we do? Use structures. Following program illustrates the use of structures for writing records of employees.

```
/* Writing records to a file using structure */
# include "stdio.h"
main( )
{
    FILE *fp ;
    char another = 'Y' ;
    struct emp
    {
        char name[40] ;
        int age ;
        float bs ;
    } ;
    struct emp e ;

    fp = fopen ( "EMPLOYEE.DAT", "w" ) ;
    if ( fp == NULL)
    {
        puts ( "Cannot open file" ) ;
        exit( ) ;
    }
```

```
    while ( another == 'Y' )
    {
        printf ( "\nEnter name, age and basic salary: " ) ;
        scanf ( "%s %d %f", e.name, &e.age, &e.bs ) ;
        fprintf ( fp, "%s %d %f\n", e.name, e.age, e.bs ) ;

        printf ( "\nAdd another record (Y/N) " ) ;
        fflush ( stdin ) ,
        another = getche( ) ;
    }

    fclose ( fp ) ;
}
```

And here is the output of the program...

```
Enter name, age and basic salary: Sunil 34 1250
Add another record (Y/N) Y
Enter name, age and basic salary: Sameer 21 1300
Add another record (Y/N) Y
Enter name, age and basic salary: Rahul 34 1400
Add another record (Y/N) N
```

I suppose the program is self explanatory. We are just reading the data into a structure variable using **scanf( )**, and dumping it into a disk file using **fprintf( )**. The user can input as many records as he desires. The procedure ends, when the user supplies 'N' for the question 'Add another record (Y/N)'

The above program has two disadvantages:

(a) The numbers (basic salary) would occupy more number of bytes, since the file has been opened in text mode. This is because when the file is opened in text mode, each number is stored as a character string.
(b) If the number of fields in the structure increase (say, by adding address, house rent allowance etc.), in that case writing struc-

tures using **fprintf( )**, or reading them using **fscanf( )**, becomes quite clumsy.

Before we go on to eliminate both these disadvantages, let us first complete the program that reads the employee records created by the above program. Here is how it can be done...

```
/* Read records from a file using structure */
#include "stdio.h"
main( )
{
    FILE *fp ;
    struct emp
    {
        char name[40] ;
        int age ;
        float bs ;
    } ;
    struct emp e ;

    fp = fopen( "EMPLOYEE.DAT", "r") ;
    if ( fp == NULL )
    {
        puts ( "Cannot open file" ) ;
        exit( ) ;
    }

    while ( fscanf ( fp, "%s %d %f", e.name, &e.age, &e.bs ) != EOF )
        printf ( "%s %d %f\n", e.name, e.age, e.bs ) ;

    fclose ( fp ) ;
}
```

And here is the output of the program...

```
Sunil 34 1250.000000
Sameer 21 1300.000000
```

```
Rahul 34 1400.000000
```

Let us now see a more efficient way of reading/writing records (structures). This makes use of two functions **fread( )** and **fwrite( )**. We will write two programs, first one would write records to the file and the second would read these records from the file and display them on the screen.

```
/* Receiving records from keyboard & writing them  to a file in binary
mode */
#include "stdio.h"
main( )
{
     FILE *fp ;
     char another = 'Y' ;
     struct emp
     {
          char name[40] ;
          int age ;
          float bs ;
     } ;
     struct emp e ;

     fp = fopen ( "EMP.DAT", "wb" ) ;
     if ( fp == NULL)
     {
          puts ( "Cannot open file" ) ;
          exit( ) ;
     }

     while ( another == 'Y' )
     {
          printf ( "\nEnter name, age and basic salary: " ) ;
          scanf ( "%s %d %f", e.name, &e.age, &e.bs ) ;
          fwrite ( &e, sizeof ( e ), 1, fp ) ;

          printf ( "\nAdd another record (Y/N) " ) ;
```

```
            fflush ( stdin ) ;
            another = getche( ) ;
        }

        fclose ( fp ) ;
    }
```

And here is the output...

```
Enter name, age and basic salary: Suresh 24 1250
Add another record (Y/N) Y
Enter name, age and basic salary: Ranjan 21 1300
Add another record (Y/N) Y
Enter name, age and basic salary: Harish 28 1400
Add another record (Y/N) N
```

Most of this program is similar to the one that we wrote earlier, which used **fprintf( )** instead of **fwrite( )**. Note, however, that the file "EMP.DAT" has now been opened in binary mode.

The information obtained about the employee from the keyboard is placed in the structure variable **e**. Then, the following statement writes the structure to the file:

```
fwrite ( &e, sizeof ( e ), 1, fp ) ;
```

Here, the first argument is the address of the structure to be written to the disk.

The second argument is the size of the structure in bytes. Instead of counting the bytes occupied by the structure ourselves, we let the program do it for us by using the **sizeof( )** operator. **sizeof( )** operator gives the size of variable in bytes. This keeps the program unchanged in event of change in the elements of the structure.

The third argument is the number of such structures that we want to write at one time. In this case, we want to write only one structure at a time. Had we had an array of structures, for example, we might have wanted to write the entire array at once.

The last argument is the pointer to the file we want to write to.

Now, let us write the program to read back the records written to the disk by the earlier program.

```
/* Read records from binary file and display them on VDU */
#include "stdio.h"
main( )
{
    FILE *fp ;
    struct emp
    {
        char name[40] ;
        int age ;
        float bs ;
    } ;
    struct emp e ;

    fp = fopen ( "EMP.DAT", "rb" ) ;
    if ( fp == NULL )
    {
        puts ( "Cannot open file" ) ;
        exit( ) ;
    }

    while ( fread ( &e, sizeof ( e ), 1, fp ) == 1 )
        printf ( "%s %d %f\n", e.name, e.age, e.bs ) ;

    fclose ( fp ) ;
}
```

Here, the **fread( )** function causes the data read from the disk to be placed in the structure variable **e**. The format of **fread( )** is same as that of **fwrite( )**. The function **fread( )** returns the number of records read. Ordinarily, this should correspond to the third argument, the number of records we asked for... 1 in this case. If we have reached the end of file, since **fread( )** cannot read anything, it returns a 0. By testing for this situation, we know when to stop reading.

As you can now appreciate, any database management application in C must make use of **fread( )** and **fwrite( )** functions, since they store numbers more efficiently, and make writing/reading of structures quite easy. Note that even if the number of elements belonging to the structure increases, the format of **fread( )** and **fwrite( )** remains same.

Making It All Make Sense

So far we have learnt record I/O in bits and pieces. However, in any serious database management application, we will have to combine all that we have learnt in a proper manner to make sense. I have attempted to do this in the following menu driven program. There is a provision to Add, Modify, List and Delete records, the operations which are imperative in any database management. Following comments would help you in understanding the program easily:

- Addition of records must always take place at the end of existing records in the file, much in the same way you would add new records in a register manually.

- Listing records means displaying the existing records on the screen. Naturally, records should be listed from first record to last record.

- In modifying records, first we must ask the user which record he intends to modify. Instead of asking the record number to be modified, it would be more meaningful to ask for the name of the employee whose record is to be modified. On modifying the record, the existing record gets overwritten by the new record.

In deleting records, except for the record to be deleted, rest of the records must first be written to a temporary file, then the original file must be deleted, and the temporary file must be renamed back to original.

Observe carefully the way the file has been opened, first for reading & writing, and if this fails (the first time you run this program it would certainly fail, because that time there is no data file existing), for writing and reading. It is imperative that file should be opened in binary mode.

Note that the file is being opened only once and closed only once, which is quite logical.

```
/* A menu-driven program for elementary database management */
#include "stdio.h"
main( )
{
    FILE *fp, *ft ;
    char another, choice ;
    struct emp
    {
        char name[40] ;
        int age ;
        float bs ;
    } ;
    struct emp e ;
    char empname[40] ;

    fp = fopen ( "EMP.DAT", "rb+" ) ;
    if ( fp == NULL )
    {
        fp = fopen ( "EMP.DAT", "wb+" ) ;
        if ( fp == NULL )
        {
            puts ( "Cannot open file" ) ;
```

```
            exit( ) ;
        }
    }

    while ( 1 )
    {
        printf ( "\n1. Add Records" ) ;
        printf ( "\n2. List Records" ) ;
        printf ( "\n3. Modify Records" ) ;
        printf ( "\n4. Delete Records" ) ;
        printf ( "\n0. Exit" ) ;
        printf ( "\n\nYour choice" ) ;

        choice = getche( ) ;

        switch ( choice )
        {
            case '1' :
                fseek ( fp, 0 , SEEK_END ) ;
                another = 'Y' ;
                while ( another == 'Y' )
                {
                    printf ( "\nEnter name, age and basic sal. " ) ;
                    scanf  ( "%s %d %f", e.name, &e.age, &e.bs ) ;
                    fwrite ( &e, sizeof ( e ), 1, fp ) ;
                    printf ( "\nAdd another Record (Y/N) " ) ;
                    fflush ( stdin ) ;
                    another = getche( ) ;
                }
                break ;

            case '2' :
                rewind ( fp ) ;

                while ( fread ( &e, sizeof ( e ), 1, fp ) == 1 )
                    printf ( "%s %d %f\n", e.name, e.age, e.bs ) ;
```

```
            break ;

        case '3' :
            another = 'Y' ;
            while ( another == 'Y' )
            {
                printf ( "\nEnter name of employee to modify " ) ;
                scanf  ( "%s", empname ) ;

                rewind ( fp ) ;
                while ( fread ( &e, sizeof ( e ), 1, fp ) == 1 )
                {
                    if ( strcmp ( e.name, empname ) == 0 )
                    {
                        printf ( "\nEnter new name, age & bs" )
                        scanf ( "%s %d %f", e.name, &e.age,
                                  &e.bs ) ;
                        fseek ( fp, -sizeof ( e ), SEEK_CUR ) ;
                        fwrite ( &e, sizeof ( e ), 1, fp ) ;
                        break ;
                    }
                }

                printf ( "\nModify another Record (Y/N) " ) ;
                fflush ( stdin ) ;
                another = getche( ) ;
            }
            break ;

        case '4' :
            another = 'Y' ;
            while ( another == 'Y' )
            {
                printf ( "\nEnter name of employee to delete " ) ;
                scanf  ( "%s", empname ) ;

                ft = fopen ( "TEMP.DAT", "wb" ) ;
```

```
                rewind ( fp ) ;
                while ( fread ( &e, sizeof ( e ), 1, fp ) == 1 )
                {
                    if ( strcmp ( e.name, empname ) != 0 )
                        fwrite ( &e, sizeof ( e ), 1, ft ) ;
                }

                fclose ( fp ) ;
                fclose ( ft ) ;

                remove ( "EMP.DAT" ) ;
                rename ( "TEMP.DAT", "EMP.DAT" ) ;

                fp = fopen ( "EMP.DAT", "rb+" ) ;

                printf ( "Delete another Record (Y/N) " ) ;
                fflush ( stdin ) ;
                another = getche( ) ;
            }
            break ;

        case '0' :
            fclose ( fp ) ;
            exit( ) ;
    }
  }
}
```

To understand how this program works, you need to be familiar with the concept of pointers. A pointer is initiated whenever we open a file. On opening a file a pointer is set up which points to the first record in the file. On using the functions **fread( )** or **fwrite( )**, the pointer moves to the beginning of next record. On closing a file the pointer is deactivated.

The **rewind( )** function places the pointer to the beginning of the file, irrespective of where it is present right now.

Note that pointer movement is of utmost importance since **fread( )** always reads that record where the file pointer is currently placed. Similarly, **fwrite( )** always writes the record where the file pointer is currently placed.

The **fseek( )** function lets us move the file pointer from one record to another. In the program above, to move the pointer to the previous record from its current position, we used the function,

```
fseek ( fp, -sizeof ( e ), SEEK_CUR ) ;
```

Here, **-sizeof (e)** moves the pointer back by **sizeof (e)** bytes from the current position. **SEEK_CUR** is a macro defined in "stdio.h".

Similarly, the following **fseek( )** would place the pointer beyond the last record in the file.

```
fseek ( fp, 0, SEEK_END ) ;
```

In fact **-sizeof (e)** or 0 are just the offsets which tell the compiler by how many bytes should the pointer be moved from a particular position. The third argument could be either **SEEK_END**, **SEEK_CUR** or **SEEK_SET**. All these act as reference from which the pointer should be offset. **SEEK_END** means move the pointer from the end of the file, **SEEK_CUR** means move the pointer with reference to its current position and **SEEK_SET** means move the pointer with reference to the beginning of the file.

If we wish to know where the pointer is positioned right now, we can use the function **ftell( )**. It returns this position as a **long int** which is an offset from the beginning of the file. The value returned by **ftell( )** can be used in subsequent calls to **fseek( )**. A sample call to **ftell( )** is shown below:

```
position = ftell ( fp ) ;
```

where **position** is a **long int**

Detecting Errors In Reading/Writing

Not at all times when we perform a read or write operation on a file are we successful in doing so. Naturally there must be a provision to test whether our attempt to read/write was successful or not.

The standard library function **ferror( )** reports any error that might have occurred during a read/write operation on a file. It returns a zero if the read/write is successful and a non-zero value in case of a failure. The following program illustrates the usage of **ferror( )**.

```
#include "stdio.h"
main( )
{
    FILE *fp ;
    char ch ;

    fp = fopen ( "TRIAL", "w" ) ;
    while ( !feof ( fp ) )
    {
        ch = getc ( fp ) ;
        if ( ferror( ) )
        {
            printf ( "Error in reading file" ) ;
            break ;
        }
        else
            printf ( "%c", ch ) ;
    }
    fclose ( fp ) ;
}
```

In this program the **getc( )** function would obviously fail first time around since the file has been opened for writing whereas **getc( )** is attempting to read from the file. The moment the error occurs **ferror( )** returns a non-zero value and the **if** block gets executed. Instead of printing the error message using **printf( )** we can use the standard library function **perror( )** which prints the error message specified by the compiler. Thus in the above program the **perror( )** function can be used as shown below.

```
if ( ferror( ) )
{
    perror ( "TRIAL" ) ;
    break ;
}
```

Note that when the error occurs the error message that is displayed is:

```
TRIAL: Permission denied
```

This means we can precede the system error message with any message of our choice. In our program we have just displayed the filename in place of the error message.

Exercise

[A] What will be the output of the following programs:

(1)
```
#include "stdio.h"
main( )
{
    char str[20] ;
    FILE *fp ;
    fp = fopen ( strcpy ( str, "ENGINE.C" ), "w" ) ;
    fclose ( fp ) ;
}
```

(2)
```
#include "stdio.h"
main( )
{
    FILE *fp ;
    char c ;

    fp = fopen ( "TRY.C", "r" ) ;
    if ( fp = NULL )
    {
        puts ( "Cannot open file" ) ;
        exit(1) ;
    }
    while ( ( c = getc ( fp ) ) != EOF )
        putch( c ) ;

    fclose ( fp ) ;
}
```

(3)
```
# include "stdio.h"
main( )
{
    FILE *fp, *fs, *ft ;
```

```
        fp = fopen ( "A.C", "r" ) ;
        fs = fopen ( "B.C", "r" ) ;
        ft = fopen ( "C.C", "r" ) ;

        fclose ( fp, fs, ft ) ;
    }
```

(4)
```
    #include "stdio.h"
    main( )
    {
        char name [20], name1[20] ;
        int age, age1 ;

        printf ( "Enter name and age\n" ) ;
        scanf ( "%s %d", name, &age ) ;
        printf ( "%s %d", name, age ) ;

        printf ( "\nEnter name and age\n" ) ;
        fscanf ( stdin, "%s %d", name1, &age1 ) ;
        fprintf ( stdout, "%s %d", name1, age1 ) ;
    }
```

(5)
```
    #include "stdio.h"
    main( )
    {
        static char str[ ] = "Triplet" ;
        char *s ;

        s = str ;
        while ( *s )
        {
            putc ( *s, stdout ) ;
            fputchar ( *s ) ;
            printf ( "%c\n", *s ) ;
            s++ ;
        }
```

```
}
```

(6)
```
/* Suppose this program is stored in the file PR.C
and its corresponding executable file PR.EXE is
executed at DOS prompt by saying,
PR CAT DOG PARROT */

main ( argc, argv )
int argc ;
char *argv[ ] ;
{
    for ( i = 0 ; i < argc ; i++ )
        printf ( "%s\n", argv[i] ) ;
}
```

(7)
```
#include "stdio.h"
main( )
{
    FILE *fp ;
    char str[80] ;

    /* TRIAL.C contains only one line Its a round, round, round world! */

    fp = fopen ( "TRIAL.C", "r" ) ;
    while ( fgets ( str, 80, fp ) != EOF )
        puts ( str ) ;
}
```

(8)
```
/* This program is stored in a file called PROB.C */
main ( x, y )
int x ;
char *y[ ] ;
{
    printf ( "%d\n", x ) ;
    printf ( "%s", y[0] ) ;
}
```

[B] Attempt the following:

(1) Write a program which would remove all comments from a C program. Your program should be capable of removing comments which occur at the beginning of a statement, at the end of a statement as well as the comments which are split over multiple lines.

(2) A file opened in Document mode in Wordstar stores each word with its last character being stored as the ascii value of the character plus 128. As against this a Non-document mode file is stored as a normal ascii file. Write a program which would convert a Document mode file into a Non-document mode file.

(3) Write a program which prints out only those lines from a file which are containing more than 80 characters. Also print out the line numbers of these lines.

(4) A file contains a C program, but by mistake a novice has typed it out in capitals. It's a long program, therefore you cannot afford to have it retyped. Write a utility which reads this program and converts it to an appropriate small-case program and writes it to a target file. Use functions fgets() and fputs().

(5) Write a program to count no of characters, words and lines in a file.

(6) Write a program that will concatenate two files: that is, append the contents of one file at the end of another file and write the result into a third file. You must be able to execute the program at command prompt as follows:

```
CONCAT source1.txt  source2.txt  target.txt
```

CHAPTER

12 The C Preprocessor

Features Of C Preprocessor
#define Directive
#include Directive
#undef Directive
Conditional Compilation Directives

The C preprocessor is exactly what its name implies. It is a program that processes our source program before it is passed to the compiler. Preprocessor commands (often known as directives) form what can almost be considered a language within C language. We can certainly write C programs without knowing anything about the preprocessor or its facilities. But preprocessor is such a great convinience that virtually all C programmers rely on it. This is a capability that does not exist in many other higher level languages. This chapter explores the preprocessor directives and discusses the pros and cons of using them in programs.

Features Of C Preprocessor

There are several steps involved from the stage of writing a C program to the stage of getting it executed. Figure 12.1 shows these different steps. You can observe from the figure that our program passes through several processors before it is ready to be executed. The input and output to each of these processors is shown in Figure 12.2.

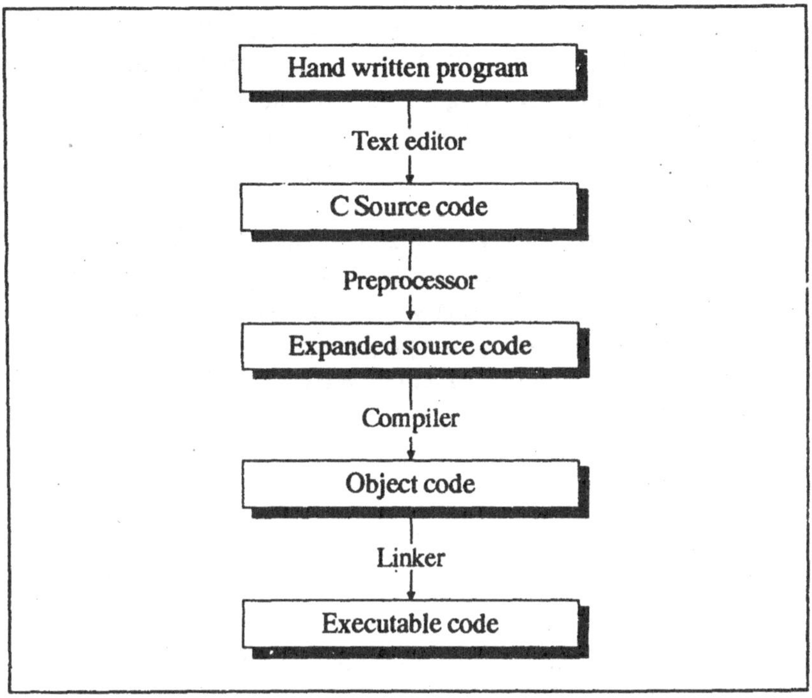

Figure 12.1

Processor	Input	Output
Editor	Program typed from keyboard	C source code file containing C source program and preprocessor commands
Prepro-cessor	C source code file	Source code file with the preprocessing commands properly sorted out
Compiler	Source code file with preprocessing commands sorted out	Relocatable object code

Figure 12.2

Whenever we want to execute our programs in Quick C, we do so by hitting the function key F5. In Turbo C the same thing can be achieved using Ctrl F9 and in Unix using the 'cc' command. When we do this, preprocessing, compiling, linking as well as execution of the program is done automatically.

The preprocessor offers several features called preprocessor directives. Each of these preprocessor directives begin with a # symbol. The directives can be placed anywhere in a program but are most often placed at the beginning of a program, before **main( )**, or before the beginning of a particular function. We would learn the following preprocessor directives here:

(a) #define directive
(b) #include directive
(c) #undef directive
(c) Conditional Compilation directives

Let us understand these features of preprocessor one by one.

#define Directive

Have a look at the following program.

```
#define UPPER 25
main( )
{
    int i ;
    for ( i = 1 ; i <= UPPER ; i++ )
        printf ( "%d", i ) ;
}
```

In this program instead of writing 25 in the **for** loop we are writing it in the form of UPPER, which has already been defined before **main( )** through the statement,

```
#define UPPER 25
```

This statement is called 'macro definition' or more commonly, just a 'macro'. What purpose does it serve? During preprocessing, the preprocessor replaces every occurrence of UPPER in the program with 25. Here is another example of macro definition.

```
#define PI 3.1415
main( )
{
    float r = 16.25 ;
    float area ;

    area = PI * r * r ;
    printf ( "Area of circle = %f", area ) ;
}
```

UPPER and PI in the above programs are often called 'macro templates', whereas, 25 and 3.1415 are called their corresponding 'macro expansions'.

When we compile the program, before the source code passes to the compiler it is examined by the C preprocessor for any macro definitions. When it sees the **#define** directive, it goes through the entire program in search of the macro templates; wherever it finds one, it replaces the macro template with the appropriate macro expansion. Only after this procedure has been completed is the program handed over to the compiler.

In C programming it is customary to use capital letters for macro template. This makes it easy for programmers to pick out all the macro templates when reading through the program.

Note that macro template and its macro expansion are separated by blanks or tabs. A space between **#** and **define** is optional. Remember that a macro definition is never to be terminated by a semicolon.

And now a million dollar question... why use **#define** in the above programs? What have we gained by substituting PI for 3.1415 in our program? Probably, we have made the program easier to read. Even though 3.1415 is such a common constant that it is easily recognizable, there are many instances where a constant doesn't reveal its purpose so readily. For example, as we will find out later, the phrase "\x1B[2J" causes the screen to clear. But which would you find easier to understand in the middle of your program "\x1B[2J" or "CLEARSCREEN"? Thus, we would use the macro definition

```
#define CLEARSCREEN "\x1B[2J"
```

Then wherever CLEARSCREEN appears in the program it would automatically be replaced by "\x1B[2J" before compilation begins.

There is perhaps a more important reason for using macro definition than mere readability. Suppose a constant like 3.1415 appears many times in your program. This value may have to be changed some day to 3.141592. Ordinarily, you would need to go through the program and manually change each occurrence of the constant. However if you have defined PI in a **#define** directive, you only need to make one change, in the **#define** directive itself:

```
#define PI 3.141592
```

The change will be made automatically to all occurrences of PI before compilation begins.

In short, it is nice to know that you would be able to change values of a constant at all the places in the program by just making a change in the **#define** directive. This convenience may not matter for small programs shown above, but with large programs macro definitions are almost indispensable.

But the same purpose could have been served had we used a variable **pi** instead of a macro template **PI**. A variable could also have provided a meaningful name for a constant and permitted one change to effect many occurrences of the constant. It's true that a variable can be used in this way. Then, why not use variables? For three reasons it's a bad idea.

Firstly, it is inefficient, since the compiler can generate faster and more compact code for constants than it can for variables. Secondly, using a variable for what is really a constant encourages sloppy thinking and makes the program more difficult to understand: if something never changes, it is hard to imagine it as a variable. And thirdly, there is always a danger that the variable may get altered somewhere in the program, inadverently; so it's no longer a constant that you think it is.

Thus, using **#define** can produce more efficient and more easily understandable programs. It is used extensively by C programmers as you will see in many programs in this book.

Following three examples show places where a **#define** directive is popularly used by C programmers.

A **#define** directive is many a times used to define operators as shown below.

```
#define AND &&
#define OR ||
main( )
{
    int f = 1, x = 4, y = 90 ;

    if ( ( f < 5 ) AND ( x <= 20 OR y <= 45 ) )
        printf ( "Your PC will always work fine..." ) ;
    else
        printf ( "In front of the maintentance man" ) ;
}
```

A **#define** directive could be used even to replace a condition, as shown below.

```
#define AND &&
#define ARANGE ( a > 25 AND a < 50 )
main( )
{
    int a = 30 ;

    if ( ARANGE )
        printf ( "within range" ) ;
    else
        printf ( "out of range" ) ;
}
```

A **#define** directive could be used to replace even an entire C statement. This is shown below.

```
#define FOUND printf("The Yankee Doodle Virus") ;
main( )
{
    char signature ;

    if ( signature == 'Y' )
        FOUND
    else
        printf ( "Safe.. as yet !" ) ;
}
```

Macros With Arguments

The macros that we have used so far are called simple macros. Macros can have arguments, just as functions can. Here is an example which illustrates this fact.

```
#define AREA(x) ( 3.14 * x * x )
main( )
{
    float r1 = 6.25, r2 = 2.5 , a ;
```

```
        a = AREA ( r1 ) ;
        printf ( "Area of circle = %f\n", a ) ;
        a = AREA ( r2 ) ;
        printf ( "Area of circle = %f", a ) ;
}
```

Here's the output of the program...

```
Area of circle = 122.656250
Area of circle = 19.625000
```

In this program wherever the preprocessor finds the phrase **AREA(x)** it expands it into the statement **(3.14 * x * x)**. However, that's not all that it does. The **x** in the macro template **AREA(x)** is an argument that matches the **x** in the macro expansion **(3.14 * x * x)**. The statement **AREA(r1)** in the program causes the variable **r1** to be substituted for **x**. Thus the statement **AREA(r1)** is equivalent to:

```
( 3.14 * r1 * r1 )
```

After the above source code has passed through the preprocessor, what the compiler gets to work on will be this:

```
main( )
{
    float r1 = 6.25, r2 = 2.5 ;
    float a ;

    a = 3.14 * 6.25 * 6.25 ;
    printf ( "area of circle = %f\n", a ) ;
    a = 3.14 * 2.5 * 2.5 ;
    printf ( "Area of circle = %f", a ) ;
}
```

Here is another example of macros with arguments:

```
#define ISDIGIT(y) ( y >= 48 && y <= 57 )
main( )
{
    char ch ;

    printf ( "Enter any digit" ) ;
    scanf ( "%c", &ch ) ;

    if ( ISDIGIT(ch) )
        printf ( "You entered a digit" ) ;
    else
        printf ( "Illegal entry" ) ;
}
```

There are two points to remember while writing macros with arguments:

(a) Be careful not to leave a blank between the macro template and its argument while defining the macro.

For example, there should be no blank between **AREA** and **(x)** in the definition,

```
#define AREA(x) ( 3.14 * x * x )
```

If we were to write **AREA (x)** instead of **AREA(x)**, the **(x)** would become a part of macro expansion, which we certainly don't want.

What would happen is, the template would be expanded to

```
( 6.25 ) ( 3.14 * 6.25 * 6.25 )
```

which won't run. Not at all what we wanted.

(b) The entire macro expansion should be enclosed within parentheses. Here is an example of what would happen if we fail to enclose the macro expansion within parentheses.

```
#define SQUARE(n) n * n
main( )
{
    int j ;

    j = 64 / SQUARE(4) ;
    printf ( "j = %d", j ) ;
}
```

The output of the above program would be:

```
j = 64
```

whereas what we expected was j = 4.

What went wrong? The macro was expanded into

```
j = 64 / 4 * 4 ;
```

which yields 64.

Macros Versus Functions

In the above example a macro was used to calculate the area of the circle. As we know, even a function can be written to calculate the area of the circle. Though macro calls are 'like' function calls, they are not really the same thing. Then what is the difference between the two?

In a macro call the preprocessor replaces the macro template with its macro expansion, in a stupid, unthinking, literal way. Whereas in a function call the control is passed to a function along with certain arguments, some calculations are performed in the function and a useful value is returned back from the function.

This brings us to a question: when is it best to use macros with arguments and when is it better to use a function? Usually macros make the program run faster but increases the program size, whereas functions make the program smaller and compact.

If we use a macro hundred times in a program, the macro expansion goes into our source code at hundred different places, thus increasing the program size. On the other hand, if a function is used, then even if it is called from hundred different places in the program, it would take the same amount of space in the program.

But passing arguments to a function and getting back the returned value does take time and would therefore slow down the program. This gets avoided with macros since they have already been expanded and placed in the source code before compilation.

Moral of the story is: if the macro is simple and sweet like in our examples, it makes a nice shorthand and avoids the overheads associated with function calls. On the other hand, if we have a fairly large macro and it is used fairly often, perhaps we ought to replace it with a function.

#include Directive

The second preprocessor directive we'll explore in this chapter is file inclusion. This directive causes one file to be included in another. The preprocessor command for file inclusion looks like this:

```
#include "filename"
```

and it simply causes the entire contents of **filename** to be inserted into the source code at that point in the program. Of course this presumes that the file being included is existing. When and why this feature is used? It can be used in two cases:

(a) If we have a very large program, the code is best divided into several different files, each containing a set of related functions. It is a good programming practise to keep different sections of a large program separate. These files are **#included** at the beginning of main program file.

(b) Many a times we need some functions or some macro definitions almost in all programs that we write. In such a case these commonly needed functions and macro definitions can be stored in a file, and that file can be included in every program we write, which would add all the statements in this file to our program as if we have typed them in. In the previous chapter we included a file called **stdio.h** in many programs.

It is common for the files which are to be included to have a .h extension. The '.h' extension stands for 'header file', possibly because it contains statements which when included go to the head of your program.

Actually there exist two ways to write **#include** statements. These are:

```
#include <filename>
#include "filename"
```

The meaning of each of these forms is given below:

#include "goto.c" — This command would look for the file **goto.c** in the current directory as well as the specified list of directories as mentioned in the include search path that might have been set up.

#include <goto.c> — This command would look for the file **goto.c** in the specified list of directories only.

#undef Directive

On some occasions it may be desirable to cause a defined name to become 'undefined'. This can be accomplished by means of the **#undef** directive. In order to undefine a macro which has been earlier **#defined**, the directive,

```
#undef macro template
```

can be used. Thus the statement

```
#undef PCAT
```

would cause the definition of PCAT to be removed from the system. All subsequent **#ifdef PCAT** statements would evaluate to false. In practise seldom are we required to undefine a macro, but for some crooked reason if you are required to, then you know that there is something to fall back upon.

Conditional Compilation Directives

We can, if we want, have the compiler skip over part of a source code by inserting the preprocessing commands **#ifdef** and **#endif**, which have the general form:

```
#ifdef macroname
    statement 1 ;
    statement 2 ;
    statement 3 ;
#endif
```

If macroname has been **#defined**, the block of code will be processed as usual; otherwise not.

Where would **#ifdef** be used? When would you like to compile only a part of your program? In two cases:

(a) It is often used to "comment out" obsolete lines of code. It often happens that a program is changed at the last minute to satisfy a client. This involves rewriting some part of source code to client's satisfaction and delete the old code. But veteran programmers are familiar with the client who changes his mind and wants the old code back again just the way it was. Now you would definitely not like to retype the deleted code again.

One solution is to put the old code within a pair of /* */ combination. But we might have already written a comment in the code that we are about to "comment out". This would mean that we are going to write nested comments. Obviously, this solution won't work since we can't nest comments in C.

The solution is therefore to use conditional compilation as shown below.

```
main( )
{
    #ifdef OKAY
        statement 1 ;
        statement 2 ; /* detects virus */
        statement 3 ;
        statement 4 ; /* specific to stone virus */
    #endif
    statement 5 ;
    statement 6 ;
    statement 7 ;
}
```

Here, statements 1, 2, 3 and 4 would get compiled only if the macro OKAY has been defined, and we have purposefully omitted the definition of the macro OKAY. At a later date if we want that these statements should also get compiled all that we are required to do is to delete **#ifdef** and **#endif**.

(b) A more sophisticated use of **#ifdef** has to do with making the programs portable, i.e. to make them work on two totally different computers. Suppose an organisation has two different types of computers and you are expected to write a program that works on both the machines. You can do so by isolating the lines of code that must be different for each machine by marking them off with **#ifdef**. For example:

```
main( )
{
    #ifdef PCAT
        code suitable for a PC/AT
    #else
        code suitable for a PC/XT
    #endif
    code common to both the computers
}
```

When you compile this program it would compile only the code suitable for a PC/XT and the common code. This is because the macro PCAT has not been defined. Note that the worling of **#ifdef - #else - #endif** is similar to the ordinary **if - else** control instruction of C.

If you want to run your program on a PC/AT, just add a statement at the top saying,

```
# define PCAT
```

Sometimes, instead of **#ifdef** the **#ifndef** directive is used. The **#ifndef** (which means: if not defined) works exactly opposite to **#ifdef**. The above example if written using **#ifndef**, would look like this:

```
main( )
{
    #ifndef PCAT
        code suitable for a PC/XT
    #else
        code suitable for a PC/AT
    #endif
    code common to both the computers
}
```

#if And #elif Directives

The **#if** directive can be used to test whether an expression evaluates to a nonzero value or not. If the result of the expression is nonzero, then subsequent lines upto a **#else**, **#elif** or **#endif** are compiled, otherwise they are skipped.

A simple example of **#if** directive is shown below:

```
main( )
{
    #if TEST <= 5
        statement 1 ;
        statement 2 ;
    #else
        statement 3 ;
        statement 4 ;
    #endif
}
```

If the expression, **TEST <= 5** evaluates to true then statements 1 and 2 are compiled otherwise statements 3 and 4 are compiled. In place of the expression **TEST <= 5** other expressions like (**LEVEL == HIGH || LEVEL == LOW**) or **ADAPTER == CGA** can also be used.

If we so desire we can have nested conditional compilation directives. An example which uses such directives is shown below.

```
#if ADAPTER == MA
    code for monochrome adapter
#else
    #if ADAPTER == CGA
        code for colour graphics adapter
    #else
        #if ADAPTER == EGA
            code for enhanced graphics adapter
        #else
            #if ADAPTER == VGA
                code for video graphics array
            #else
                code for super video graphics array
            #endif
        #endif
    #endif
#endif
```

The above program can be made more compact by using another conditional compilation directive called **#elif**. The same program using this directive can be rewritten as shown below. Observe that by using the **#elif** directives the number of **endifs** used in the program get reduced.

```
#if ADAPTER == MA
    code for monochrome adapter
#elif ADAPTER == CGA
    code for colour graphics adapter
#elif ADAPTER == EGA
    code for enhanced graphics adapter
#elif ADAPTER == VGA
    code for video graphics array
```

```
#else
    code for super video graphics array
#endif
```

Exercise

[A] Answer the following:

(1) What is a preprocessor directive?

1. a message from compiler to the programmer
2. a message from compiler to the linker
3. a message from programmer to the compiler
4. a message from programmer to the microprocessor

(2) Which of the following are correctly formed **#define** statements

```
#define INCH PER FEET 12
#define SQR (X) ( X * X )
#define SQR(X) X * X
#define SQR(X) ( X * X )
```

(3) State True or False:

A macro must always be written in capital letters.
A macro should always be accomodated in a single line.

(4) How many **#include** directives may be there in a given program file ?

(5) What is the difference between the following two **#include** directives:

```
#include "conio.h"
#include <conio.h>
```

(6) A header file is:

1. A file that must contains standard library functions
2. A file that contains definitions and macros
3. A file that contains user defined functions
4. A file that is present in current working directory

[B] What will be the output of the following programs:

(1)
```
main( )
{
    int i = 2 ;
    #ifdef DEF
        i *= i ;
    #else
        printf ( "%d", i ) ;
    #endif
}
```

(2)
```
#define PRODUCT(x) ( x * x )
main( )
{
    int i = 3, j ;
    j = PRODUCT(i+1) ;
    printf ( "%d", j ) ;
}
```

(3)
```
#define MESS(m) printf( "m")
#define GOTONEXTLINE printf( "\n" )
main( )
{
    MESS( "A galaxy of persons were born on this day..." ) ;
    GOTONEXTLINE ;
    MESS( "But somehow you seem to be the best!!" ) ;
}
```

(4)
```
#define ISUPPER(x) (x >= 65 && x <= 90)
#define ISLOWER(x) (x >= 97 && x <= 122)
```

```
#define ISALPHA(x) (ISUPPER(x) || ISLOWER(x))
main( )
{
    char ch = '+' ;

    if (ISALPHA(ch))
        printf ( "ch contains an alphabet" ) ;
    else
        printf ( "ch doesn't contain an alphabet" ) ;
}
```

(5)
```
#define MEAN( a, b, c, d,e ) ( a + b + c + d + e )/5
main( )
{
    int a, b, c, d, e, m ;

    a = 1;
    b = 2 ;
    c = 3 ;
    d = 4 ;
    e = 5 ;

    m = MEAN(a, b, c, d, e) ;
    printf ( "Mean of the five numbers is = %d" );
}
```

(6)
```
#define CUBE(X) (X*X*X)
main( )
{
    int a ;

    a = 27 / CUBE(3) ;
    printf ( "%d", a ) ;
}
```

(7)
```
#define CUBE(X) (X*X*X)
```

```
main( )
{
    int a, b ;

    b = 3 ;
    a = CUBE(b++) / b++ ;
    printf ( "a = %d b = %d", a, b ) ;
}
```

(8)
```
#define INTEGER int
main( )
{
    INTEGER a =10, b = 20 ;
    printf ( "a = %d b = %d", a, b );
}
```

(9)
```
#define MAX(a, b) ((a) > (b) ? (a) : (b) )
main( )
{
    int m, x = 5, y = 6 ;

    m = MAX( x + y, 10 ) ;
    printf ( "%d", m ) ;

    m = MAX(x,y) * 100 ;
    printf ( "\n%d", m ) ;
}
```

[C] Attempt the following:

(1) Write down macro definitions for the following

(a) To test whether a character entered is a small case letter or not.
(b) To test whether a character entered is a upper case letter or not.

(c) To test whether a character is an alphabet or not. Make use of the macros you defined in (a) and (b) above.
(d) To obtain the bigger of two numbers.

[2] Write macros definitions with arguments for calculation of area and perimeter of a triangle, a square & a circle. Store these macro definitions in a file called "areaperi.h". Include this file in your program, and call the macro definitions for calculating area and perimeter for different squares, triangles and circles.

CHAPTER

13 Header Files And Standard Library Functions

Header Files
Standard Library Functions
Utility Functions
Standard I/O Functions
Character Class Test Functions

Each C compiler provides a Library of around 200 predefined functions and macros designed for use in C programs. These library functions make programming easier by providing the follwing:

(a) An interface to the operating system functions (such as opening and closing files).

(b) Fast and efficient functions to perform common programming tasks (such as string manipulation), sparing the programmer the time and effort needed to write such functions.

These library functions are especially important in C programming because C programmers rely on the library for basic functions that are not provided in the language. These functions include, among others, input and output, storage allocation, and process control.

For using most of these functions certain files need to be included in the programs which makes call to these functions. These files are often known as header files and they contain macro definitions, type definitions and function declarations. These header files usually have an extension **.h**, as in **stdio.h, ctype.h, string.h** etc. A few commonly required header files and the Standard Library functions that they support are discussed int the following sections.

Header Files

Usually header files have an extension **.h** just to distinguish them from the C program files which commonly use the extension **.c**. There are several header files available with a C compiler. Here we would briefly touch upon the imortant ones.

stdio.h

The header file **stdio.h** contains definitions of constants, macros and types, along with function declarations for standard I/O functions. These functions are listed below.

calloc	fgetchar	fputchar	getc	remove
fclose	fgetpos	fputs	getchar	rename
fcloseall	fgets	fread	gets	rewind
feof	flushall	fscanf	printf	scanf
ferror	fopen	fseek	putc	ungetc
fflush	fprintf	ftell	putchar	
fgetc	fputc	fwrite	puts	

ctype.h

The **ctype.h** header file defines macros and constants and declares a global array used in character classification. The macros defined in **ctype.h** are listed below.

isalnum	isdigit	ispunct	toascii	_toupper
isalpha	isgraph	isspace	tolower	
isascii	islower	isupper	toupper	

iscntrl	isprint	isxdigit	_tolower

string.h

The **string.h** header file declares the string manipulation functions, as listed below.

memccpy	memmove	strcmpi	strlwr	strchr
memchr	memset	strcpy	strncat	strrev
memcmp	strcat	strdup	strncmp	strset
memcpy	strchr	stricmp	strncpy	strstr
memicmp	strcmp	strlen	strnicmp	strupr

math.h

The header file **math.h** contains function declarations for all floating point math routines as listed below.

abs	atof	cosh	log	sinh
acos	cabs	exp	log10	sqrt
asin	ceil	fabs	pow	tan
atan	cos	floor	sin	tanh

stdlib.h

The **stdlib.h** header file contains function declarations for the following functions.

abort	bsearch	itoa	rand	system
abs	calloc	labs	realloc	tolower
atof	exit	malloc	srand	toupper
atoi	free	perror	strtod	
atol	gcvt	qsort	strtol	

stdarg.h

The include file **stdarg.h** defines macros that allow you to access arguments in functions which are passed variable number of arguments, such as **vprintf( )**. These macros are defined to be machine independent and portable. These macros are listed below.

va_arg	va_end	va_start

time.h

The **time.h** header file declares the following time related functions.

asctime	difftime
clock	gmtime
ctime	time

Standard Library Functions

Discussing all the functions given above in all their garbs would call for a separate book by itself. Therefore, we have decided just to give in brief the purpose of each commonly used function, the arguments that are passed to it and the value that the function returns.

For easy reference these functions have been categorised as per their purpose and have been listed here in alphabetical order.

String Functions

memccpy( ) Copies a block of **n** bytes
Syntax: void *memccpy (void *dest, void *src, int c, unsigned n) ;

memchr( ) searches **n** bytes for a character **c**.

	Syntax: void *memchr (void *s, int c, unsigned n) ;
memcmp( )	Compares two blocks for a length of exactly **n** bytes. Syntax: memcmp (void *s1, void *s2, unsigned n) ;
memcpy( )	Copies a block of **n** bytes. Syntax: memcpy (void *dest, void *src, unsigned n) ;
memicmp( )	Compares **n** bytes of two character arrays, ignoring case. Syntax: int memicmp (void *s1, void *s2, unsigned n) ;
memmove( )	Copies a block of specified number of bytes. Syntax: void *memmove (void *dest, void *src, unsigned n) ;
memset( )	Sets a given block of memory to specified byte. Syntax: void *memset (void *s, int c, unsigned n) ;
strcat( )	Appends one string to another. Syntax: char *strcat (char *dest, char *src) ;
strchr( )	Scans a string for the first occurrence of a given character. Syntax: char *strchr (char *s, int c);
strcmp( )	Compares one string with another. Syntax: char *strcmp (char *s1, char *s2) ;
strcmpi( )	Compares one string with another, without case sensitivity. Syntax: int strcmpi (char *s1, char *s2) ;
strcpy( )	Copies one string into another. Syntax: char *strcpy (char *dest, char *src) ;
strdup( )	Copies a string into a newly created location. Syntax: char *strdup (char *s) ;
stricmp( )	Compares one string to another, without case sensitivity. Syntax: int stricmp (char *s1, char *s2) ;
strlen( )	Calculates the length of a string.

	Syntax: unsigned strlen (char *s) ;
strlwr( )	Converts uppercase letters in a string to lowercase. Syntax: char *strlwr (char *s) ;
strncat( )	Appends a portion of one string to another. Syntax: char *strncat (char * dest, char *src, unsigned maxlen) ;
strncmp( )	Compares a portion of one string to a portion of another. Syntax: strncmp (char *s1, char *s2, unsigned maxlen) ;
strncpy( )	Copies a given number of bytes from one string into another. Syntax: char *strncpy (char *dest, char *src, unsigned maxlen) ;
strrev( )	Reverses a string. Syntax: char *strrev (char *s) ;
strnset( )	Sets a specified number of characters in a string to a given character. Syntax: char *strnset (char *s, int ch, unsigned n) ;
strstr( )	Scans a string for the occurrence of a given substring. Syntax: char *strstr (char *s1, char *s2) ;
strupr( )	Converts lowercase letters in a string to upper case. Syntax: char *strupr (char *s) ;

Mathematical Functions

abs( )	Returns the absolute value of an integer. Syntax: abs (int x) ;
acos( )	Calculates the arc cosine. Syntax: double acos (double x) ;
asin( )	Calculates the arc sine. Syntax: double asin (double x) ;

atan( )	Calculates the arc tangent. Syntax:double atan (double x) ;
atof( )	Converts a string to a floating point number. Syntax: double atof (char *s) ;
cabs( )	Absolute value of complex number. Syntax: double cabs (struct complex z) ;
ceil( )	Rounds up. Syntax: double ceil (double x) ;
cos( )	Calculates the cosine. Syntax: double cos (double x) ;
cosh( )	Calculates the hyperbolic cosine. Syntax: double cosh (double x) ;
exp( )	Calculates the exponential e to the x'th power. Syntax: double exp (double x) ;
fabs( )	Returns the absolute value of a floating point number. Syntax: double fabs (double x) ;
floor( )	Rounds down. Syntax: double floor (double x) ;
log( )	Calculates the natural logarithm of x. Syntax: double log (double x) ;
log10( )	calculates log(x) to the base 10. Syntax: double log10 (double x) ;
pow( )	Calculates x to the power of y. Syntax: double pow (double x, double y) ;
sin( )	Calculates the sine of the angle specified in radians. Syntax: double sin (double x) ;
sinh( )	Calculates hyperbolic sine. Syntax: double sinh (double x) ;
sqrt( )	Calculates the positive square root of input value. Syntax: double sqrt (double x) ;
tan( )	Calculates the tangent. Syntax· double tan (double x) ;
tanh( )	Calculates the hyperbolic tangent. Syntax: double tanh (double x) ;

Time And Date Functions

asctime( )	Converts date and time to ASCII Syntax: char *asctime (struct tm *tblock) ;
clock( )	Determines the processor time Syntax: long clock( ) ;
ctime( )	Converts date and time to a string. Syntax: char *ctime (long *time) ;
difftime( )	Computes the difference between the two times. Syntax: double difftime (long time2, long time1) ;
gmtime( )	Converts date and time to Greenwich Mean Time (GMT). Syntax: struct tm *gmtime (long *timer) ;
time( )	Gets time of day. Syntax: long time (long *timer) ;

Variable Argument List Functions

va_arg( )	Implements a variable argument list. Syntax: type va_arg (va_list param, type) ;
va_end( )	Implements a variable argument list. Syntax: void va_end (va_list param) ;
va_start( )	Implements a variable argument list. Syntax: void va_start (va_list param, lastfix) ;

Utility Functions

abort( )	Abnormally terminates a process. Syntax: void abort( ) ;
abs( )	Returns the absolute value of an integer Syntax: int abs (int x) ;
atof( )	Converts a string to a floating point number. Syntax: double atof (char *s) ;
atoi( )	Converts a string to an integer.

	Syntax: int atoi (char *s) ;
atol( )	Converts a string to a long. Syntax: long atol (char *s) ;
bsearch( )	Binary search of an array. Syntax: void bsearch (void *key, void *base, unsigned nelem, unsigned width, int (*fcmp) (void*, CONST void*)) ;
calloc( )	Allocates main memory. Syntax: void *calloc (unsigned nitems, unsigned size) ;
exit( )	Terminates execution of a program. Syntax: void exit (int status) ;
free( )	Frees allocated block. Syntax: void free (void *block) ;
gcvt( )	Converts a floating point number to a string. Syntax: char *gcvt (double value, int ndec, int *buf) ;
itoa( )	Converts an int to a string. Syntax: char *itoa (int value, char *string, int radix) ;
labs( )	Gives the absolute value. Syntax: long labs (long x) ;
malloc( )	Allocates main memory. Syntax: void malloc (unsigned size) ;
perror( )	Prints a system error message. Syntax: void perror (char *s) ;
qsort( )	Sorts using the quicksort algorithm. Syntax: void qsort (void *base, unsigned nelem, unsigned width, int (*fcmp) (void *, void *)) ;
rand( )	Random number generator. Syntax: rand( ) ;
realloc( )	Reallocates the main memory. Syntax: void *realloc (void * block, unsigned size) ;
srand( )	Initialises the random number generator. Syntax: void srand (unsigned seed) ;
strtod( )	Converts a string to a double value.

	Syntax: double strtod (char *s, char **endptr) ;
strtol( )	Converts a string to a long value. Syntax: long strtol (char *s, char **endptr, in radix) ;
system( )	Issues a DOS command. Syntax: int system (char *command) ;
tolower( )	Translates characters to lowercase. Syntax: int tolower (int ch) ;
toupper( )	Translates characters to uppercase. Syntax: int toupper (int ch) ;

Standard I/O Functions

calloc( )	Allocates main memory. Syntax: void *calloc (unsigned nitems, unsigned size) ;
fclose( )	Closes a stream. Syntax: int fclose (FILE *stream) ;
fcloseall( )	Closes open streams. Syntax: int fcloseall( )
feof( )	Detects end-of-file on a stream. Syntax: int feof (FILE *stream) ;
ferror( )	Detects errors on stream. Syntax: int ferror (FILE *stream) ;
fflush( )	Flushes a stream Syntax: int fflush (FILE *stream) ,
flushall( )	Flushes all streams. Syntax: int flushall( ) ;
fgetc( )	Gets a character from stream. Syntax: int fgetc (FILE *stream) ;
fgetchar( )	Gets character from stdin. Syntax: int fgetchar( ) ;
fgetpos( )	Gets the current file pointer. Syntax: int fgetpos (FILE *stream, long *pos) ;
fgets( )	Gets A string from a stream.

	Syntax: char *fgets (char *s, int n, FILE *stream);
fopen( )	Opens a stream. Syntax: FILE *fopen (char *filename, char *mode);
fprintf( )	Writes formatted output to a stream. Syntax: int fprintf (FILE *stream, char *format[,argument...]);
fputc( )	Puts a character on a stream. Syntax: int fputc (int c, FILE *stream);
fputchar(	Outputs a character on stdout. Syntax: int fputchar (int c);
fputs( )	Outputs a string on stream. Syntax: int fputs (char *s, FILE *stream);
fread( )	Reads data from a stream. Syntax: unsigned fread (void *ptr, unsigned size, unsigned n, FILE *stream);
fscanf( )	Scans and formats inputs from a stream. Syntax: int fscanf (FILE *stream, char *format[,address...]);
fseek( )	Repositions a file pointer on a stream. Syntax: int fseek (FILE *stream, long int offset, int whence);
ftell( )	Returns the current file pointer. Syntax: long int ftell (FILE *stream);
fwrite( )	Writes to a stream. Syntax: unsigned fwrite (void *ptr, unsigned size,unsigned n, FILE *stream);
getc( )	Gets character from stream. Syntax: int getc (FILE *stream);
getchar( )	Gets character from stdin. Syntax: int getchar( );
gets( )	Gets a string from stdin. Syntax: char *gets (char *s);
printf( )	Writes formatted output to stdout. Syntax: int printf (char *format[,argument,...]);
putc( )	Outputs a character to a stream.

	Syntax: int putc (int c, FILE *stream) ;
putchar( )	Outputs character on stdout. Syntax: int putchar(int c) ;
puts( )	Outputs a string on the screen. Syntax: int puts (char *s) ;
remove( )	Removes a file. Syntax: int remove (char *filename) ;
rename( )	Renames a file. Syntax: int rename (char *oldname, char *newname) ;
rewind( )	Repositions a file pointer to the begining of a stream. Syntax: void rewind (FILE *stream) ;
scanf( )	Scans and formats input from the stdin stream. Syntax: int scanf (char *format[, address,...]) ;
ungetc( )	Pushes a character back into input stream. Syntax: int ungetc (int c, FILE *stream) ;

Character Class Test Functions

isalnum( )	Tests whether a character is an alphabet or a number. Syntax: isalnum (int c) ;
isalpha( )	Character classification macro that returns non-zero if **c** is a letter (A-Z or a-z). Syntax: int isalpha (int c) ;
isascii( )	Tests whether a character is an ascii (0 to 127) character. Syntax: iasascii (int c) ;
iscntrl( )	Tests whether a character is a control character. Syntax: iscntrl (int c) ;
isdigit( )	Character classification macro that returns non-zero value if **c** is a digit ('0'-'9'). Syntax: int isdigit (int c) ;

isgraph( )	Character classification macro that returns non-zero if **c** is a printing character, space character is excluded Syntax: int isgraph (int c) ;
islower( )	Character classification macro that returns non-zero value if **c** is a lower case alphabet and zero otherwise. Syntax: int islower (int c) ;
isprint( )	Character classification macro that returns value if **c** is a printable characte (ascii 32 to 126) and non-zero otherwise. Syntax: int isprint (int c) ;
ispunct( )	Character classification macro that returns non-zero value if **c** is a punctuation character (iscntrl or isspace). Syntax: int ispunct (int c) ;
isspace( )	Character classification macro that returns non-zero if **c** is a space, tab, carriage return, newline, vertical tab, formfeed. Syntax: int isspace (int c) ;
isupper( )	Character classification macro that returns non-zero if **c** is an uppercase letter (A-Z). Syntax: int isupper (int c) ;
isxdigit( )	Character classification macro that returnsnon-zero if **c** is a hexadecimal digit (0-9, A-F, a-f).
toascii( )	Translates character to ASCII format. Syntax: int toascii (int ch) ;
tolower( )	Translates character to lowercase. Syntax: int tolower (int ch) ;
toupper( )	Translates character to uppercase. Syntax: int toupper (int ch) ;
_tolower( )	Translates character to lowercase. Syntax: int _tolower (int ch) ;
_toupper( )	Translates character to uppercase. Syntax: int _toupper (int ch) ;

Miscellaneous Functions

absread( )	Reads absolute disk sectors. Syntax: int absread (int drive, int numsect, int beginsect, void *buffer) ;
abswrite( )	Writes absolute disk sectors. Syntax: int abswrite (int drive, int numsect, int beginsect, void *buffer) ;
access( )	Determines accesibility of a file. Syntax: int access (char *filename, int amode) ;
biosdisk( )	Performs BIOS disk services. Syntax: int biosdisk (int cmd, int drive, int head, int track, int sector, int numsect, void *buffer) ;
chmod( )	Changes file access mode. Syntax: int chmod (char *path, int amode) ;
clrscr( )	Clears the text mode screen. Syntax: void clrscr( ) ;
getch( )	Gets character from keyboard, does not echo it to screen. Syntax: int getch( ) ;
getdate( )	Gets system date. Syntax: void getdate (struct date *datep) ;
gettime( )	Gets system time. Syntax: void gettime (struct time *timep) ;
gotoxy( )	Positions cursor at specified position on screen. Syntax: void gotoxy (int x, int y) ;
inport( )	Reads a word from a hardware port. Syntax: int inport (int portid) ;
inportb( )	Reads a byte from a hardware port. Syntax: unsigned char inportb (int portid) ;
kbhit( )	Checks for currently available keystroke. Syntax: int kbhit( ) ;
outport( )	Outputs a word to a hardware port. Syntax: void outport (int portid, int value) ;
outportb( )	Outputs a byte to a hardware port.

	Syntax: void outportb (int portid, unsigned char value) ;
setdate( )	Sets DOS date. Syntax: void setdate (struct date *datep) ;
settime( )	Sets system time. Syntax: void settime (struct time *timep) ;
sprintf( )	Writes formatted output to a string. Syntax: sprintf (char *buffer, char *format[, argument, ...]) ;

APPENDIX

A Summary Of C Language

In this appendix, we will briefly discuss the most frequently used parts of C. It is not intended that this appendix be a complete definition of the language, but rather a concise summary of all its features. You are advised to thoroughly read the material in this section after you have completed the text. Doing so will not only reinforce the material you have read but will also provide a better understanding of C. The subsections have been listed in alphabetical order as given below:

Arrays	Escape Sequences	return
break	for	sizeof
case	Functions	Storage Classes
Cast	goto	Structures
Comments	if	switch
Constants	Keywords	typedef
continue	Labels	Unions
Data Types	Null Statement	void
do-while	Pointers	while
enum	Precedence of Operators	

Arrays

An array is a collection of similar elements stored in contiguous memory locations. An array is declared by writing the data type followed by the array name followed by the size (dimension) in brackets. For example,

```
int x[20] ;
```

On declaring this array forty memory locations are reserved (since each **int** is 2 bytes long). Each location can be referred to by using **x[0]**, **x[1]**, **x[2]** etc. If the array is initialised where it is declared, then mentioning the dimension is optional.

There can exist an array of **ints**, an array of **floats**, an array of **longs**, an array of **doubles**, an array of pointers, an array of structures etc.; in general, an array of any data type.

break

When the statement

```
break ;
```

is encountered during execution, the control immediately comes out of the corresponding **while**, **do-while**, **for** or **switch** and reaches the statement immediately after the **while**, **do-while**, **for** or **switch**.

case

Used in conjunction with **switch**, so kindly refer **switch** statement.

cast

The typecast operator is written as

```
( type )
```

where **type** is any data type. When the typecast operator is executed, the operand is converted to the specified data type. For example, if we write,

```
int k = 35 ;  float a ;
a = ( float ) k / 3 ;
```

the value of **k** will be first converted to **float** before division is performed. As a result division would be performed between two **floats** and hence the fractional part obtained on division will be preserved which would have otherwise been truncated.

Comment

Anything enclosed within a pair of /* and */ is treated as a comment. Note the following points about the comments:

- There can be any number of comments in a program.
- A comment can be split over two lines.
- A comment can occur anywhere in a program.
- Comments cannot be nested.

Constants

Integer constants do not contain a decimal point. For example,

```
123   450   -32767
```

An integer constant that begins with zero is treated as an octal number. For example,

```
023   045   0112
```

A constant that begins with 0x or 0X is treated as a hexadecimal number. For example,

```
0x66   0Xb800   0X5c
```

In hexadecimal numbers, small case letter from **a** to **f** or a capital letter from **A** to **F** is acceptable.

An integer constant that is followed by **l** or **L** is of the type **long**. For example,

```
730l   0730l   0x90AL
```

A floating point constant is the one which contains a decimal point. For example,

```
2.22   4.3e4   113.4e-3   .67
```

A character constant is a character enclosed within a pair of single quotes. For example,

```
'a'   'A'   '!'   '7'
```

A string constant is any combination of characters, digits and special symbols enclosed within a pair of double quotes. For example,

```
"Hello"   "good bye"   "plot - 10"
```

continue

When the statement

```
continue ;
```

is encountered in a **while, do-while** or a **for** loop, control passes to the condition that determines whether to execute the body of the loop again or not. **continue** cannot be used with **switch**, the way **break** can be.

For example,

```
for ( i = 12 ; i <= 45 ; i++ )
{
    k = i * 7 + b ;
    if ( k < 1000 )
        continue ;
    else
        printf ( "%d", k ) ;
}
```

Here, on encountering **continue** control passes to **i++**, which increments the value of **i** and then passes control to **i <= 45**, which determines whether the body of the loop should be executed or not.

Data Types

There are two fundamentally different types of data in C programming - integer and floating point. From these two we can derive two others - character and double precision. There also exists one more data type called void, which isn't used as often as the other four. The bytes occupied by each of these data types as well as the name used to refer to them is shown in the following figure:

Data type	Meaning	Size (bytes)
char	a character	1
int	an integer	2
float	a single precision real number	4
double	a double precision real number	8
void	valueless	0

do-while

When we execute,

```
do
{
    statement 1 ;
    statement 2 ;
    statement 3 ;
    statement 4 ;
} while ( condition ) ;
```

as long as the condition is true (evaluates to a non-zero value), the statements get executed. The condition is tested after the statements have been executed, ensuring that the statements are executed at least once. Note that the condition must be terminated by a semicolon.

enum

An enumerated data type is the one which has user specified values. For example, the declaration

```
enum player { Manjrekar, Tendulkar, Vengsarkar } ;
```

describes the data type **enum player.** Following this a variable of the type **enum player** should take one of the values Manjrekar, Tendulkar, or Vengsarkar. To define a variable of the type **enum player,** we write

```
enum player name ;
```

Escape Sequences

C recognises the following escape sequences. When used with output functions like **printf( ), putc( ), fprintf( ), puts( ), puchar( )** etc. the escape sequences help in formatting the output. Following escape sequences are available.

Escape Seq.	Meaning	Escape Seq.	Meaning
\n	newline	\\	back slash
\t	tab	\'	single quote
\b	backspace	\"	double quote
\r	carriage return	\f	form feed
\a	alert		

for

When we execute

```
for ( expresssion 1 ; expression 2 ; expression 3 )
{
    statement 1 ;
    statement 2 ;
    statement 3 ;
}
```

we first execute **expression 1**. Then, as long as **expression 2** is true (has a non-zero value), the statements are executed, followed by **expression 3**. If there is only one statement in the body of the loop, then the pair of braces may be dropped.

Functions

The following example illustrates two things:

(a) How a function is called
(b) How a function is defined

```
main( )
{
    int i = 3 ;
    float a = 12.5 ;
    display ( i, a ) ;
}

display ( j, b ) ;
int j ;
float b ;
```

```
{
    printf ( "%d %f", j, b ) ;
}
```

From **main( )** the function **display( )** is being called since **display( )** is followed by a semicolon. While calling the **display( )** function the values of variables **i** and **a** are being passed to it. **i** and **a** are called actual arguments, whereas **j** and **b** are called formal arguments.

There are many more features about a function like call by reference, call by value, returning values, returning non-integer values, recursion etc. which have not been discussed here for want of space.

goto

When the statement

```
goto label ;
```

is executed, control passes to the line

```
label:
```

For example, in the following program control passes to the label **out** if the condition is satisfied.

```
main( )
{
    int i = 3 ;

    if ( i == 3 )
        goto out ;
    else
        printf ( "%d", i ) ;
```

```
        out :
            printf ( "sudden death of the program" ) ;
    }
```

if

When we execute

```
if ( condition )
    statement 1 ;
    statement 2 ;
```

if condition is true (evaluates to a non-zero value), the statement 1 is executed followed by statement 2, otherwise straightaway statement 2 is executed.

When we execute

```
if ( condition )
{
    statement 1 ;
    statement 2 ;
}
else
{
    statement 3 ;
    statement 4 ;
}
statement 5 ;
```

if condition is true (non-zero), statements 1 and 2 are executed followed by statement 5, otherwise statements 3 and 4 are executed followed by statement 5.

keywords

These are also known as reserved words. They should never be used as variable names. There are totally 32 keywords in C. A list of these keywords is given in Figure 3.7. in Chapter 3.

Labels

A label is the identifier for a statement or a group of statements. It must be followed by a colon. A statement or a set of statements that begin with label are a target of a **goto** statement. Please refer **goto** as well.

Null Statement

A null statement is one which contains only a semicolon. The following **for** loop executes a null statement 10 times.

```
for ( i = 1 ; i <= 10 ; i++ )
```

Pointers

A pointer must be defined so as to point to a particular data type. For example, if we write,

```
int *p ;
float *k ;
char *ch ;
```

p can hold the address of an **int**, **k** can hold the address of a **float**, whereas **ch** can hold the address of a **char**. Note that the addresses are always whole numbers, hence any pointer can contain only a whole number. The only arithmetic operations that can be performed on pointers are as follows:

(a) addition of a number to a pointer
(b) subtraction of a number from a pointer
(c) subtraction of a pointer from another pointer

Never attempt the following operations on pointers:

(a) addition of two pointers
(b) multiplication of two pointers
(c) division of two pointers

Precedence of operators

Precedence decides which operation would be performed first in a given expression. Figure 4.10 in Chapter 4 shows a full list of operators along with their precedence and associativity. The function expression operator has the highest precedence, whereas the comma operator has the lowest precedence.

return

When the statement

```
return ;
```

is executed, the control returns to the calling function along with a garbage integer value.

When the statement

```
return ( expression ) ;
```

is executed, the control returns to the calling function along with the value of the expression. If not specifically mentioned **return** returns an integer value. To return a non-integer value from a function the function has to be so defined.

sizeof

The sizeof operator gives the size of its operand in bytes. For example, if the following program is run

```
main( )
{
    int i ;
    float a ;
    int arr[10] ;
    printf ( "%d %d %d ", sizeof ( i ), sizeof ( a ), sizeof ( arr ) ) ;
}
```

it would print the output as,

```
2 4 20
```

Storage Classes

The various storage classes are **auto, register, static, extern**. Since the details about these storage classes are too involved, the reader is referred to Chapter 3 in the text.

Structures

A structure declaration consists of the keyword **struct** followed by an optional structure name, followed by structure elements in braces. The terminating brace must be followed by a semicolon. For example,

```
struct employee
{
    char name[30] ;
    int age ;
    char sex ;
} ;
```

Once a structure data type has been defined, we can define variables to have this data type. For example,

```
struct employee e1, e2 ;
```

declares two variables **e1** and **e2** to be of the type **struct employee**.It's possible to define, declare and initiate structures simultaneously, as in,

```
struct employee
{
    char name[30] ;
    int age ;
    char sex ;
} e1 = { "Rahul", 21, 'M' } ;
```

Structures can be passed from one function to another just as other data types. While passing structures either a call by value or a call by reference can be made. Two structure variables can be equated to assign value of one to another, as in,

```
e1 = e2 ;
```

switch

The switch statement has the form

```
switch ( expression )
{
    case c1 :
        stat 1 ;
        stat 2 ;
    case c2 :
        stat 3 ;
        stat 4 ;
    default :
        stat 5 ;
        stat 6 ;
}
```

- When **switch** is executed the 'expression' is evaluated, and control passes to that **case** whose value is same as that of the expression.

- If expression's value doesn't equal any of the cases then the control goes to the default block.

- Usually each set of statements in a case is followed by the **break** statement. If **break** statement is executed control passes to the statement immediately after the closing brace of **switch**. If **break** is not present, execution will continue through all the statements, beginning with the the first case which equals the value of the expression.

- Each of **c1**, **c2** etc. must be integers. The **default** clause is optional.

typedef

The use of **typedef** creates a synonym for some other data type. For example, if we write

```
typedef struct employee
{
    char name[30] ;
    int age ;
    char sex ;
} emp ;
```

the type **struct employee** and **emp** would be synonyms. For example once the above type definition has been done, writing

```
emp e1 ;
```

is same as writing

```
struct employee
{
    char name[30] ;
    int age ;
    char sex ;
} e1 ;
```

union

A union is syntactically (grammatically) identical to a structure. A element of a **union** is accessed in the same way as the element of a structure. A **union** provides a way to look at the same memory location's contents in more than one way.

For example, in the following program, we can look at two memory locations simultaneously using **key.i**, and at individual bytes of these two bytes using **key.ch[0]** and **key.ch[1]**.

```
main( )
{
    union a
    {
        int i ;
        char ch[2] ;
    } key ;
    key.i = 145 ;
    printf ( "%d %d %d", key.i, key.ch[0], key.ch[1] ) ;
}
```

void

The keyword **void** is used to define or declare a function that returns no value. For example, the definition

```
void func ( i, j )
int i, j ;
```

defines a function that receives two integer values but returns no value.

while

When we execute

```
while ( condition )
{
    statement 1 ;
```

```
        statement 2 ;
    }
```

so long as the condition is true (evaluates to a non-zero value), the statements are executed. Note that the condition is tested before the statements are executed. If there is only one statement in the body of the **while** loop then the pair of braces may be dropped.

APPENDIX B

Chasing The Bugs

C programmers are great innovators of our times. Unhappily, among their most enduring accomplishments are several new techniques for wasting time. There is no shortage of horror stories about programs that took twenty times to 'debug' as they did to 'write'. And one hears again and again about programs that had to be rewritten all over again because the bugs present in it could not be located.

A typical C programmer's 'morning after' is red eyes, biue face and a pile of crumpled printouts and dozens of reference books all over the floor. Bugs are C programmer's birth right. But how do we chase them away. No sure-shot way for that. Possibly if I make a list of more common programming mistakes it might be of help. They are not arranged in any particular order. But as you would realise surely a great help!

[1] Omitting the ampersand before the variables used in **scanf( )**

```
int choice ;
scanf ( "%d", choice ) ;
```

Here, the **&** before the variable **choice** is missing. Another common mistake with **scanf( )** is to give blanks either just before the format string or immediately after the format string as in,

```
int choice ;
scanf ( " %d ", choice ) ;
```

Note that this is not a mistake, but till you don't understand **scanf( )** thoroughly, this is going to cause trouble. Safety is in eliminating the blanks. Thus, correct form would be,

```
int choice ;
scanf ( "%d", &choice ) ;
```

[2] Using the operator = instead of the operator ==.

What do you think will be the output of the following program?

```
main( )
{
    int i = 10 ;

    while ( i = 10 )
    {
        printf ( "got to get out" ) ;
        i++ ;
    }
}
```

At first glance it appears the message will be printed once and the control will come out of the loop when **i** becomes 11. But, actually we have fallen in an indefinite loop. This is because the = used in the condition always assigns the value 10 to **i**, and since **i** is non-zero the condition is satisfied and the body of the loop is executed over and over again.

[3] Ending a loop with a semicolon.

```
main( )
{
    int j = 1 ;
    while ( j <= 100 ) ;
    {
        printf ( "Compguard" ) ;
        j++ ;
    }
}
```

Inadverently, we have fallen in an indefinite loop. Cause is the semicolon after **while**. This in effect makes the compiler feel that you wanted the loop to work in the following manner:

```
while ( j <= 100 )
```

By all means an indefinite loop since **j** never gets incremented and hence eternally remains less that 100.

[4] Omitting the **break** statement at the end of a **case** in a **switch** statement. Remember that if a **break** is not included at the end of a **case**, then execution will continue into the next **case**.

```
main( )
{
    int ch = 1 ;
    switch ( ch )
    {
        case 1 :
            printf ( "Goodbye" ) ;
        case 2 :
            printf ( "Lieutenant" ) ;
    }
}
```

Here, since the **break** statement has not been given after **printf( )** in **case 1**, the control runs into **case 2** and executes the second **printf( )** as well.

However, this sometimes turns out to be a blessing in disguise. Especially, in cases when we are checking whether the value of a variable equals a capital letter or a small case letter. This example has been succinctly explained in Chapter 5.

[5] Using **continue** in a **switch**. It is a common error to believe that the way the keyword **break** is used with **while**, **for**, **do-while** and a **switch**, similarly the keyword **continue** can also be used with them. Remember, **cotinue** works only in loops, never with a **switch**.

[6] A mismatch in the number, type and order of actual and formal arguments.

```
yr = romanise ( year, 1000, 'm' ) ;
```

Here, three arguments in the order **int**, **int** and **char** are being passed to **romanise( )**. When **romanise( )** receives these arguments they must be received in the same order by the formal arguments. A careless mismatch might give strange results.

[7] Omitting provisions for returning non-integer value from a function. Look at the following function call:

```
area = area_circle ( 1.5 ) ;
```

When **area_circle( )** function is defined later in the program, care should be taken to make it capable of returning a **float** value. Note that unless otherwise mentioned the compiler will assume that a function returns a value of type **int**.

[8] Inserting a semicolon at the end of macro definition.

How do you recognise a C programmer? Ask him to write a paragraph in English and watch whether he ends each sentence with a semicolon. This usually happens because a C programmer becomes habitual to ending all statements with a semicolon.

However, a semicolon at the end of a macro definition might create a problem. For example,

```
#define UPPER 25 999;
```

would lead to a syntax error if used in an expression such as

```
if ( counter == UPPER )
```

This is because on preprocessing, the **if** statement would take the form

```
if ( counter == UPPER; )
```

[9] Omitting parentheses around macro expansion.

```
#define SQR(x)  x * x
main( )
{
    int a ;
    a = 25 / SQR(5) ;
    printf ( "%d", a ) ;
}
```

In this example we expect the value of **a** to be 1, whereas it turns out to be 25. This so happens because on preprocessing the arithmetic statement takes the following form:

```
a = 25 / 5 * 5 ;
```

[10] Leaving a blank space between the macro template and the macro expansion. Consider the following macro,

```
#define ABS (a) ( ( (a) (0) ) ? (a) : (-a) )
```

Here, the space between **ABS** and **(a)** makes the preprocessor believe that you want to expand **ABS** into **(a)**, which is certainly not what you want.

[11] Using an expression that has side-effects in a macro.

```
#define SUM(a)  ( a + a )
main( )
{
    int w, b = 5 ;
    w = SUM ( b++ ) ;
    printf ( "%d", w ) ;
}
```

On preprocessing the macro would be expanded to,

```
w = ( b++ ) + ( b++ ) ;
```

If you are wanting to get first sum of 5 and 5 and then increment **b** to 6, that would not happen using the above macro definition.

[12] Confusing a character constant and a character string.

In the statement

```
letter = 'z' ;
```

a single character is assigned to **letter**. In the statement

```
letter = "z" ;
```

a pointer to the character string "z" is assigned to **letter**.

Note that in the first case, the declaration of **letter** would be,

```
char letter ;
```

whereas in the second case it would be,

```
char *letter ;
```

[13] Forgetting the bounds of an array.

```
main( )
{
    int num[50], i ;

    for ( i = 1 ; i <= 50 ; i++ )
        num[i] = i * i ;
}
```

In the array **num**, there is no such element as **num[50]**, since array counting begins with 0 and not 1. Compiler would give no warning if our program exceeds the bounds. If not taken care of, in extreme cases the computer might even hang.

[14] Forgetting to reserve an extra location in a character array for the null terminator.

Remember each character array ends with a '\0', therefore its dimension should be declared big enough to hold the normal characters as well as the '\0'.

For example, the dimension of the array **word[ ]** should be 9 if a string "Jamboree" is to be stored in it.

[15] Confusing the precedences of the various operators.

Consider the following program:

```
#include "stdio.h"
main( )
{
    char ch ;
    FILE *fp ;

    fp = fopen ( "text.c", "r" ) ;
    while ( ch = getc ( fp ) != EOF )
        putch ( ch ) ;

    fclose ( fp ) ;
}
```

Here, the value returned by **getc( )** will be first compared with EOF, since **!=** has a higher priority than **=**. As a result the value that is assigned to **ch** will be the True/False result of the test: 1 if the value returned by **getc( )** is not equal to EOF, and 0 otherwise. The correct form of the above **while** would be,

```
while ( ( ch = getc ( fp ) ) != EOF )
```

[16] Confusing the operator '->' with the operator '.' while referring to a structure element.

Remember, on the left of the operator '.' only a structure variable can occur, whereas on the left of operator '->' only a pointer to a structure can occur. This is illustrated in the following program.

```
main( )
{
    struct emp
    {
        char name[35] ;
        int age ;
    } ;
    static struct emp e = { "Dubhashi", 40 } ;
```

```
        struct emp *ee ;

        printf ( "%d", e.age ) ;
        ee = &e ;
        printf ( "%d", ee->age ) ;
}
```

[17] Exceeding the range of integers and chars.

```
main( )
{
        char ch ;

        for ( ch = 0 ; ch <= 255 ; ch++ )
            printf ( "%c %d\n", ch, ch ) ;
}
```

Can you believe that this is an indefinite loop. Probably, a closer look would confirm it. Reason is, **ch** has been declared as a **char** and the valid range of **char** constant is -128 to +127. Here, the moment **ch** tries to become 128 (through **ch++**), the value of character range is exceeded, it goes to the other side and becomes -127, which is certainly less than 255.

APPENDIX C Hexadecimal Numbering

While working with computers we are very often required to use hexadecimal numbers. The reason for this is: everything a computer does is based on binary numbers, and hexadecimal notation is a convenient way of expressing binary numbers. Before justifying this statement let us first discuss what numbering systems are, why computers use binary numbering system, how binary numbering system and hexadecimal numbering systems are related and how to use hexadecimal numbering system in everyday life.

Numbering Systems

When we talk about different numbering systems we are really speaking about the base of the numbering systems. For example, binary numbering system has base 2 and hexdecimal numbering system has base 16, just the way decimal numbering system has a base 10. What in fact is the 'base' of a numbering system? Base represents number of digits you can use before you run out of digits. For example, in decimal numbering system, when we have used digits from 0 to 9, we run out of digits. And the moment we run out of digits, we put a 1 in the column to the left - the ten's column - and start again in the one's column with 0, as shown below :

0
1
2
3
4
5
6
7
8
9 last available digit
10 start using a new column
11
12
13
14
...
...

Thus, decimal numbering system has base 10 since it constructs any number using some out of the ten digits from 0 to 9. This seems perfectly natural. However, the choice of 10 as a base is quite arbitrary, having its origin possibly in the fact that man has 10 fingers. It is very easy to use other bases as well. For example, if we wanted to use base 8 or octal numbering system, which uses only eight digits (0 to 7), here's how counting would look like :

0
1
2
3
4
5
6
7 last available digit

10 start using a new column
11
12
...
...

Similarly, a hexadecimal numbering system has a base 16. In hex notation, the ten symbols 0 through 9 are used to represent the ten values zero through nine, and the remaining six values, ten through fifteen, are represented by the symbols A through F. The hex digits A through F are usually written in capitals, but lowercase letters are also perfectly acceptable. Here is how the counting would look like.

0
1
2
3
4
5
6
7
8
9
A
B
C
D
E
F last available digit
10 start using a new column
11
...
...

Many other numbering systems can also be imagined. For example, we use a base 60 numbering system, for measuring minutes and seconds. From the base 12 system we retain our 12 hour system for time, the number of inches in a foot and so on. The moral is that any base can be used in a numbering system, although some bases are convenient than others.

The hex numbers are built out of hex digits the same way that decimal numbers are built. For example, when we write the decimal number 342, we mean,

```
  3 times 100 (square of 10)
+ 4 times 10
+ 2 times 1
```

Similarly, if we use number 342 as a hex number, we mean,

```
  3 times 256 (square of 16)
+ 4 times 16
+ 2 times 1
```

Computers And Binary & Its Relation With Hex

As it turns out, computers are more comfortable with binary numbering system. In a binary system, there are only two digits 0 and 1. This means you can't count very far before you need to start using the next column:

```
 0
 1  last available digit
10  start using a new column
11
...
...
```

Binary numbering system is a natural system for computers because each of the thousands of electronic circuits in the computer can be in one of the two states: on or off. Thus, binary numbering system corresponds nicely with the circuits in the computer: 0 means off, and 1 means on. 0 and 1 are called as bits, a short-form of binary digits.

Hex numbers are used primarily as a shorthand for binary numbers that the computers work with. Every hex digit represents four bits of binary information (Refer table given below). In the binary numbering system, 4 bits taken at a time can give rise to sixteen different numbers, so the only way to represent each of these sixteen 4 bit binary numbers in a simple and short way is to use a base sixteen numbering system.

Hex	Binary	Hex	Binary
0	0000	8	1000
1	0001	9	1001
2	0010	A	1010
3	0011	B	1011
4	0100	C	1100
5	0101	D	1101
6	0110	E	1110
7	0111	F	1111

Now suppose we want to represent a binary number 11000101 in a short way. One way is to find it deimal equivalent as follows :

```
  1 times 128
+ 1 times 64
+ 0 times 32
+ 0 times 16
+ 0 times  8
```

+ 1 times 4
+ 0 times 2
+ 1 times 1

197

Another method is much simpler. Just look at the table given above. From it find out the hex digits for 2 sets of four bits (1100 and 0101) from the binary number. These happen to be C and 5. Therefore, the binary number's hex equivalent is C5, a much easier way to represent the binary number than to find its decimal equivalent. Multiplication is not needed neither is addition. All we need to do is look up the above table.

In fact, since there are only 16 hex digits, it's fairly easy to memorise the binary equivalent of each one. Quick now, what's binary 1011 in hex? That's right B. You are already getting the feel of it. With a little practice it is easy to translate even long numbers into hex. Thus, 1100 0101 0011 1010 binary is C53A hex.

As it happens with many unfamiliar subjects, learning hexadecimal requires a little practice. Try your hand at converting some binary numbers to hex and vice versa. Soon you will be talking hexadecimal as if you have known it all you life.

APPENDIX

D ASCII Chart

There are 256 distinct characters used by IBM compatible family of microcomputers. Their values range from 0 to 255. These can be grouped as under:

Character Type	No. Of Characters
Capital Letters	26
Small-case Letters	26
Digits	10
Special Symbols	32
Control Characters	34
Graphic Characters	128
Total	256

Out of the 256 character set, the first 128 are often called Ascii characters and the next 128 as Extended Ascii characters. Each Ascii character has a unique appearence. The following simple program can generate the Ascii chart :

```
main()
{
    int ch ;

    for ( ch = 0 ; ch <= 255 ; ch++ )
        printf ( "%d %c\n", ch, ch ) ;
}
```

This chart is shown on the following page. Out of the 128 graphic characters (Extended Ascii characters), there are characters which are used for drawing single line and double line boxes in text mode. For convenience these characters are shown below:

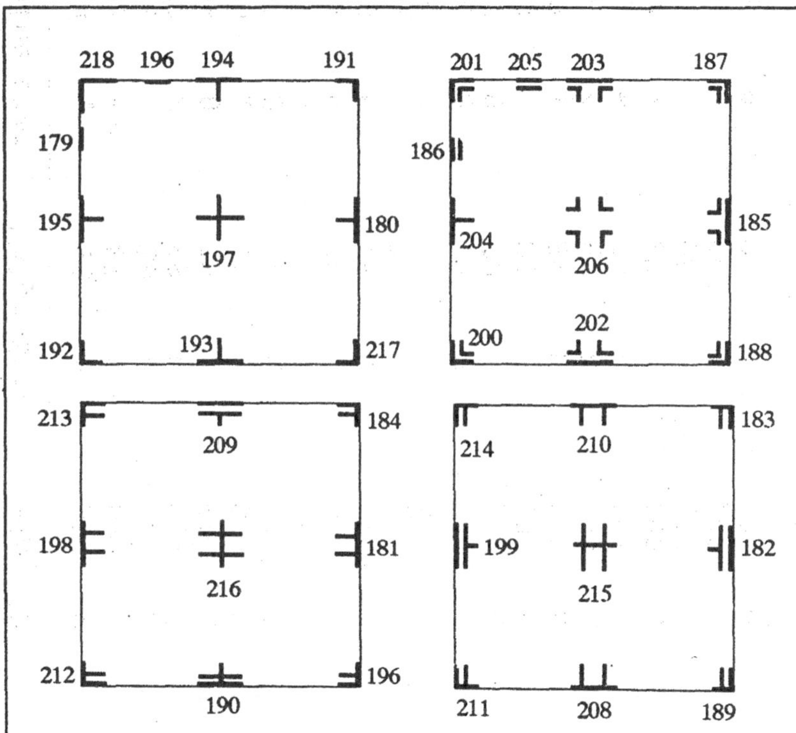

Value	Char	Value	Char	Value	Char	Value	Char	Value	Char	Value	Char
0		22	▬	44	,	66	B	88	X	110	n
1	☺	23	↨	45	-	67	C	89	Y	111	o
2	☻	24	↑	46	.	68	D	90	Z	112	p
3	♥	25	↓	47	/	69	E	91	[	113	q
4	♦	26	→	48	0	70	F	92	\	114	r
5	♣	27	←	49	1	71	G	93	]	115	s
6	♠	28	∟	50	2	72	H	94	^	116	t
7	•	29	↔	51	3	73	I	95	_	117	u
8	◘	30	▲	52	4	74	J	96	`	118	v
9	○	31	▼	53	5	75	K	97	a	119	w
10	◙	32		54	6	76	L	98	b	120	x
11	♂	33	!	55	7	77	M	99	c	121	y
12	♀	34	"	56	8	78	N	100	d	122	z
13	♪	35	#	57	9	79	O	101	e	123	{
14	♫	36	$	58	:	80	P	102	f	124	|
15	☼	37	%	59	;	81	Q	103	g	125	}
16	►	38	&	60	<	82	R	104	h	126	~
17	◄	39	'	61	=	83	S	105	i	127	MH
18	↕	40	(	62	>	84	T	106	j	128	Ç
19	‼	41	)	63	?	85	U	107	k	129	ü
20	¶	42	*	64	@	86	V	108	l	130	é
21	§	43	+	65	A	87	W	109	m	131	â

APPENDIX

E DOEACC Solved Papers

The solutions given in this publication of solutions for 'A&B' level papers are not endorsed by the CSI education directorate. There can be differences between these solutions and official version.

DOEACC - 'A' LEVEL EXAMINATION - FEBRUARY 1993
INTRODUCTION TO PROGRAMMING LANGUAGE THROUGH 'C'

Total time: 3 Hours

Marks: Part I 40
Part II 60
Total marks: 100

PART - I

I. Choose the correct answer among the alternatives indicated.
(8 x 2.5 = 20 marks)

1.
```
main( )
{
    int counter = 40 ;
    for ( ; counter; )
        counter-- ;
    printf ( "%d\n", counter ) ;
}
```

In the above program, the output is

(a) 40 (b) -40 (c) 0 (d) None of the above

2.
```
#define max (a,b) (a  b ? a : b)
main( )
{
    int m ;
    m = max (123, 456) ;
    /* more program lines */
}
```

The above program

(a) Assigns 456 to m (b) Assigns 123 to m
(c) Assigns the string "(a,b)" to m (d) None of the above

3.
```
main( )
{
    int i, j, r ;
    i = 100 ; j = 5 ; r = 20 ;
    printf ( "Value of i + j - r is %o \n", i + j - r ) ;
}
```

When the above program segment is run, it prints

(a) 55 (b) 85 (c) 125 (d) None of the above

4. Consider the following program:

```
char oadd ( char c )
{
    return &c ;
}
void ost ( char *cad, char vai )
{
    *cad = val ;
}
main( )
{
    char a = 'A', b = 'B' ;
    ost ( oadd ( a ), b ) ;
    printf ( "Value of a = %c \n", a ) ;
}
```

Which of the following is true for the above program?

(a) This program contains a syntax error
(b) Program prints "Value of a = A"
(c) Program prints "Value of a = B"
(d) None of the above

5. What does the following program segment print?

```
main( )
{
    int i ;
    int iarray[4] = { 1, 2, 3, 4 } ;
    #define SIZE (sizeof(iarray) / sizeof(int))
    for (i = 0 ; i < SIZE ; ++i)
        iarray[i] += 2 ;
    printf ( "Value is %d\n", iarray[3] ) ;
}
```

(a) 3
(b) 6
(c) Compilation error because of **#define** within main module
(d) None of the above

6. Find out the error in the following program:

```
main( )
{
    int mark ;
    char grade ;
    switch ( mark )
    {
        case 5 : grade = 'A' ; break ;
        case 4 : grade = 'B' ; break ;
        case 4 : grade = 'B' ; break ;
        default : grade = 'c' ; break ;
    } /* switch */
}
```

(a) **switch** statement cannot have more than three labels
(b) **case** labels cannot be numbers
(c) No two labels may be identical
(d) None of the above

7.

```
main( )
{
```

```
    int buf[5] ;
    int *btr = &buf[2] ;
    btr[-1] = 20 ;
    btr[-2] = 10 ;
    btr[-3] = 0 ;
    printf ( "buf[1] = %d\n", buf[1] ) ;
}
```

The above program prints

(a) buf[1] = 20 (b) buf[1] = 10
(c) buf[1] = 0 (d) None of the above

8. What is the output of the following program?

```
#define ROWS 3
#define COLUMNS 4
int z[ROWS][COLUMNS] = {1, 2, 3, 4, 5, 6, 7, 8, 9, 10, 11, 12}
main( )
{
    int a, b, c = 999 ;
    for ( a = 0 ; a < ROWS ; ++a )
    for ( b = 0 ; b < COLUMNS ; ++b )
    if ( z[a][b] < c )
        c = z[a][b] ;
    printf ( "%d", c ) ;
}
```

(a) 999 (b) 12 (c) 1 (d) None of the above

II MATCH THE FOLLOWING

Write only appropriate alphabet as answer against question numbers 9 to 18. (10 Marks)

Consider the following program segment:

```
int i, j = 25 ;
int *pi, *pj = &j ;
......
...... /* more lines of program */
......
*pj = j + 5 ;
i = *pj + 5 ;
pi = pj ;
*pi = i + j ;
```

Each integer quantity occupies 2 bytes on memory. The value assigned to **i** begins at (hexadecimal) address F9C and the value assigned to **j** begins at address F9E. Match the value represented by Left Hand Side quantities with the Right.

9. &i	a. 30
10. &j	b. F9E
11. pj	c. 35
12. *pj	d. FA2
13. i	e. F9C
14. pi	f. 67
15. *pi	g. unspecified
16. (pi + 2)	h. 65
17. (*pi + 2)	j. F9E
18. * (pi + 2)	k. F9E
	m. FAO
	n. F9D

III With respect to the following program segment, say whether the subsequent remarks are true or false. (5 marks)

```
typedef struct {
                int month ;
                int day ;
                int year ;
            } date ;

struct {
```

```
        int acct_no ;
        char acct_type ;
        char name [80] ;
        float balance ;
        date lastpayment ;
    } customer, *pc = &customer ;
```

(19) **customer.balance** and (***pc**).**balance** refers to the same value
(20) **pc -> lastpayment.month** is syntactically valid
(21) ***(pc.lastpayment.month**) is syntactically invalid
(22) ***(customer.name + 2**) and **customer.name[2]** both refer to **pc -> (name + 2)**
(23) ***((*pc).name + 2**) refers to the second character of customer's name

IV Fill in the blanks (5 marks)

In the following questions by choosing the most appropriate word or phrase from the following list. Enter only the alphabet corresponding to the answer. (e.g. if for a question, the correct answer is third in the list, then enter only 'C' in the blank space provided for that question).

(a) address	(b) char	(c) extern	(d) void
(e) preprocessor	(f) pointer	(g) getchar()	(h) recursive
(j) hexadecimal	(k) octal	(m) union	(n) FILE

(24) 0x7FFF refers to a ________ constant.
(25) ________ is a structure used to conserve memory.
(26) ________ is a structure type defined within a system include file, typically stdio.h.
(27) **#define** is a typical ____________ directive.
(28) A ________________ as a return data type in a function indicates that the function does not return anything.

PART II

(29) You are given a data file EMPLOYEE.DAT with the following record structure:

```
struct employee {
                    int empno ;
                    char name[30] ;
                    int basic, grade ;
            } ;
```

Every employee has a unique empno and there are no gaps. Records are entered into the data file in ascending order of employee number, 'empno'. It is intended to check whether there are missing employee numbers. Write a program segment to read the data file records sequentially and display the list of missing employee numbers.

(30) Write a program to accept any 3 digit integer and display it in words. For example,

134 One Hundred And Thirty Four
301 Three Hundred And One
518 Five Hubdred And Eighteen

(31) Write a program to carry out the following:

(i) to read a text file "TRIAL.TXT" consisting of a maximum of 50 lines of text, each line with a maximum of 80 characters.
(ii) Count and display the number of words contained in the file.
(iii) Display the total number of four letter words in the text file.

(Assume that the end of a word may be a space, a comma or a fullstop followed by one or more spaces or a anew line character)

(32) Write a program to read a list of words, sort the words in alphabetical order and display them one word per line. Also give the total number of words in the list. Output format should be:

Total Number of words in the list is ------------
Alphabetical listing of words

Assume the end of the list is indicated by ZZZZZZ and there are maximum of 25 words in the Text file.

DOEACC Solutions

Part 1

1. (c)
2. (a)
3. (c)
4. (b)
5. (b)
6. (c)
7. (a)
8. (d)
9. (e)
10. (b)
11. (j)
12. (h)
13. (c)
14. (k)
15. (h)
16. (d)
17. (f)
18. (g)
19. T
20. T
21. T
22. F
23. F
24. (j)
25. (m)
26. (n)
27. (e)
28. (d)

Part II

(29)
```
#include"stdio.h"
main( )
{
    int counter = 1 ;
    struct employee
    {
        int empno ;
        char name[30] ;
        int basic, grade ;
    } e ;
    FILE *fp ;

    if ( ( fp = fopen ( "employee.dat", "rb" ) ) == NULL )
    {
        printf ( "\nCan not open file ..." ) ;
        exit (1) ;
    }

    while ( fread ( &e, sizeof(e), 1, fp ) )
    {
        for ( ; counter < e.empno ; counter++ )
            printf ( "\n%d", counter ) ;

        counter++ ;
    }

    fclose ( fp ) ;
}
```

(30)
```
main( )
{
    char *arr1[ ] = {
                        "One",
                        "Two",
```

```
                    "Three",
                    "Four",
                    "Five",
                    "Six",
                    "Seven",
                    "Eight",
                    "Nine",
                    "Ten",
                    "Eleven",
                    "Twelve",
                    "Thirteen",
                    "Fourteen",
                    "Fifteen",
                    "Sixteen",
                    "Seventeen",
                    "Eighteen",
                    "Nineteen"
                } ;
char *arr2[ ] = {
                    "Twenty",
                    "Thirty",
                    "Forty",
                    "Fifty",
                    "Sixty",
                    "Seventy",
                    "Eighty",
                    "Ninety"
                } ;
int num ;

printf ( "\nEnter any 3 digit number" ) ;
scanf ( "%d", &num ) ;

if ( num > 999 || num <= 0 )
{
    printf ( "\nNumber is invalid" ) ;
    exit ( 1 ) ;
```

```
    }

    if ( num / 100 )
        printf ( "\n%s Hundered and", arr1[ num / 100 - 1 ] ) ;

    num %= 100 ;
    if ( num > 19 )
    {
        printf ( "%s", arr2[ num / 10 - 2 ] ) ;
        num %= 10 ;
    }

    if ( num )
        printf ( "%s", arr1[ num - 1 ] ) ;
}
```

(31)
```
#include "stdio.h"
main( )
{
    int words = 0, words4 = 0, wlen, i ;
    char str[81] ;
    FILE *fp ;

    if ( ( fp = fopen ( "TRIAL.TXT", "r" ) ) == NULL )
    {
        printf ( "\nCan not open file" ) ;
        exit ( 1 ) ;
    }

    while ( ( fgets ( str, 81, fp ) ) != NULL )
    {
        i = 0 ;
        while ( 1 )
        {
            while ( str[i] == ' ' || str[i] == '\n' )
                i++ ;
```

```
                if ( str[i] == '\0' )
                    break ;

                wlen = 0 ;
                while ( str[i] != ',' && str[i] != '.' && str[i] != ' ')
                {
                    i++ ;
                    wlen++ ;
                }

                i++ ;

                if ( wlen )
                {
                    words++ ;
                    if ( wlen == 4 )
                        words4++ ;
                }
            }
        }

        fclose ( fp ) ;
        printf ( "\nTotal number of words in TRIAL.TXT = %d", words ) ;
        printf ( "\nNumber of 4 letter words in TRIAL.TXT = %d", words4 ) ;
    }
```

(32)
```
    # include "stdio.n"
    main( )
    {
        int wc = 0, i = 0, j, cmp, ch ;
        char words[25][30], temp[30] ;
        FILE *fp ;

        if ( ( fp = fopen ( "TRIAL.TXT", "r" ) ) == NULL )
        {
            puts ( "Unable to open trial.txt file" ) ;
            exit ( 1 ) ;
```

```
    }

    while ( 1 )
    {
        words [wc][i++] = ch = getc ( fp ) ;
        if ( ch == ' ' || ch == '\n' || ch == '.' || ch == EOF )
        {
            words[wc][i - 1] = '\0' ;
            i = 0 ;

            if ( ! ( strcmp ( words[wc], "ZZZZZZ" ) ) )
                break ;

            wc++ ;
            while ( ( ch = getc ( fp ) ) == ' ' )
                ;
            ungetc ( ch, fp ) ;
        }
    }

    for ( i = 0 ; i < wc-1 ; i++ )
    {
        for ( j = i + 1 ; j < wc ; j++ )
        {
            cmp = strcmp ( words[i], words[j] ) ;
            if ( cmp > 0 )
            {
                strcpy ( temp, words[i] ) ;
                strcpy ( words[i], words[j] ) ;
                strcpy ( words[j], temp ) ;
            }
        }
    }

    for ( i = 0 ; i < wc ; i++ )
        printf ( "\n%s", words[i] ) ;
}
```

DOEACC - 'A' LEVEL EXAMINATION - JULY 1993
INTRODUCTION TO PROGRAMMING LANGUAGE THROUGH 'C'

Total time: 3 Hours

Marks: Part I 40
Part II 60
Total marks: 100

PART -I

I. Choose the appropriate answer among the alternatives indicated. (8 x 2.5 = 20 Marks)

1. Consider the following program segment:

```
main( )
{
    int fa;
    fa = fac ( 5 ) ;
    /* more program lines */
}
fac ( num )
int num ;
{
    if ( num == 1 )
        return 1 ;
    return ( num * fac ( num - 1 ) ) ;
}
```

The above program segment

(a) Assigns 5 to **fa** (b) Assigns 120 to **fa**
(c) Assigns 1 to **fa** (d) None of the above

2. Consider the program segment:

```
main( )
{
```

```
    printf ( "Hello\n" ) ;
    main( ) ;
}
```

Which of the following is true for the above program segment?

(a) Prints only once
(b) Infinite loop
(c) Compilation error because of main within main module
(d) None of the above

3. Consider the program segment:

```
#define SQUARE(x)=(x * x)
#define csi(m,n) ( SQUARE(m) > SQUARE(n) ? n : m )
main( )
{
    int s ;
    s = csi(2,-3) ;
    printf ( "%d\n", a ) ;
    /* more program lines */
}
```

In the above program segment, the output is

(a) 2 (b) -3 (c) 4 (d) None of the above

4. Consider the program segment:

```
main( )
{
    char c_arry[ ] = { 'A', 'B', 'C', 'D' }, *ptr ;
    *ptr = c_arry ;
    *++ptr = *( c_arry + 2 ) ;
    printf ( "c = %c", *ptr + 1 ) ;
}
```

The Output of the above program segment is

(a) A (b) D (c) C (d) None of the above

5. Consider the program segment:

```
main( )
{
    int n = 2, *ptr ;
    ptr = &n ;
    n *= 3 ;
    printf ( "%d\n", *ptr**ptr ) ;
}
```

The above program segments prints

(a) 6 (b) 36 (c) 4 (d) None of the above

6. Consider the program segment:

```
main( )
{
    int i, j = 1 ;
    for ( i = j - 2 ; i < 5 ; i++ )
        j += j ;
    printf ( "The Value of j is : %d\n", j ) ;
}
```

The Output of the above program segment is:

(a) 5 (b) 13 (c) 12 (d) None of the above

7. What is the output of the following program segment?

```
main( )
{
    int val, x ;
```

```
    val = 5 ;
    call_funct1 ( val ) ;
    printf ( "The Output is : %d\n", val ) ;
}
call_funct1 ( val )
int val ;
{
    return ( call_funct2 ( val * 2 ) ) ;
}
call_funct2 ( val )
int val ;
{
    val *= 2 ;
    return ( val ) ;
}
```

(a) 5 (b) 10 (c) 20 (d) None of the abo\

8. Consider the following program segment:

```
func ( a, b )
int a, b ;
{
    return ( a = ( a == b ) ) ;
}
main( )
{
    int process( ), func( ) ;
    printf ( "The value of process: %d\n", process ( func, 3, 4 ) ) ;
}
process ( pf, val1, val2 )
int ( *pf )( ) ;
int val1, val2 ;
{
    return ( ( *pf )( val1, val2) ) ;
}
```

The above program segment prints:

(a) 3 (b) 4 (c) 0 (d) None of the above

II MATCH THE FOLLOWING

Write only appropriate alphabet as answer against question numbers 9 to 18. (10 Marks)

In the following program segment

```
int x[3][5] = {
                { 1, 2, 3, 4, 5 },
                { 6, 7, 8, 9, 10 },
                { 11, 12, 13, 14, 15 }
            }, *n = &x ;
```

9. *(*(x + 2) + 1)	a. 9
10. *(*x + 2) + 5	b. 13
11. *(*(x + 1))	c. 4
12. *(*(x) + 2) + 1	d. 3
13. *(*(x + 1) + 3)	e. 2
14. *n	f. 12
15. *(n + 2)	g. 14
16. (*(n + 3) + 1)	h. 7
17. *(n + 5) + 1	i. 1
18. ++*n	j. 8
	k. 5
	l. 10
	m. 6

III. State whether the following statements are True or False. (5 Marks)

19. 'C' functions need not necessarily have arguments.
20. A **switch** statement can always be replaced by a series of **if-else** statements.
21. **printf( )** always begins printing on new line.

22. Every Function should have a 'return' statement.
23. **do..while( )** statement will always be executed atleast once.

IV. Fill in the blanks. (5 Marks)

In the following questions by choosing the most appropriate word or pharse from following list. Enter only the alphabet corresponding to the answer.

24. A _____ performs macro substitution, and conditional compilation.
25. **&&** is a logical _____ operator.
26. Buffering is a software technique designed to make _____ operations more efficient.
27. Function returns _____ value by default.
28. A _____ is a file that contains a list of filenames.

(a) scheduler	(b) directory	(c) and	(d) integer
(e) or	(f) control	(g) preprocessor	(h) void
(i) not	(j) device	(k) I/O	

Part II

Answer all Questions. Each Questions carries 10 Marks.

1. Generate the following "pyramid" of digits, using **for** loops for a given input. Input range should be between 0 and 9. For example, if input is 5, the output would be:

```
        1
      2   2
    3   3   3
  4   4   4   4
5   5   5   5   5
```

2. Write a program to carry out the following:

(i) To read a text file 'INPUT.TXT'.
(ii) Print each word in reverse order.

Note : Assume that each word length is maximum of 10 characters and each word is separated by new line/blank character.

For example,

Input : INDIA IS MY COUNTRY
Output : AIDNI SI MY YRTNUOC

3. The Problem of Tower of Hanoi:'n' disks are to be moved from a peg 'A' to peg 'C' via peg 'B' if necessary. The disks must be moved one at a time and a larger disk may never be placed on top of a smaller one.

Solution : To obtain a solution for the above problem, we adopt the following algorithm.

- First move the first set of (n - 1) disks from 'A' to 'B' via 'C'.
- Move the nth disk to 'C'.
- Move the first set of (n-1) disks from 'B' to 'C' via 'A'.

The following program segment is written for the above algorithm for the Tower of Hanoi Problem, with one blank line. Study the program and fill up the blank line completing the program.

```
main( )
{
    int n ;
    printf ( "How many Disks ? : " ) ;
    scanf ( "%d", &n ) ;
    move ( n, 'A', 'B', 'C' ) ;
}
move ( i, source, aux, dest )
```

```
int i ;
char source, aux, dest ;
{
     if ( i > 0 )
     {
          move ( i - 1, source, dest, aux ) ;
          printf ( "Move disk %d from peg %c to peg %c\n", i, source, dest ) ;
          ............................
     }
}
```

4. The following program is intended to print the list of all prime numbers less than or equal to a given number. The portion of the program detailing the function gcd (greatest common divisor - the largest number dividing two given numbers - for example gcd of 24 and 64 is 8) is missing. Complete the statements pertaining to this function.

```
# include "math.h"
int gcd ( u, v )
int u, v ;
{
     ............
     ............
     return ( gcd ) ,
}
main( )
{
     int n, i, j, m ;
     printf ( "Enter a given number :" ) ;
     scanf ( "%d", n ) ;
     for ( i = 1 ; i <= n ; i++ )
     {
          m = ( int ) ( sqrt(i) ) ;
          for ( j = 1 ; j <= m ; ++j )
          {
               if ( gcd ( i, j ) != 1 )
```

```
                break ;
            if ( j == m + 1 )
            printf ( "%d", i ) ;
        }
    }
```

5. The output of the following program segment is

```
1 4 8 10 12 23 45 65 76 98
```

Modify the program segment suitably (indicating only the changes made, without rewriting the program) so that the output will be

```
1 4 8 65 12 23 45 76 98 10
```

```
main( )
{
    int i, first = 0, last = 9 ;
    int list[ ] = { 12, 65, 1, 4, 8, 23, 45, 76, 98, 10 } ;
    qt ( first, last, list ) ;
    for ( i = 0 ; i <= 9 ; ++i )
        printf ( "%d ", list[i] ) ;
}
qt ( first, last, list )
int first, last, list[10] ;
{
    int i, j, divline, temp;
    i = first ;
    j = last ;
    divline = list [ ( first + last ) / 2 ] ;
    while ( i <= j )
    {
        while ( list[i] < divline ) i = i + 1 ;
        while ( list[j] > divline ) j = j - 1 ;
        if ( i <= j )
        {
```

```
                temp = list[i] ;
                list[i] = list[j] ;
                list[j] = temp ;
                i = i + 1 ;
                j = j - 1 ;
            }
        }

        if ( first < j )
            qt ( first, j, list ) ;

        if ( i < last )
            qt ( i, last, list ) ;
    }
```

6. Write a C program to read a large text file 'NOTES.TXT' and print it on the printer in cut-sheets, introducing page breaks at the end of every 50 lines and a pause message on the screen at the end of every page for the user to change the paper.

DOEACC Solutions

Part I

1. (b)
2. (b)
3. (d)
4. (b)
5. (b)
6. (d)
7. (a)
8. (c)
9. (f)
10. (j)
11. (m)
12. (c)
13. (a)
14. (i)
15. (d)
16. (k)
17. (h)
18. (e)
19. T
20. T
21. F
22. F
23. T
24. (g)
25. (c)
26. (k)
27. (d)
28. (b)

Part II

(1)
```
main( )
{
    int i = 1, l, r ;

    for ( l = 0 ; l <= 4 ; l++, i++ )
    {
        printf ( "\n" ) ;
        for ( r = 3 - l ; r >= 0 ; r-- )
            printf ( "  " ) ;

        for ( r = 0 ; r < l + 1 ; r++ )
            printf ( "%d   ", i ) ;
    }
}
```

(2)
```
# include "stdio.h"
main( )
{
    FILE *fs ;
    char arr[11] ;
    int ch, i = 0 ;

    if ( ( fs = fopen ( "INPUT.TXT", "r" ) ) == NULL )
    {
        printf ( "Cannot open INPUT.TXT\n" ) ;
        exit( ) ;
    }

    while ( ( ch = getc ( fs ) ) != EOF )
    {
        if ( ch != '\n' && ch != ' ' )
        {
            arr[i] = ch ;
            i++ ;
```

```
		}
		else
		{
			arr[i] = '\0' ;
			strrev ( arr ) ;

			printf ( "%s", arr ) ;
			printf ( "%c", ch ) ;

			i = 0 ;
		}
	}
}
```

(3) move (i - 1, aux, source, dest) ;

(4)

```
# include "math.h"
main( )
{
	int n, i, j, m ;

	printf ( "Enter any number \n" ) ;
	scanf ( "%d", &n ) ;

	for ( i = 1 ; i <= n ; i++ )
	{
		m = ( int ) ( sqrt( i ) ) ;

		for ( j = 1 ; j <= m ; ++j )
			if ( gcd ( i, j ) != 1 )
				break ;

		if ( j == m + 1 )
			printf ( "%d\t", i ) ;
	}
}
int gcd ( u, v )
```

```
int u, v ;
{
    int min, i, gcd ;
    min = ( u < v ? u : v ) ;
    for ( i = 1 ; i <= min ; i++ )
        if ( u % i == 0 && v % i == 0 )
            gcd = i ;

    return ( gcd ) ;
}
```

(5) Comment out the iast two lines in the **qt( )** function as shown below:

```
/* if ( i < last )
    qt ( i, last, list ) ; */
```

(6)

```
# include "stdio.h"
main( )
{
    char arr[132], ch ;
    int i = 0, j = 0 ;
    FILE *fs ;

    if ( ( fs = fopen ( "NOTES.TXT", "r" ) ) == NULL )
    {
        printf ( "Cannot open NOTES.TXT" ) ;
        exit( ) ;
    }

    while ( ( fgets ( arr, 80, fs ) ) != NULL )
    {
        fputs ( arr, stdprn ) ;
        j++ ;

        if ( ( j % 50 ) == 0 )
        {
```

```
            puts ( "Change paper & hit any key " ) ;
            getch( ) ;
            putc ( '\f', stdprn ) ;
        }
    }
}
```

Index

A

argc 256, 366
arguments
  actual 228
  formal 228
argv 256, 366
array 196, 441
  bounds checking in 202
  declaration 199
  initialisation 201, 209
  memory map of 202, 210
  multi dimensional 210
  of pointers 286
  of structures 319
  single dimensional 196
  two dimensional 207
ascii
  extended 479
ascii chart 478
assignment
  statement 97
  type conversion in 100

B

break 158, 441

C

C
- character set 31
- constants 34
- variables 39

call
- by reference 242
- by value 241

case 132, 441
cast 442
characters
- box drawing 479

chars
- signed & unsigned 49

comment 43, 442
compiler 11
conditional compilation 412
constants 34, 442
- character 36
- integer 34
- logical 37
- range of 38
- real 35
- string 37

continue 160, 444
conversion specifications 183

D

data types 31, 51, 444
- enumerated 339

default 132
#define 402

isk I/O
binary mode 377
formatted 374
text mode 377
lo-while 445

E

#elif 415
#else 414
enum 340, 446
uses of 341
enumerated data types 339
EOF 379
errors
in disk i/o 393
programming 460
escape sequences 187, 446
exit( ) 161
expressions
definition 93
type conversion in 94, 95

F

fclose( ) 362
feof( )370
fflush( ) 376
fgets( ) 373
file
closing 362
opening 359
opening modes 362
reading from 360
string i/o in 371
fopen( ) 360
for 147, 447

multiple initialisations in 154
fprintf( ) 375
fputs( ) 371
fread( ) 384
fscanf( ) 377
fseek( ) 389, 392
ftell( ) 392
function
call 222
call by reference 235
call by value 235
declaration 232
definition 222
general form of 218
passing array to 253
passing structure elements to 321
passing structure to 322
pointers to 292
prototypes 232
scope rules 244
variable no. of arguments 297
with arguments 226
functions 447
character class test 435
disk i/o 356
math 429
miscellaneous 437
standard i/o 433
standard library 427
string 427
time and date 431
utility 431
variable argument list 431
fwrite( ) 384

G

getc( ) 360
getchar( ) 179
gets( ) 180
goto 162, 448

H

header files 425
  ctype.h 425
  math.h 426
  stdarg.h 427
  stdio.h 425
  string.h 426
  time.h 427
header files
  stdlib.h 426
hexadecimal 472

I

I/O
  console 177, 178
  disk 177
  formatted, console 182, 374
  port 177
  record 381
  types of 176
  unformatted, console 179
if 113, 415, 449
  general form 113
  nested 121
  summary of 130
  with multiple statements 117
if-else 119
#ifdef 413
#include 418

integers
    long & short 47
    signed & unsigned 48
interpreter 11

K

keywords 41, 450

L

labels 450
language
    assembly 6
    characteristics of 9
    fourth generation 8
    history of C 21
    machine 5
    steps in learning 30
    third generation 7
loop
    do-while 156
    for 147
    while 141
loops 140
    nesting of 153

M

macro 406
    versus functions 409
    with arguments 406
memory
    dynamic allocation 279

N

null statement 450

numbering
- binary 473
- hexadecimal 472

numbering systems 470

O

object code 400, 401

operators
- address of 237, 271
- arithmetic 69
- bitwise 76
- bitwise AND 82
- bitwise OR 85
- bitwise XOR 86
- comma 88
- conditional 87, 129
- decrement 69
- increment 69, 152
- left shift 81
- logical 74
- modulo division 71
- one's complement 78
- precedence of 90, 91, 451
- relational 72
- right shift 80
- sizeof 89, 452
- structure 316
- types of 68
- value at address 271
- value at address 237

P

pointer
- arithmetic 275
- assignment 273

comparison 279
expressions 273
pointers 235, 450
array of 286
returning 295
to functions 292
to pointers 290
to strings 290
to structures 324
preprocessor 400
printf( ) 44, 183
program
structure of C 23
steps in development 2
programming
bottom-up 12
modular 12
structured 14
techniques 12
top-down 12
programming language
classification 4
putchar( ) 179
puts( ) 180

R

recursion 257
return 229, 451
rewind( ) 392

S

scanf( ) 45, 190
sizeof 452
sprintf( ) 190

statement
- assignment 97
- break 158
- continue 160
- goto 162
- if 113
- if-else 119
- if-else-if 122
- loop 140
- null 450
- return 229
- switch 131
- typedef 343

storage class
- automatic 52
- external 58
- register 55
- static 56

storage classes 51, 452
strings 203
structure
- declaration of 313
- elements 316
- memory map of 317
- operator 316
- passing to functions 322
- pointers 324

structures 310, 453
- array of 319
- nested 326
- union of 334
- uses of 327

switch 131, 454

T

translators 10

type casting 96
type modifiers 46
typedef 343

U

#undef 412
unions 328, 455
    of structures 334
    memory map of 330
    uses of 335

V

variable
    declaration 40
    initialisation 101
    no. of arguments 297
variables 39
    global 40
    local 40
    scope of 40
void 234, 456

W

while 141, 456